dancing prophets

CHICAGO STUDIES

IN ETHNOMUSICOLOGY

EDITED BY

PHILIP V. BOHLMAN AND

BRUNO NETTL

STEVEN M. FRIEDSON

dancing prophets

MUSICAL EXPERIENCE IN

TUMBUKA HEALING

THE UNIVERSITY OF CHICAGO PRESS

CHICAGO & LONDON

Steven Friedson is associate professor of music and adjunct associate professor of anthropology at the University of North Texas.

The University of Chicago Press, Chicago 60637
The University of Chicago Press, Ltd., London
©1996 by The University of Chicago
All rights reserved. Published 1996
Printed in the United States of America
05 04 03 02 01 00 99 98 97 96   1 2 3 4 5
ISBN (cloth): 0-226-26501-3
ISBN (paper):0-226-26502-1

Library of Congress Cataloging-in-Publication Data

Friedson, Steven M. (Steven Michael), 1948–
    Dancing prophets : musical experience in Tum-
buka healing / Steven M. Friedson.
        p.   cm. — (Chicago studies in ethnomusicology)
    Includes bibliographical references and index.
    1. Tumbuka (African people)—Music. 2. Tum-
buka (African people)—Rites and ceremonies. 3.
Healing—Malawi. 4. Music therapy—Malawi. 5.
Ethnology—Malawi. 6. Music and dance. I. Title.
II. Series.
    ML350.F75   1996
    615.8'82'096897—dc20   95-44931
                                            CIP
                                            MN

> *. . . you are the music*
> *While the music lasts.*
> T. S. ELIOT,
> ''THE DRY SALVAGES,''
> FOUR QUARTETS

CONTENTS

ILLUSTRATIONS

Questioning builds a way. . . . The way is a way of thinking.
—MARTIN HEIDEGGER,
"THE QUESTION CONCERNING TECHNOLOGY"

This book is a way of thinking about Tumbuka healing. It is a way of understanding a health care system populated by dancing prophets, singing patients, and drummed spirits. In Tumbuka medical praxis, the healing arts have not been separated—as they have been in the West—into mutually exclusive categories of medical care and aesthetic experience. Healing is still an art form in northern Malawi. From all-night divination sessions, with their virtually continuous singing and drumming, to the internal experience of spirit possession, music gives form to a sacred clinical reality.[1] What follows is a questioning of that lived experience. Such an inquiry builds the way of this ethnography.

What is it to dance a disease, to drum a diagnosis, and, in doing so, to embody the spirits? How do we come to understand ways of "being-in-the-world" so radically different from our own experience? If "we cannot live other people's lives" (Geertz 1986: 373)—which would be its own form of possession—what kinds of understandings can we have of such modes of existence?

Musical experience in clinical settings can be as superficial as a Western surgeon's listening to Mozart while performing surgery or as intricate and complex as the musical transaction that takes place between a Tumbuka healer and his patient. In the West, music simply is not part of the biomedically driven clinical reality encountered in doctors' offices, clinics, and hospitals. Muzak may be piped into a doctor's waiting room, but these sounds have nothing to do with clinical practice, let alone with an active musical experience. Throughout Africa, however, traditional diagnostics and therapeutics are saturated with musical phenomena.

Azande "witch-doctors" eat special divinatory medicines activated by drumming, singing, and dancing (Evans-Pritchard 1937: 148–82). More reliable than rubbing-board divination but less trustworthy than oracular poison, these human oracles "dance the question," that is, diagnose the ills and misfortunes of those who seek their help. Among the Hausa of northern Nigeria, the sounds of the *garaya* (two-stringed plucked lute) and *buta* (gourd rattle) call the "divine horsemen" of the sacred city of Jangare to descend into the heads of *bori* adepts, thus healing the very people they have made sick (Besmer 1983). Similarly, the various *orisha* (Barber 1981; Bascom 1944) and *vodu* (Herskovits 1938) spirits of the Guinea coast, called by their particular drum motto, mount their horses (possess their devotees). The resultant spirit-possession dance, though religious in nature, is, in the first instance, often a therapy for those afflicted by the same spirits. Spirit affliction is healed through music and dance in Ethiopia and Sudan wherever *zar* cults occur (Boddy 1989; Lewis 1971). For the coastal Swahili-speaking peoples of East Africa, it is the *shetani* spirits who possess and afflict (Cory 1936; Gray 1969), and for the Tonga of Zambia (Colson 1969) and the Shona of Zimbabwe (Gelfand 1956, 1964b), it is the foreign *mashave*[2]—a class that includes spirits as diverse as lion, European, guitar, and airplane. Central, southern, and parts of equatorial Africa all have examples of the *ng'oma* type of healing complex (Janzen 1992; Turner 1968), whose name points to the centrality of music in curative rites (*ng'oma* means drum, among many other things). In North Africa, members of the Hamadsha brotherhood obtain the healing power of *baraka* by a dance of self-mutilation, which itself is a meditation on Allah (Crapanzano 1973). And at the other end of the continent, in perhaps one of the oldest forms of music and healing in Africa, !Kung bushmen dance to boil their *num*, the source of a spiritual energy that heals both individual and group (Katz 1982; Marshall 1969).

In each of these cases (and these are only a few of the documented ones), people experience sickness and healing through rituals of consciousness-transformation whose experiential core is musical. And while ethnographers often interpret these types of experiences as religious, the types are, nonetheless, part of long-standing indigenous health care practices.

It is impossible to separate the phenomenal reality of music, trance, and healing in Africa into neatly defined categories of Western epistemological thought such as aesthetics, religion, and medicine. Trance that involves spirits is inherently religious, at least according to E. B. Tylor's minimum definition of the term (1920: 424); yet in many instances, this kind of trance ultimately has to do with sickness and health mediated through musical performance. Music, trance, and healing form a continuum that is often functionally irreducible into constituent parts.

The Silent Drum

Although analyses of these kinds of diagnostic and therapeutic processes cover a wide range of diverse perspectives—the functionalist approaches of Evans-Pritchard (1937) and Elizabeth Colson (1969); I. M. Lewis's (1971) deprivation theories of peripheral cults; Janice Boddy's (1989) analysis of the same cults as women's discourse; the symbolic dramaturgy of Victor Turner's (1968) work on Ndembu "cults of affliction"; the ethnopsychiatric perspectives taken by Vincent Crapanzano (1973), to name but a few—ethnographers have not given musical experience a correspondingly prominent place in their research.[3] Music is usually treated as an epiphenomenon, something that accompanies other, more important ritual activities.

I am not saying, of course, that every ethnographer working with these healing traditions should be an ethnomusicologist, or that the work others have done on this aspect of culture has not been valuable. But when a particular phenomenon—in this case, music—is repeatedly mentioned in the literature as a prominent element of indigenous healing systems in Africa and yet is still given only perfunctory treatment, then an important dimension of the cultural experience being studied is silenced.[4] In Western society, which reduces music to "the secondary realms of 'art,' 'entertainment,' and occasional 'religious music' " (Ellingson 1987: 163), it seems to be difficult for researchers to overcome this cultural bias and *hear* the significance of music in a clinical context.

I have always found it ironic—even paradigmatic—that Victor Turner's seminal study on Ndembu ritual, *The Drums of Affliction* (1968), actually has very little to say about either drums or drumming.[5] We get tantalizing hints and passing references to musical phenomena, but Turner never elaborates on musical material as he does on matrilineal kinship ties, the symbolic meanings of various trees, or the sociological implications of witchcraft accusations. Yet in Turner's own writings there is abundant evidence that Ndembu curative rites are saturated with musical experience. Each ritual has its own special drum rhythms, dance, and songs (Turner 1968: 14); patients "tremble" when the correct drum rhythm is sounded (p. 63); diviners use drumming and singing as part of "physiological stimuli" to "heighten [their] intuitive awareness" (p. 43); songs are sung when medicines are collected, prepared, and applied (p. 65); and drums are often played at shrine trees (p. 73), those dominant symbols par excellence in Ndembu ritual. In Turner's ethnography of the Ndembu, however, we get a more detailed description of the symbolic contents of leather wallets worn by Ndembu hunters than we do of drumming.

This is not to say that Turner's concern with the operational meanings and multivocal interpretations of Ndembu symbols (1968: 17) is unimportant. Hunters' wallets do contain a complex of symbolic material—red medicines, magic bullets to kill were-lions, the incisor tooth of a dead hunter who was an ancestor (pp. 177–78)—and Turner's scheme of dominant and instrumental symbols (1967: 30–32), with their opposing ideological and sensory poles, reflects well how this domain of the Ndembu world is actualized. In fact, Turner focuses more on aspects of ritual media than most other ethnographers, which, given the turn in his later work (1985, 1986) toward an anthropology of experience—with its emphasis on performance—makes the title of his book doubly ironic.

But what Turner cannot get to through his symbolic analyses, regardless of their virtuosity, is the phenomenal surface of things, where understanding initially unfolds. Searching deeper and deeper into cultural symbols, peeling off layers of interconnected meaning, is a metaphor for going the wrong direction. Instead, we need initially to move farther and farther out into a phenomenology of what is given first. For the Ndembu, the phenomenal surface of things—that which is given first and foremost—is musical experience. There is a reason why they call their rituals of affliction "drums."

Ng'oma, the Ndembu word for drum, means much more than merely a particular kind of membranophone. Indeed, we have no gloss that comes close to conveying adequately the fullness of its associations and meanings. For scholars such as John Janzen (1992), this term is a "proto-Bantu cognate" that speaks of an ancient healing institution found throughout central and southern Africa.[6] For the purposes of this book, it points to the long history and importance of musical experience in African diagnostics and therapeutics.

Musical performance in rituals of affliction like those found among the Ndembu and the Tumbuka is not ancillary to the proceedings. For much of the ritual time, it *is* the proceedings. In order to describe the phenomenological surface of these kinds of healing rituals and thus gain an ontological insight into the phenomenon under investigation, one must delve further into the musical, or else risk mistaking partial descriptions for more complete ones.

Even a researcher such as Bruce Kapferer (1983, 1986), who has dealt extensively with aesthetic forms in rituals of healing, stops at what seems to be the wall of musical description. Drumming in Sinhalese exorcism, as in Ndembu rituals of affliction, is a prominent feature of the soundscape, but, like Turner, Kapferer fails to provide any meaningful music-specific description. He tells us that drumming is constituted from a combination of five basic sounds, which are equivalent to the five elemental substances of all matter (1983: 188). He does not tell us, however, what these five sounds are, as he undoubtedly would if these were five basic plants or animals, for example. Identification of symbolic referents seems to be standard practice for most domains; music is a glaring exception.

In some ways this lack of ethnographic material on music is even more frustrating in Kapferer's work than it is in Turner's, because Kapferer brings into bold relief the significance of musical phenomena in Sinhalese exorcism: "In the music and dance of exorcism, both deities and demons are constituted of the same fundamental units of sound and gesture. They are made coexistent in the single and continuous flowing motion of music and dance" (1986: 199). Moreover, "the deity can emerge from a rhythmic recombination of sounds evocative of demons but equally, through a quick combinational change, the music can revert to the demonic" (1983: 188). Kapferer seems to be saying that the demons and deities that populate the world of Sinhalese Buddhism exist in the world of exorcism as musical sound—not sound as a symbol of these beings, but these beings literally manifested as music. If demons and deities are indeed combinations and recombinations of the same basic sonic material, then a description of this material is not secondary, but essential.

For Kapferer (1986: 202), music and dance are aesthetic forms capable of "structuring the structure" of ritual. To investigate them as lived experience is to begin to uncover the ontological meaning of ritual. I take Kapferer literally when he states that "music and dance have their meaning constituted in the directly revealed experience of them" (1983: 181). For Sinhalese exorcism, as for Tumbuka healing, it is nothing less than a phenomenological turn *to the things themselves*. Music in these situations is a core experience, perhaps even a root paradigm in Turner's sense, for it structures clinical reality in all its immediacy. To forsake the reality of the musical in rituals of transformation such as those found in Ndembu cults of affliction, Tumbuka healing, or Sinhalese exorcism is to render silent the very essentials of the phenomenon under investigation.

Tumbuka Healing

For the Tumbuka-speaking peoples of northern Malawi, musical experience is the structural nexus where healer, patient, and spirit meet. A structural nexus draws phenomena within its *presence*. It structures the "qualitatively determined reality that constitutes lived experience" (Dilthey 1985: 226). The sound of the *ng'oma* drum invoking the rhythmic mode particular to a spirit, the clapping of the choir (*kwaya*), call and response singing, the sound of trance dancing, the jangle of tin belts and iron anklets—these are not epiphenomena, something that accompanies other, more important ritual activities, but the very substance of a sacred clinical reality. This aspect of Tumbuka life—the sheer intensity of musical experience in a clinical setting—is the connecting thread that runs throughout this book.

To approach such phenomena from an analytical model—one that inherently reduces experience to a reflected and sometimes deflected synthesis—is insufficient to adequately grasp and deal with the musical reality encountered in the temple of a Tumbuka healer. It is phenomenology that must serve the purpose, a phenomenology that seeks its ground in specific lifeworlds: thus, ethnography. And if ethnography, then the lived experience of research is essential to understanding. Specificity is no hindrance here, no constraining and limiting factor; it is the locus of concrete possibilities.

The essential question is not what *is* this musical experience, but how is this musical experience possible? To answer this kind of question demands an ethnography that is itself phenomenological. Such a phenomenology of musical experience—by its very nature an ethnomusicology—lies not in a "theory of the real" (Heidegger 1977: 157) but in the possibilities of an event, where tradition unfolds. To investigate possibilities—as opposed to actualities—requires participation and openness, not manipulation and control; experience, not knowledge; dialectic, not methodology (Palmer 1969: 215). Essentially, it requires *doing phenomenology*.[7]

ACKNOWLEDGMENTS

All the old men begin at the beginning.
—MAYA DEREN, *DIVINE HORSEMEN:*
THE LIVING GODS OF HAITI

An ethnography—unlike the myths of old men—never really begins at the beginning. Ethnographers always find themselves already in a situation, and all situations have a history. This is not to deny myths a history, as some structuralist interpretations would have it, but rather to remember that all ethnography, by its very nature, is localized.

This book is the final act of a project that started in 1986 while I was teaching at the University of Malawi. In the interim—a return to the United States, then a return to Malawi in 1987 under a Fulbright research grant—the book has gone through several transformations. Many people have helped along the way, both in Africa and in the United States, and to each one I owe a debt. Part of this debt is being repaid in the fact of this book's existence. But part needs to be repaid with more specificity.

I would like to thank Barbara Lundquist, who was responsible for getting me to Malawi in the first place and for putting me in the good hands of Mitch Strumph. In Malawi, Mitch eased my path in ways too numerous to mention. While I was in the North, the home of Mupha Shumba and his family provided a welcome respite from my work. I would also like to acknowledge the Centre for Social Research in Malawi for graciously extending me an affiliation as a research fellow.

In one incarnation this book was a dissertation, and grateful appreciation goes to my doctoral committee—Ter Ellingson, Chris Waterman, Simon Ottenberg, Barbara Lundquist, and Carol Eastman. All of them have been important and valued teachers. The main debt for this book, however, is owed to Ter Ellingson. While maintaining the standard disclaimer—whatever shortcomings the present work has are indeed my own—it is largely through his suggestions, criticisms, and encouragement that this work is in its present form.

To my wife, Elise, a thank-you is insufficient to express my appreciation for your being there throughout this long process. To my daughter, Sophia, I ask for your understanding in the years to come for my sometimes not being there.

Finally, to write these last words, and thus both finish and begin this book at the same time, calls for a "paying of respects to the ancestors," as the Tumbuka would put it. Paying respects always begins with an apology to those who have departed—to Sipho, my research assistant, who, tragically, died at the age of thirty; to Chikanga, *nchimi ya uchimi*, the healer of healers, who I thought would live to an old age of biblical proportions; to my father, who died long before; and to my grandmother, who gave me the gift of music—*pepani, pepani.*

I conclude by paying respects to the *nchimi*—Chikanje, Chikanga, Edita, Lußemba, Mseka, Mulaula, Muswahili, and Ziloya—the dancing prophets of Malawi, who opened up their world and invited me in. The debt I owe you cannot be repaid, only carried forward in this book.

NOTE ON

ORTHOGRAPHY

The Tumbuka language can be read phonetically with little difficulty using standard English pronunciation. All syllables end in a vowel, with a stress on the penultimate syllable. Tumbuka speakers use two consonant forms not generally found in English. Greek beta (β), following IPA usage, represents a voiced bilabial fricative (open "b") pronounced somewhere between "w" and "v." In other works this sound is represented as either a circumflexed "ŵ" (Young 1932a), or the symbol "v" (Turner 1952; International African Institute 1930). "Ng'" denotes a nasalized velar stop, as in the sound "ng" in "singing." Although this sound is found in English, it does not appear at the beginning of words as in chiTumbuka.

For the names of ethnic groups such as the Bemba and Biza, I am following stylistic convention by using Roman "B" to represent the voiced bilabial fricative used in chiTumbuka. When reference is made to these groups as spirit types (e.g., *ßaßemba, ßaßiza*), the "ß" symbol is retained, reflecting Tumbuka pronunciation.

Ethnography as Possibility

Higher than actuality stands possibility.
—MARTIN HEIDEGGER,
BEING AND TIME

Writing an ethnography often has more to do with what to leave out than with what to put in. Ethnographers, to paraphrase Clifford Geertz (1986: 373), always have more experience than they know what to do with. Research is typically a messy business, and in spite of how much we sometimes try to force them, field experiences rarely fit into the neat categories of our predetermined epistemologies. The lived experience of fieldwork tends to overflow these Procrustean beds of knowledge, creating intensities that can be exhilarating and frustrating at the same time. Instead of editing out the intensities, and along with them much of the veracity of fieldwork, coming to terms with these experiences—translating the experiential into the phenomenological—is the ethnographic task at hand. Something is always lost in translation, yet this loss need not be a deficit, for what is lost says much about what remains. What remains here are the possibilities inherent in the lived experience of ethnographic research.

Ethnography as possibility precludes the investigative focus of searching for a fixed reality functioning within a social field. Neither does the "possible" dwell in an abstract, timeless structure hidden beneath the distractions of concrete tales. Ethnography as an "objective" account offered from some privileged position—regardless of the ethnographer's orientation—no longer holds sway. The mirror has long been broken (Ruby 1982); the "experimental moment" (Marcus and Fischer 1986) is no longer so experimental.

If an ethnography of the "real" is no longer tenable—or at the very least is under suspicion—then how do we translate the ethnographic field into a phenomenological writing that is not merely the reflection of our own projections masquerading as ethnographic truths? Are we doomed, ironically, to a resurrection of the Cartesian subject? In phenomenological inquiry, introspection of self-experience, regardless of how insightful, is, by itself, a blinding light. Doing phenomenology—as opposed to merely claiming one—goes beyond a naive subjectivism; it requires a reflexive engagement with *the things themselves* (Husserl 1960: 12), which are the touchstone of any phenomenological investigation. In ethnography, the things themselves call for an openness to the possibilities inherent in the field, possibilities that, by their very nature, include (and are circumscribed by) that of the ethnographer.

Whether the fact is acknowledged or ignored, ethnography always begins in the simultaneity *and historicality* of the lived experience of fieldwork—all questions are asked of someone, and all answers are embodied. I refer to the historical here not as part of a totalizing political and economic contextualization but in its phenomenological and ontological meaning as a temporality that conditions understanding. The rationalizing discourse in ethnography that brackets out this temporal dimension, that postulates a detached analytical knowledge arising from an ahistorical objective standpoint—a stance somehow outside of lived experience—conveniently overlooks the very ground from which ethnographic understanding issues forth. It is within historicality, the passage of time with all its relativizing implications, that human beings endeavor to find one another. And yet as time passes, in simultaneity we are coeval (Fabian 1983) with those with whom we live and study. It is other subjects we deal with, not objective personas; people are also gazing at us. Ethnography is constituted in the interactions and transactions of consociates—researcher and researched encountering each other face-to-face in the mundane and sometimes extra-ordinary realities of everyday life.[1]

This boundary of transactions between consociates rests in the liminal moment[2]—between tradition and possibility, between the particular and the universal—when the horizonal future plays out into the historical past. Tradition is the recurrence of the possible, not merely the handing down of ways to do things, and the possible always resides in a mode of anticipation and hence in the future.[3] Ontologically, we are always projecting our future out in front of us as a possible horizon of action, thus throwing a perspective on our past as presently experienced. Fieldwork, like all lived experience, has this quality of thrown projection. Research consociates bring their own temporal, and thus interpretive, nexus of past-present-future to events. It is there that the

ethnographic enterprise unfolds, for this temporal unfolding into experience is where meaning emerges.

Understanding at the onto-phenomenological level subsumes this
background of prior interpretation, the very prejudice that an analytical
ethnography seeks to overcome.[4] Prejudice—in Hans-Georg Gadamer's
(1976) literal sense—is not something to overcome but the essential
condition for understanding. This kind of ethnographic understanding
comes not from the encounter of a perceiving subject (ethnographer)
with the world of the "other"—a trap into which any number of writers
have fallen—but is more in the nature of what Gadamer refers to as a
fusion of horizons. In such a fusion, the lived experience of fieldwork
goes beyond an objective interrogation by an inquiring subject, as it has
so often been constructed. To quote Richard Palmer's (1969: 185) reading of Gadamer's nontranscendental hermeneutics, it is rather "a matter of placing oneself in a tradition and then in an 'event' that transmits
tradition." To question in this way is to grasp a tradition within the
realm of the everyday. In ethnographic terms, it is to hold a dialogue
with other ways of understanding the world. Phenomenologically, it is
to approach a world that is already given.

Being-There[5]

For the Tumbuka people who knew of me, I was at first merely another
in a long line of Mzungu—medical missionaries, colonialist officers,
militarists, capitalist entrepreneurs—in a word, "Europeans." Although
I did not quite fit into any of the foregoing categories—I was an anomaly, a white man who lived at a healer's compound in one of the huts
reserved for patients—initially I was, nevertheless, just one more
Mzungu to the Tumbuka.

In a similar vein, the Tumbuka were typecast for me through
my readings: a Bantu-speaking people of southeastern Africa; subsistence farmers inhabiting the "dead North," a place politically repressed
and economically ignored by the post-independence government of
President Banda (McCracken 1977; Vail and White 1989). Most importantly for my research, they were a people known throughout this
part of Africa for their powerful healers (Redmayne 1970) and strong
drummers.

The Tumbuka, however, did not fit the preconceived mold I had
shaped for them, especially concerning music. In healer's compounds,
I had not planned on hearing Top 40 South African pop music on bat-

tery-powered radios or to hear healer and patient alike refer to music of the spirits in such technological terms as the equivalent of batteries for radios (see chapter 1). There is no doubt that the Tumbuka and I were "strangers" in Alfred Schutz's (1964: 91–105) sense of the term.

As is the case for most researchers, my typicalities—those things which are "taken for granted," my "trustworthy recipes" for social action (ibid.: 95)—were fundamentally different from the typicalities of those with whom I found myself living at the beginning of my research. Simply put, the Tumbuka and I did not share an intersubjective social world of any consequence. Over an extended period of time, however—such as most fieldwork entails—one cannot help but become somewhat more "familiar." The Tumbuka and I did eventually engage certain typicalities that situated us within a field of researcher and researched, though the boundaries of who was whom were not always clear. Our typicalities were not a given but were something we built on over a period of time, both consciously and, as it turned out, unconsciously. Not only did we encounter each other face-to-face in our wakefulness, but as I learned from Tumbuka healers, we did so no less in our dreams (a theme I take up in chapter 1). Both kinds of encounters are part of the research field and worthy of our attention.

I never did, of course, completely lose my status as stranger. "Graves and reminiscences," as Schutz (1964: 97) reminds us, "can neither be transferred nor conquered." I did, however, come to experience a world with those among whom I lived, drummed, and eventually danced. It is this lifeworld that I explore in this book.

Lifeworlds are filled not with substance but with existence. To get at existence requires more than a search for objective facts to be interpreted into synthetic analyses, more than uncovering ethnographic truths from the debris of field experiences. Neither endeavor is adequate for investigating the phenomenal content of the specific lifeworld of an ethnography—and even less so when one is studying the immediacies of musical experience in a clinical context.

I am not advocating some kind of rapprochement; empathy is insufficient to the task, and rapport often succumbs to narcissism. We must be wary of ethnographic heroes (Clifford 1988) who, in transcending cultural distances, do violence to existential space. The ethnographic present demands more than Cartesian metaphysics or subjective tellings of "being there." Victor Turner and Edward Bruner (1986; Bruner 1993), in their call for an anthropology of experience, rightly warn us not to let the pendulum swing too far in the other direction and end up with stories about researchers whose subjects are merely foils for the telling of their own experience. When reflexivity falls into reminiscence, it is no longer ethnography.

The problem intensifies when we attempt to translate and thus interpret such virtuoso and potentially alienated displays of culture as dancing prophets and drummed spirits. The difficulty lies not so much in a problematic division between experience and interpretation, as Clifford (1988: 211–54) would have it, but in the symptomatic intensification of the illusion that the two are somehow separate entities, chronologically distinct. Interpretation does not arise from or flow out of experience—lived experience is, at its very inception, an interpretation. This does not mean that an ethnography of lived experience results in a free-floating analysis of psychical states and personal behaviors, all duly classified; it is, rather, an uncovering, an unconcealing of the interpretation inherent in the ethnographic situation itself.

But what do we make of worlds possessed by spirits, spirits moved by music? How do we interpret a world that is neither given nor experienced in Cartesian duality? This oppositional structure breaks down in the face of such porous corporealities as dancing prophets. There the body has an ontological status different from its status in Western conceptions of the individual, with their connotations of a bounded, delimited, and inviolate space. When Tumbuka healers dance, they reach beyond and place themselves through subject-object distinctions, into a fundamental relationship with *the things themselves.*

Tumbuka healers, in an ontological sense, dance an authentic existence, an openness to Being, which must be understood first and foremost in its existential status as a mode of being-in-the-world. In what follows, the term "mode" is to be taken not only in its general ontological meaning as a way of Being, but also in a more strictly musical sense as a tonal/rhythmic structuration. In trance dancing there is no separation between the two: lived experience *is* a musical mode of being-in-the-world.

A Phenomenology of Musical Experience

Being-in-the-world in a musical way can be a particularly powerful mode of lived experience, what Dilthey (1976) terms *Erlebnis,*[6] that which is lived through. It is a field of action before subject and object, a realm in which the world and our experience of it are given together. This does not mean that lived experiences are amorphous events, diffuse and boundless, seamlessly flowing into one another. Lived experiences are structured, with determinate beginnings and endings. The distinction is between "mere" experience, "simply the passive endurance and acceptance of events," and "an experience," which, "like a rock in a Zen sand garden, stands out from the evenness of passing hours and years" (Turner 1986: 35). *Erlebnis* carries the connotation of a framed temporal process—a "structure of experience" (Dilthey, quoted in Turner 1986: 35).

Structured experiences are never isolated affairs but are interconnected to previous experiences of the same nature. In this way *Erlebnis* transcends its temporal immediacy, each particular experience containing sedimentations of previous like experiences. Appropriately for our purposes here, Dilthey (1985: 227) uses a musical metaphor to make the point: "Lived experiences are related to each other like motifs in the andante of a symphony: they are unfolded (explication) and what has been unfolded is then recapitulated or taken together (implication). Here music expresses the form of a rich lived experience." This relational quality of lived experience does not involve reflection and representation, a conscious synthesis of past experiences, but is "a reality that manifests itself immediately, that we are reflexively aware of in its entirety" (ibid.: 224).

Repeated encounters with the music and dance of Tumbuka healing similarly coalesce into a rich lived experience, one that is manifested in its entirety immediately. Awareness of this immediacy *in its entirety* is precisely what forms the musical tradition of trance dancing in northern Malawi. This is not a matter of a subject (trancer) encountering an object (music). A musical tradition is not fixed—regardless of its degree of professed rigidity—but rather is made up of projected possibilities. Music dwells in these possibilities of *having been*.

Music is not given here as an object of reflection, something that points beyond itself. It is there in immediacy, before the distinctions—between act and content, subject and object—"that characterize representational consciousness" (Makkreel and Rodi 1989: 26). Musical experience is *reflexive*, not reflective: "There is no duality of lived experience and music, no double world, no carry-over from one into the other. Genius involves simply living in the tonal sphere as though this sphere alone existed" (Dilthey 1985: 17). Although Dilthey is discussing the genius of a "composer" in the Western art music tradition, he might as well be describing trance experience for Tumbuka healers and their patients, for it is in that experience that the "genius" of Tumbuka music is most evident. This is the genius not of an individual but of a people. For Tumbuka gathered inside a temple, making music together is an intense, intersubjective experience that brings healer, patient, and spirit into an existential immediacy unparalleled in quotidian or ritual life. Through music, with its resultant trance, Tumbuka have the possibility of experiencing the present—and thus each other—in complete "fulfillness."

This given world is not where an individual—whether ethnographer or "native"—meets tradition. Tradition is not a static construct, a thing to be met, but the liminal moment itself. Boundaries are not ideological here, they are experiential; they are not rigid but fluid possibilities. It is the possibilities inherent in the research situation that open this world to investigation—hence the ontological priority of questioning. Nowhere in Tumbuka culture are tradition and event, question and possibility transmitted more powerfully than in the drama of sickness and health—often life and death—that unfolds through music and dance in the *thempli* (temple) of an *nchimi* (lit. "prophet") healer.

Being-in-the-World

"Questioning builds a way," writes Heidegger (1977: 3). Building a way is a way of "being-in-the-world" that itself is a mode of experience which grounds understanding. Heidegger uses this hyphenated, prepositional terminology to move away from the metaphysics of interiority and point to the equiprimordiality of human Being and world—both are always given together. *Things*—both naturally occurring and humanly constructed—can be within a world, but they cannot have a world in the ontological sense of Being-there (Heidegger's *Dasein*). Only human beings can have a world in this sense. This does not mean that *Dasein* is merely a more subtle, phenomenological form of the conscious subject, a consciousness that constitutes the world. On the contrary, "consciousness always finds itself already at work in the world" (Merleau-Ponty 1962: 432). Solipsistic constructs have no claim for precisely this reason: being-in-the-world is *always a being-with others, which* by its very nature is a cultural mode of existence.

Being-in-the-world involves relationships of intention, of concern, "of meaning radiating from the only kind of being capable of grouping, relating, using, willing things" (Langan 1959: 22), that is, human beings. In a way this is all fairly obvious and seems merely to be a description of cognitive processes, but more is going on here. Being-in-the-world is fundamentally a self-interpreting activity enmeshed in those

much-cited Weberian "webs of significance." This interpretive significance is not something applied to a world, part of some superstructure
of which human beings partake, but the very essence of human existence—hence the ontological priority of culture, and thus Heidegger's
relevance to ethnography.[7] As Geertz (1973: 68) puts it, a "cultureless"
human being would not be an "intrinsically talented though unfulfilled
ape, but a wholly mindless and consequently unworkable monstrosity."
Geertz and Heidegger seem to agree that it is interpretation all the way
down. For Heidegger, however, this is not a matter of delving deeper
and deeper until finally reaching the *right* interpretation. "The only
deep interpretation . . . is that there is no deep interpretation" (Dreyfus
1991: 157).

Although parts of this world, such as kinship systems, political
economies, and aesthetic modes of production, can be classified and
studied—whether by approximating scientific methods or by turning
to interpretive strategies—being-in-the-world cannot be understood ontologically in objectivistic terms as a collection of facts to be gathered,
categorized, and analyzed or, for that matter, as a set of cultural texts
to be interpreted and rendered meaningful. There is no question that
these approaches contribute to the ethnographic enterprise, but they
are ultimately only signposts along the way. In themselves, they cannot
explicate the way of lived experience that is at the center of phenomenological ethnographic inquiry.

If we are to build a way through questioning—that is, investigating
possibilities—then Heidegger (1977: 3) advises us "to pay heed to the
way, and not to fix our attention on isolated sentences and topics." I
ask the same of readers of this book—to pay heed to the way, to understand the following ethnography as a questioning and thus as an expression of the possibilities of the *Erlebnis* of fieldwork.

Ironically, physics—that "hardest" of sciences—offers an apt metaphor for this kind of ethnomusicological inquiry. In a quantum world,
reality is filled with the in-between: "something standing in the middle
between the idea of an event and the actual event, a strange kind of
physical reality just in the middle between possibility and reality"
(Heisenberg 1958: 41). Writing ethnography is a kind of standing in the
middle. It is not the actual event but an expression of it. Similarly, it
depicts a reality that is merely one of many possibilities. My experience
of the Tumbuka had much to do with their experience of me. This
book is an ethnography of that dialectic.

To Dance and To Dream

At my last research site, the compound of a woman named Lußemba, I danced *vimbuza* for the first time. I had met Lußemba the year before and had been planning to stay with her for some time, because I wanted to include a woman healer as part of my research. In the patrilineal society of the Tumbuka, it is difficult for a woman to set up her own business, and therefore someone like Lußemba, with her own compound, is a rarity.

Lußemba is not her birth name but one the spirits conferred on her when she became an *nchimi* ("prophet"), a special class of healers among the Tumbuka. As both herbalists and diviners, *nchimi* are considered to be the most powerful of the indigenous healers of northern Malawi. Not only do they effect cures for all types of illnesses with their extensive pharmacopoeias, but they also smell out witches, neutralize witchcraft, and, most importantly, divine their patients' ills and misfortunes.

When she divines, Lußemba "dances her disease" (*kuvina nthenda*). Like all *nchimi* healers, she dances to transform an initiatory illness into a divinatory trance blessed with diagnostic power. While entranced, Lußemba divines the causality of the past and the consequences of potential futures for those who seek her help. In a health care system such as the Tumbuka's, where therapeutic intervention is based on etiology, these prophetic diagnoses are crucial to clinical efficacy.

For the past twenty years Lußemba had been practicing her healing art. She was now forty-three and divorced for the third time. It is hard for a woman to be a full-time *nchimi* and also fulfill her obligations as a Tumbuka wife. Lußemba had recently moved her compound to land that her uncle had left her. Only one building had been completed so far, but it was fairly large by Tumbuka standards. It had enough space to house Lußemba and her assistants—at that time there were three women and one young man "in training"—plus a large room for dancing *vimbuza* and receiving patients. The compound, however, was nowhere near the size of her previous *chipatala* (lit. "hospital") in Nkhata Bay on the shores of Lake Malawi. There, among the lakeshore Tonga, she was well known for her abilities as a diviner-healer, and many people sought her services. But at her current site on her uncle's land, she had yet to establish her reputation.

Lußemba's compound was located in the Henga Valley, the heart of Tumbuka country, some 100 kilometers from Nkhata Bay. The Henga is well known for its powerful healers, and early on I decided to make it the center of my research activity. Bounded by the Nyika Plateau to the west and the Vipyia Mountains in the east, it has within its borders a number of sacred geographical sites. Where the South Rukuru River turns northeast to enter the valley, there is the Njakwa Gorge, a dramatic formation of large boulders that since ancient times has been used as a place to pay respects to the *mizimu* (ancestors). Next to this gorge is Njakwa Hill, which is said to be frequented by many spirits and is regularly visited by healers searching for powerful medicines. Farther north are the Pwezi Falls, the location of an ancient and important rainmaking shrine that is still in use today.[1] The ancient sites and long history of settlement in the Henga Valley—Bantuspeakers first came there some seventeen hundred years ago,[2] accounting for the valley's abundance of ancestral spirits—along with the belief that the surrounding hills and mountains are the favorite haunts of spirits of all kinds, have imparted a kind of sacred geography to the whole valley. People from all over this part of Africa travel to the Henga and its environs in order to consult with and receive treatment from one of the many *nchimi* who live there.[3]

By moving to the Henga, Lußemba was returning to her ancestral land and, in a sense, to the wellspring of her spiritual power. It was there that she first was struck with the "disease of the prophets" (*nthenda ya uchimi*). Her symptoms included severe headaches and general body malaise, and she began having dreams of the ancestors, a sure sign of the healer's calling. Given the concentration of healers in this area, when Lußemba became sick it was fairly obvious, and not in the least unusual, that she had been stricken with the healer's disease.

The illness began while she was married to Chikanje, her first husband, an *nchimi* healer himself, who at the time was just beginning to establish his own business along the main tarmac road that cuts the Henga Valley from north to south.[4] When Lußemba didn't respond to conventional treatment, Chikanje danced the question—divined the cause of her illness—and confirmed that she was indeed afflicted with the disease of the prophets. Reluctantly, considering the problems entailed in having his spouse as a patient, Chikanje took his wife on as a *mutwasa*, a "new moon." Thus Lußemba started on the path toward becoming a prophet healer, learning about the many medicines a healer must know, about how to interpret and direct her dreams, and, above all, about how to dance her disease. These developments put a severe strain on her marriage, and within a year she and Chikanje divorced. It was shortly after the divorce that she left the Henga Valley and began her own business in Nkhata Bay.

Ten years had passed there, along with two more marriages, when Lußemba's ancestors came to her in a dream and told her to move to the land that had been left to her by her uncle. The land was not far from her first husband's compound, and given her previous history with Chikanje and her successful business in Nkhata Bay, she understandably resisted the move. But the *mizimu*, the ancestors, are demanding, and if one does not obey their wishes then one risks illness or worse (see chapter 2). Shortly after this dream, Lußemba became ill—she felt "a big lump" in her stomach that was "pulling her heart," making it difficult to breathe—and had to cease her practice. She quickly realized that the only road to recovery was the road to her ancestral home.

When I arrived at Lußemba's compound, her illness had stabilized, but she was still subject to serious relapses, sometimes lasting for days. Although she had yet to establish herself firmly as an *nchimi* at her new location, within a relatively short time she had already begun to attract a substantial following.

About a week after I settled in, I approached Lußemba about the possibility of dancing. For the past year I had been spending at least two and often three nights a week attending all-night sessions of *vimbuza* dancing. At last I wanted to try "doing" what I had been watching. It was not as though I had not been an active participant in *vimbuza* before this: by the time I asked to dance, I had learned enough drumming to be able to play for the spirits, had taken dream medicine to be able to "see" in my dreams, had had those dreams interpreted by *nchimi* as portents for the future and as indicators of witch activity by locals, had been given special *mboni* beads to wear around my wrist to serve as a "telephone to the spirits," and, in general, was considered by most Tumbuka to be someone who was afflicted by the spirits.

For the most part, my transactions with the Tumbuka I lived and worked with were based on their perception of me as an Mzungu, a European, who was learning to become an *nchimi*, a dancing prophet. Most villagers believed that I, too, had the "disease of the prophets" and was living in the compounds of *nchimi* in order to learn their healing art. It was generally assumed that I would go back to America and start my own "business." By dancing *vimbuza* that night, I was merely confirming the fact.

Nchimi such as Lußemba were well aware of my research intentions but nonetheless often pushed me in the direction of becoming a healer. On more than one occasion they interpreted events as signs of the power of my ancestors, of the spirits inside me, and of their desire that I learn the "business" of *nchimi*. On my part, I neither promoted nor discouraged this perception, but accepted events as they unfolded.

Until I came to Lußemba's, I had never danced, though for some time I had been interested in trying. For whatever reasons, before my arrival at Lußemba's the circumstances had never seemed right. Perhaps by the time I was at her compound, I felt my position in the community of healers was secure, and since this was my last research stay, I had nothing to lose. I had not reached the decision to dance prior to my arrival, but once at Lußemba's, I made a firm commitment to myself that I would dance *vimbuza*.

Vimbuza—a multivocal term, a complex of meanings and references—encompasses a class of spirits, the illnesses they cause, and the music and dance used to treat the illnesses. As spirit, *vimbuza* is the numinous energy of foreign peoples and wild animals; as illness, it is both a spirit affliction and an initiatory sickness; as musical experience, it is a mode of trance. For patients possessed by *vimbuza* spirits, trance dancing is a cooling therapy; for adepts, it is the means for transforming a disease into a vocation; and for healers, it is the source of an energizing heat that fuels the divination trance. Although I was neither afflicted by the spirits nor about to divine anything, when I approached Lußemba about dancing, she was receptive to the idea and arranged for me to dance that night.

Word travels fast in the North, and by sunset a good-sized crowd had gathered at Lußemba's to watch the Mzungu dance *vimbuza*. I started to have second thoughts about what I was doing, but in the name of research I decided to swallow my pride, let go of my inhibitions, and participate in the dance as fully as possible, even if it meant making a fool of myself. This was a distinct possibility, consider that I had never tried to dance *vimbuza* before and had no idea exactly what I was going to do.

I had heard and seen more than enough *vimbuza*, however, to know the progression of events and generally what kind of behavior was expected from a dancer. After the drums had been tuned by being heated over an outside fire and then brought inside the main building, a few songs were raised by women in the crowd. As these songs were sung, and as the master drum, *ng'oma*, began to sound the spirit-specific rhythmic mode of one of the *vimbuza* spirits, several of Lußemba's assistants began to dress me in the standard *vimbuza* dance outfit. This kit consists of a number of pieces of dangling metal (idiophones) wrapped around the waist and legs, and a skirt, *mazamba*, made out of either animal skins or cloth that has been cut into many thin strips. The dance paraphernalia both enhances the visual movement of the dance (the skirt sways to the movement of the hips) and transforms this movement into sound through the strategic placement of the idiophones. Iron jingles (*nyisi*) are strapped around the ankles, which gives sound to the rhythmic movement of the feet, and a belt (*mang'wanda*) with many triangular pieces of folded tin hanging from it is worn around the waist. When the hips are shaken, which is the central movement of most *vimbuza* dances, the *mang'wanda* sounds, adding a loud and distinctive timbre to the overall musical texture. In essence, the dancer's body, through these idiophones, is transformed into a musical instrument. This aspect of music making in rituals of affliction such as *vimbuza* has been virtually ignored by ethnographers—including ethnomusicologists—even though it is often an essential part of the performance matrix—but more about this later.

I did not possess a healer's special dress—the most common form being a short red skirt and a top embroidered with white crosses—so I improvised as best I could. Wearing red gym shorts, a black tank top, and the full *vimbuza* kit, I must have been quite a sight. I sat down in front of the drums with my legs outstretched before me, as I had seen so many other patients do, and waited for the music to heat up the spirits.

From the very beginning of this "fieldwork exercise," I held no illusions that the *vimbuza* spirits would actually heat up and possess me. It was not that I questioned the phenomenon of possession by the *vimbuza* spirits, for I had been a witness to that experience, but rather that I questioned what kind of access I could have to this world while still carrying a considerable load of my own cultural baggage. I couldn't

imagine letting go of my ego to the extent necessary to be able to let
the *vimbuza* in. My goal was not to become possessed but to approach
the experience as an opportunity to encounter at least some of the
physical manifestations of dancing *vimbuza*. It had become increasingly clear to me during my research that in order to gain a better
understanding of this bodily mode of awareness, I must somehow enter
into—as best I could given my limitations as researcher—the physical
reality of this danced experience.

As I sat in front of the drums, I felt a bit nervous, not so much
about dancing in front of so many people—that was a given—but about
the possibility that somehow I would be surprised and in fact the *vimbuza* would come. Somehow, having been immersed in the healing
culture of *vimbuza* for the past year, I might have been unconsciously
converted to a new way of seeing—or, more appropriately for *vimbuza*,
hearing—a new way of being-in-the-world that included possession by
the *vimbuza*. Like Maya Deren (1953: 259–60), in her experience with
the *loa*, I might begin to feel my body sink into the music. The cultural
expectations generated by the context of the performance in which I
found myself were so strong that my skepticism about possession by
the *vimbuza* was weakened.

I had been aware of the considerable pressure, both covert and
overt, applied to new patients in these situations to fulfill cultural expectations of becoming possessed. But to experience these pressures
through the filter of my own experience gave them an immediacy and
reality that they had lacked in my speculations about the experiences
of others. There were well over one hundred people crammed into the
thempli that night, and as is the case with any new patient, I was the
focus of this focused gathering (to use Goffman's [1961] terminology of
the everyday). Regardless of what I thought I was doing at the time,
people were singing, clapping, and drumming for the explicit purpose
of heating the spirits within me.

As I listened to the music, I concentrated my attention on the
drums. I tried to recapture previous moments when, late at night, the
drumming seemed to transcend its existential space. At those times,
distinctions between subject and object began to break down. If I let
myself become immersed in the sound of the drums, in the metrical
shifting of two- and three-beat rhythmic configurations (see chapter 5),
the drumming would sound close to my ears. Within that experience,
I would no longer be able to tell whether the sound was coming from
inside or outside of my head. But as I listened, nothing changed. Waiting
for the spirits, obviously, was going to be a fruitless gesture, and al-

though it wasn't exactly a Kierkegaardian leap of faith, it was with a certain amount of belief that I stood up to dance.

The majority of *vimbuza* dances are centered on a core kinesthetic movement that involves shaking the hips in rhythmic synchroneity with the lead drumming. The purpose of this dance movement does not seem to be purely dance oriented, for it is aimed partly at sounding the *mang'wanda* idiophones that are tied around the waist—hence my earlier designation of the human body as musical instrument. This hip shaking is usually done in a stationary position, with the balls of both feet in contact with the ground while the heels move up and down in time to the drums. The heel movement, of course, causes the *nyisi* (ankle jingles) to sound.

My first attempts at dancing were based on this core movement. To my surprise, and I believe to the surprise of most people in attendance, I began giving a fairly credible performance of the basic *vimbuza* dance. Two things struck me almost immediately: dancing *vimbuza* was physically taxing, and it felt good to dance. When I got my hips to synchronize with the basic six-pulse pattern of the drums, I felt as if the drums were moving my hips for me. Although the dancing was physically exhausting, it nevertheless seemed effortless while I was doing it.

As I gained some confidence in my dancing ability, I began to try different styles that related to different types of *vimbuza* spirits. Often a *vimbuza* dancer will walk over to the master drum and begin playing the rhythmic signature of the spirit that wants to dance next. Trying to "act" in accordance with standard *vimbuza* behavior, I went over to the *ng'oma* and began playing the distinctive rhythmic motto for *vyanusi* (see chapter 5), one of the most important of the *vimbuza* spirits. By playing this rhythmic motto, I was doing more than indicating a spirit type; I was calling forth an entire historical field of action for the Tumbuka.

Vyanusi is the spirit of Ngoni warriors, an Nguni-speaking people from the Natal region of South Africa who invaded Malawi in the nineteenth century.[5] They were warrior herders who left their homeland, fleeing the upheavals caused by Shaka, the military chief who forged the Zulu nation. The nineteenth century was a period of turmoil throughout this part of Africa, with the Ngoni raiding and conquering peoples as they made their way to the northern region of Malawi, where they eventually subjugated most of the Tumbuka population.[6] There they found good pasture for their cattle and began to build permanent villages. But as so often happens with conquering peoples, as time passed the Ngoni were gradually incorporated into the local traditions.

Today, Ngoni culture has, for the most part, disappeared in the Henga Valley.[7] Much of what remains is manifested through the *vyanusi* spirits.

When *vyanusi* possesses someone, the person dances in *vyanusi* style, which is modeled loosely on the dances that were performed by Ngoni warriors in the royal cattle kräal (Friedson 1994a). Before giving a verbal report to the paramount chief on the details of a battle, warriors would enter the kräal and recount their heroic deeds through the *ingoma* dance. Only those who had entered the enemy's stockade or who had killed a man were allowed to dance. Often warriors would receive promotions or rewards based on their dancing.

As I played the rhythmic signature of *vyanusi* on the *ng'oma* drum, and as the *mphiningu* supporting drum joined in with its characteristic invariant rhythmic pattern, the women began to raise one of the *vyanusi* songs. Typical of these songs, it was sung in chiNgoni, a language virtually no one could speak any longer, and so no one understood the meaning of the words they were singing:

> *Mugwede unandi we*
> *Unandi Mugwede uyasula mazilikani*
> *unandi Mugwede*

Content in *vimbuza* songs for the most part—and despite the emphasis and importance given to the texts of songs by folklorists, anthropologists, and historians—is not nearly so important to the Tumbuka as the fact of singing, of making music together, something I deal with in more detail later.

It was only just before I left the field that I met one of Lußemba's "elder fathers" (uncle), a wizened old Ngoni man in his late eighties or early nineties, who could translate the song. He had the traditional elongated earlobes that were physical markers of Ngoni men who had worn large beads of ivory wedged into holes slit in their ears. When I played him the song on my tape recorder, he immediately recognized it and explained:

> solo *Mugwede unandi we*
> Mugwede is too much.

> chorus *Unandi Mugwede uyasula mazilikani unandi Mugwede*
> Mugwede troubles the white soldiers too much.

Mugwede was a famous *isanusi*, an Ngoni witchsmeller and diviner. The name *vyanusi* is taken from this chiNgoni word, and there is a rich association *nchimi* make with the divinatory powers of these Ngoni diviner-healers.

It seems that in the 1920s, the British commissioner for the North, a Mr. MacDonald, decided to expose the "witchdoctors" in his district as frauds. He called all of them together at his station and asked them to explain the blood on his front door and what had happened to his money that was missing. As part of their duties as diviners, *izanusi* (plural of *isanusi)* were often called on to find lost or stolen objects. Of all the *izanusi* gathered, only Mugwede correctly divined that the commissioner himself had put the blood of a goat on the door and hidden a coin in his wife's shoe. It is said that all the other *izanusi* were banned from practicing their vocation, but not Mugwede, who on that day was "too much."

As the *kwaya* ("choir," a term taken from the church), sang about Mugwede and the drummers sounded the mode of *vyanusi*, I was handed a short stabbing spear, which is symbolic of the Ngoni and, in a deeper sense, of the upheavals of all of southern Africa resulting from Shaka's conquests.[8] I had seen this dance performed many times and had a fairly good idea of what to do. As I danced *vyanusi* and stabbed at the air with the spear, I caused quite a sensation in the crowd. There was much ululation (*nthunguru*) from the women and good-natured laughter from the men. From this point onward, there was a palpable rise in the excitement level inside the *thempli*.

About half an hour into the dance, the special *nkufi* clapping was performed for me.[9] Clapping in African music is much more than merely an accompaniment to singing; in *vimbuza* it is further differentiated into particular styles that have symbolic import. When singing, most people clap with their hands held flat and parallel to each other. This is generally referred to as *mapi*. For clapping in the *nkufi* style, the hands are cupped and held at a 90-degree angle to each other. This clapping style is traditionally done to pay respects to chiefs and other important personages, and it can be found throughout central, southern, and southeastern Africa (see Wills 1985: 24, 71). In the context of *vimbuza*, it is used to pay respects to the spirits.

While I was dancing, two of Lußemba's assistants grabbed my hands and pulled me down to the floor. The assistants and Lußemba gathered around me and began to clap in the *nkufi* style in order to talk to the spirits within me. Clapping in a slow, steady rhythm, Lußemba apologized to the spirits:

> *Pepani, pepani*
> Sorry, sorry,
> *Nthenda ya mphepo zinai*
> Disease of the four winds.

As is always done, she asked them not to come harshly but to be gentle. Lußemba told them that they should not "bind the feet" but feel free "to come play with their children." Then, following standard procedure, as an offering to the spirits, a silver coin was placed in a plate of maize flour (*ufu*), which was then covered with another plate that had a red cross painted on it.[10] These plates are called *mboni* (lit. "witness"), which is also the name for the beads healers wear around their wrists to keep open the lines of communication to the spirit world. As the plates were taken away, a new song was raised, and I began to dance again.

People were singing about the *vimbuza umphanda*, a spirit from Zambia:

> solo *ßanyimirachi morozi*
> Why have you dug me [wild tree]?
> *ndiyo mphanda ßaliranga*
> That's the *mphanda* you were crying for.

> chorus *Hele yayi, Zanga undirye*
> Hele yayi, come and eat me.

This song is very old (*kale chomeni*), and no one was really sure what it meant. Some Tumbuka thought that eating the *mphanda* might be about possession by the *umphanda* spirits, while others suggested that the song was about a medicine for this kind of spirit possession.[11] Once again, the lyrical content and meaning of *vimbuza* songs do not seem to be a main focus for those who are singing.

The dance of this *vimbuza* is fairly complicated and involves a crossing of the feet. Although I had seen the dance many times before, I was unsure whether I could perform it. After standing up from the *nkufi*, however, I found myself doing the dance without really thinking about it. My body just sort of took over and followed the distinct rhythmic motto of the *umphanda* spirits (see appendix B). I can remember dancing and feeling that my perception was becoming detached from my body. It was almost as if I were watching someone else dance.

When reflecting back upon dancing *umphanda*, it occurred to me that I perhaps reflexively experienced something similar to the way Tumbuka learn to dance *vimbuza*. In a way, no one *learns* to dance *vimbuza* in that no one practices dancing or has someone show him or her how to do it. Children may play at being possessed and simulate the *vimbuza* dance, which may be construed as a kind of practice, but there is no systematic training involved in *vimbuza*. When you become possessed, you dance. In my case, I believe it was a matter of having watched this dance for over a year and, through a process of osmosis, having learned how to do it without rehearsal. From the time they are babies, most Tumbuka are exposed to the world of *vimbuza*, which is simply a part of everyday life. By the time they are adults, Tumbuka are ready to participate fully in this world without the benefit or need of "practice," itself a Western concept not applicable to much African performance.

In the context of *vimbuza* dancing, competence in performance needs to be understood as part of an everyday, generalized, background understanding. And although the content of this everyday background is very different from that of everyday life in the Western postindustrial world, it nevertheless has the same kind of ontological status and function. The difference, of course, is in the kind of world that it reveals.

For the next hour I shifted back and forth between several different kinds of *vimbuza* dance, until I became so exhausted I could no longer stand, let alone continue to dance. The *vimbuza* kit was removed and I sat down in the chair next to Lußemba, exhausted, drenched in sweat, but feeling a calmness that I had never felt before. Dancing *vimbuza* was an intense, cathartic experience that had left me physically and emotionally drained.

As I sat there, I became aware that my internal dialogue, that voice of consciousness, had stopped. My conscious awareness seemed to be much more diffused throughout my entire body, as opposed to being centered in my head. It seems that my physical body had experienced *vimbuza* as much as my thinking self had, if not more. But this is a way of interpreting experience which assumes that the mind and body are somehow separate entities, and implicit in this assumption is the priority of the mind over the body. If anything—at least according to Merleau-Ponty's (1962) phenomenology—in actuality the body always has priority, for conscious awareness comes out of this realm of existence. Nevertheless, for those of us inculcated in the metaphysics of a split between mind and body, it is hard *not* to interpret experience in these terms. I often—though not always—experience myself as a thinking subject. On the night I danced *vimbuza*, however, I experienced not so much the absence of this phenomenon but its transformation.

After I danced, several other people donned the *vimbuza* kit and danced to cool the *vimbuza* spirits inside them. The whole session lasted until the early morning hours, when people left to return to their home villages or found places to sleep at the compound until daylight. I returned to my room, looking forward to a restful sleep.

As I was about to go to sleep, Lußemba unexpectedly came into my room, handed me the *mboni* plates with the flour and coin in them, and instructed me to put them under my pillow. She told me that by sleeping with the plates beneath my head, I would have powerful dreams, which I should be sure to remember in order to tell her the next day. That night I had a dream I did not understand but which I now believe was pointing toward the reality of the *vimbuza*—a reality I did not realize until well after I had returned to the United States.

The dream had no plot per se, only one concentrated action, but it was packed with emotional content. In the dream I am standing in a featureless landscape, an unformed darkness. Someone comes up behind me, someone I can't see, and whispers in my ear one word, "Mulaula," the name of a *vimbuza* spirit from the eastern shores of Lake Malawi and also the name of one of the most famous *nchimi* in the North. The instant this name is whispered, my whole body seems to leap out in front of me. It is as if my body space is elastic, with the front part stretching outward and upward.[12] Along with the expansion of my body, I feel a tremendous exhilaration. I immediately woke up, feeling this exhilaration but also feeling somewhat anxious, as if I were about to lose part of myself.

The next morning I told Lußemba my dream. She smiled and told me it was the *vimbuza*, that this was the way the spirits came. I wasn't quite sure what she meant, but I had learned to accept an *nchimi*'s explanation at face value. For the next several days I found myself returning frequently to the scene in my dream and puzzling over what it had meant.

The dream, for me, was an expression of unconscious contents in symbolic form, but at the time, nothing came to me about what those contents were or what meaning was embedded in the symbols. Of course, many psychoanalytical interpretations could be read into the dream—inflation of the ego, for one—which may well have been applicable. But whether applicable or not, they would still be unintelligible within the *vimbuza* idiom. I wasn't sure of the significance of the dream, but what did stay with me was the vivid memory of the intense feeling of exhilaration and anxiety I had felt.

For Lußemba, my dream was not a symbolic process but an actual encounter with the *vimbuza*. Dreams do not have the same ontological status for the Tumbuka that they have for those of us in the West whose perceptions of the psyche have been shaped by depth psychologies. For the Tumbuka, dreams are *real*. When a Tumbuka dreams of a visit from his dead grandfather or of traveling to a neighboring village, or when an *nchimi* dreams of going into the bush to be shown medicinal herbs by an ancestor, it is not taken as a fiction of the mind but as a reality of the soul. According to the Tumbuka, a person has multiple souls, some of which are detachable from the physical body. One of these souls, a kind of dream soul, can leave the body through the ear when a person is asleep and can travel about.[13] This is why one must be careful when waking someone up. If the soul hasn't returned before the person awakes, the person could die or become seriously ill. For the Tumbuka, there is no sharp demarcation between the reality of waking consciousness and the reality of dreams. Events in both realms have the same status of reality.

Having the same status does not mean, however, that they share the same reality. The Tumbuka are not lost in a Lévy-Bruhlian *participation mystique* (1923). There is no question that they clearly differentiate between the reality of waking consciousness and that of dreams. They do not, however, dichotomize the two into real and unreal (hallucinatory phenomena), as we tend to do in the West. For the Tumbuka, these two realities have an equal ontological status.

In this context, someone really did speak the name Mulaula, and my body actually did begin to expand. I eventually began to realize that what Lußemba was telling me was that the meaning of the dream was not hidden in some deep symbolic content but was, in a sense, on the phenomenal surface of the dream, in the reality of the action. And when I finally began to think of the dream in those terms—which is not a psychological thinking but essentially a phenomenological one—the meaning of the dream became clear to me, at least within the confines of *vimbuza*.

In the dream, the whisperings of the invisible *vimbuza* caused my "self" to expand, creating a space within me, an opening, a clearing. Significantly, it was the *sound* of the word Mulaula that caused this expansion. Reflecting on this experience now, I believe that the dream was an expression of the dynamics of spirit possession. In order to be possessed by the *vimbuza* spirits, there must be a space created in oneself in order to accommodate the possession. The logic of the trance of spirit possession dictates that another personality takes over the will, and for this to be accomplished, I realized, there must be an opening, or clearing, of interior space in oneself to accommodate the new spirit personality. In other words, I had to be willing to displace myself, my ego consciousness, and the space created by this sacrifice would be filled by the *vimbuza*.[14] The phenomenon of spirit possession is an opening of interior space: the resulting possession is a being-in-it. In *vimbuza*, this space is projected through musical means.

During my stay at Lußemba's, I had several more of these dreams. In each dream I seemed to be expanding a little further, letting go a little more, but also becoming more concerned about what was going on. I had only a short time left in the field, and one day I found myself deciding that my research was becoming redundant and I had more than enough material to serve my purposes, and therefore it was time to leave. Perhaps the *vimbuza* were becoming too much of a reality for me, and subconsciously I decided I needed to distance myself from the situation in order to maintain my balance as a researcher—to remain a participant-observer and not become wholly immersed in the first part of the equation.

I often think now that eventually, if I had stayed longer at Lußemba's, one night when I danced I would have taken the final step of letting go, and the *vimbuza* would have entered. The thought has crossed my mind lately, however, that perhaps this already had happened the first night I danced, but I was unaware of the new reality I had encountered.

Kulota/*To Dream*

My dreaming and dancing, of course, were not the dreaming and dancing of an *nchimi* healer. For an *nchimi* like Lußemba, to dream is to communicate with the ancestral *mizimu* spirits, and to dance *vimbuza* is to enter a divinatory trance where potential futures are revealed and the causality of the past is disclosed. The power of a healer rests in this ability to gain access to, and maintain contact with, the invisible world of the spirits. To dream and to dance are essential to an *nchimi*'s healing art.

Every Wednesday and Saturday night, Lußemba dances *vimbuza* at her compound in order to "heat" (*kutukizga*) her spirits (fig. 1). For

Fig. 1. Lußemba dancing *vimbuza* for divination

nchimi, musical heat has alchemical-like abilities in its power to transform phenomenal reality. It is in the act of dancing *vimbuza* that the ancestral *mizimu* and foreign *vimbuza* spirits are "melded together" (the term the Tumbuka use), creating the necessary conditions for an *nchimi* to "see" (*kuwona*).[15] Through the divination trance, Lußemba diagnoses the illnesses of patients who have come to her for help, and most importantly, she determines the causes of those illnesses—in other words, establishes etiologies. In the indigenous health care system of the Tumbuka, therapeutic intervention is shaped by the discovery of which pathogenic agent is responsible for the illness (see chapter 2).

During the day, before a session of *vimbuza* dancing, Lußemba spends some time sleeping in order to dream about what will happen that night. According to Lußemba, dreaming is not something that *she* does, it is something done by the *mizimu:* "Everyone has mizimu because you dream—that's what makes you dream. What makes me see in dreams of home is the mizimu goes there and brings me pictures of what is there." Dreams confirm the reality of the *mizimu,* and the *mizimu* confirm the reality of dreams.

From the very beginning of an *nchimi's* career, dreams play an important role. Special dreams about the ancestors differentiate *nchimi* from ordinary Tumbuka afflicted by the spirits and are one of the first signs that a person has been called by the spirits to become a healer. Sometimes these dreams are straightforward: Lußemba's *mizimu* simply came to her in a dream and told her she would become an *nchimi.* But sometimes these initial dreams can be extraordinary, having an almost visionary or religious quality about them. Such was the case with Mulaula, the healer whose name was whispered in my dream.

When Mulaula was nineteen he died for the first time. This wasn't a complete death but a "small death," or what we would call a coma. One morning on his way to school he unwittingly stepped over *nyanga* (witch medicine) hidden at a crossroads. By the time he reached school he was very ill, and by the time his father arrived to take him home he was already in a coma. During this small death, Mulaula relates, he had the following vision/dream:

> A white dove came from the direction of the sunrise, right from the rays. When it got close its wings changed into the hands of a person. A cloud came and covered the dove, and when the cloud opened there was a man dressed in white robes. The cloud closed again and when it opened a second time, once again there was a dove. A third time the cloud closed, and when it opened the man reappeared but this time he was standing over my head. He turned back into a dove and flew away west.

When I asked Mulaula what this dream meant, he explained that it was his first encounter with the *mizimu,* the ancestors, who were calling him to become an *nchimi.*

Shortly after this dream, Mulaula "died" again and had a second vision: "Upstairs in a house, doves were nested in reeds. The doves had necks like sheep." This dream was, for Mulaula, a further indication that he was to be an "mzimu man" (*mzimu* is the singular of *mizimu*)—in other words, a prophet healer.

If doves, sheep, and white-robed men suggest a kind of biblical imagery, it is no coincidence. Christianity, which missionaries introduced to northern Malawi over a century ago, is now a deep part of Tumbuka culture. Virtually all Tumbuka believe in the Father, the Son, and the Holy Ghost, in an everlasting heavenly peace for the righteous, and in damnation in hell for the wicked. Although these beliefs are now universal among the Tumbuka, their application to, and their degree of syncretism with, an indigenous Tumbuka worldview is not uniform. Religious syncretism operates along a continuum from the total rejection of traditional beliefs by conservative members of the Church of Central African Presbyterian (CCAP) to the highly syncretic models professed by most *nchimi*. The word *nchimi*, in fact, is glossed as "prophet" in the chiTumbuka translation of the Bible, and healers make a direct connection between themselves and the biblical prophets.[16] *Nchimi* are the ones who are carrying on the tradition of the Old Testament prophets.[17]

Mulaula certainly sees himself this way, and so do many of the people who come to him for help. He was well known beyond the confines of the Henga Valley as a powerful healer, for he was the heir apparent to Nchimi Chikanga, *nchimi ya uchimi*, the prophet of prophets, who for the past thirty years had been the most famous and feared healer and witchfinder in this part of Africa. His *chipatala* (hospital) is even labeled on the official Malawian map of the North (Government of Malawi 1983: map 7).

When I was in the North, Chikanga had just returned from having been exiled for seven years by the central government to the southern city of Blantyre. The authorities had been concerned that he was acquiring too much power, and there were persistent rumors that rebels were infiltrating from the north and west through his compound. Chikanga had literally become a one-man antiwitchcraft movement—seven thousand people had come to see him in one day alone when he traveled to Zimbabwe—and the last thing President Banda's government wanted was another Alice Lenshina, a prophet and witchfinder who had started a virtual revolution in Zambia (van Binsbergen 1981). Chikanga had been back in the Henga Valley for only a month when I first met him, but already thousands of people were coming to his compound every week. But more about Chikanga later; here I want to concentrate on his relationship to biblical prophets, which was even more explicit than Mulaula's.

When Chikanga was nineteen, he, too, died and had a vision. But according to Chikanga and other people I interviewed, he did not die a little death, like Mulaula, but died completely for one day. In fact,

when he awoke (was resurrected?) he found his parents mourning over
his body. While he was dead, Chikanga had the following dream:

> I went to heaven and there were two ministers from the church.
> One of the ministers asked me what I was doing there, and I
> told him I had come to see God. He told me to go with the
> other minister who took me to another place where I found
> Daniel, Joseph, Elijah, and some others which I don't know.
> They gave me a chair, a very good chair, but before I sit down
> to that chair my grandfather came and said, what have you
> come to do here? I said I have come to see God, and he said
> no, no, this is not your time to see God. So my grandfather told
> those people, no, I want this man to go back. I didn't stop there.
> I said no, I want to see God. So those people took me to where
> my grandfather stayed, and then they showed me where God
> stayed, but it was very far and I could barely see. I was just
> seeing something funny there. But then I could see that Moses
> was staying next to God. Then I came back to that place, and
> those people there gave me an old Bible [Old Testament], a
> song, and a stick. At that time my name was Brighton, but
> those people told me now you are Chikanga [lit. "brave"], do
> not fear anything. When I woke up there were many people in
> the house crying.

This dream seems to have a veracity to it—significantly, he did not see
the face of God, which, according to the Jungian theory of archetypes,
is an impossibility—that transcended his individuality, initiating a life
transformation. The young man named Brighton became Chikanga,
nchimi ya uchimi, the prophet of prophets.

All *nchimi* attest that their ultimate power comes from God. Christian prayers are said before each session of divination, and crosses are
as common at an *nchimi*'s compound as at the local church. Mulaula
wears a rosary around his neck, Lußemba sometimes holds a Bible
while she is divining a patient's troubles, and Chikanje, Lußemba's
first husband, frequently quotes chapter and verse from the Bible to
explain to a patient what he has "seen." When I asked Chikanje why
he used music and dance when he divined, he replied simply, "Psalms
one hundred fifty."[18]

Most *nchimi*, when asked why they became healers, responded that
they had no choice, that it was the will of God. But God in this context
must be understood as a synthesis of the Old Testament Jehovah and

the traditional Tumbuka supreme deity, Chiuta. God is almighty, but just as Chiuta created the world and then removed himself from the concerns of everyday life, so has Jehovah.[19] If God is ultimately responsible for who becomes or does not become a healer, it is only in the sense of a "first cause." The spirits, the *mizimu* and *vimbuza,* are the active players in the world of human beings.

In northern Malawi, one does not choose to become a healer; one is chosen. The elect are called to their vocation—it is much more than a profession—through an affliction caused by the spirits. This affliction takes on the basic form that Eliade (1964: ch. 2) calls an "initiatory sickness"; the person so afflicted will not get well until the calling is heeded.

Once elected by the spirits, most *nchimi* undergo a relatively long apprenticeship—usually from one to two years—with an established healer. The choice of the healer under whom to serve one's apprenticeship is most often revealed to the novice by the *mizimu* ancestors in a dream. If an *nchimi* divines that the person is, in fact, being called by the spirits to become a healer, then the person will move into the compound and become a member of the healer's community. Although many are called—at Mulaula's alone there were twelve novices in training—only a few actually become full-time professional healers.

As novices progress in their training, dreams take on an increasingly important role. Dreams may reveal new medicines (usually herbal compounds, which sometimes also include animal parts), where to find the ingredients in the bush, and for what purposes they may be used. In this manner, new compounds are continually added to the largely shared pharmacopoeia of *nchimi,* keeping it an open-ended system. Dreams may also begin to foretell the future—the spirits may reveal a death that is soon to happen, or warn of an attack by one of the foes of all *nchimi,* an *mfwiti* (witch). One morning, for example, Lußemba told me that the night before she had seen in her dream two witches who were trying to enter the compound but who were turned away because her medicine protecting the compound was too strong. This medicine was itself revealed to Lußemba by her late mother, who, in a dream, told her to get a white stone from Lake Malawi and special medicines from Tanzania and bury them in her compound. In dreams, one may also take journeys to discover what is happening at other villages or to find out who is responsible for certain illnesses—in other words, who bewitched whom. And, importantly, given the focus of this book, in dreams come many of the *vimbuza* songs that will be used to heat the *vimbuza* spirits and fuel the divination trance. For *nchimi* who maintain a correct relationship to their spirits, unparalleled knowledge is revealed through dreams. Future, past, and present are collapsed in dreamtime, giving *nchimi* access to a wider and deeper world than that of their fellow human beings.

Coterminous with this expanded world, and in many respects the gravitational center of the entire healing complex of the *nchimi*, is the *vimbuza* dance. Through the music and dance of *vimbuza*, the *nchimi* gains another entry point or opening to the numinous world of the spirits. It is from this opening that *nchimi* acquire the gift of "seeing." Dreaming is an internal and perforce a private process, whereas dancing is the public enactment of a healer's power and access to the spiritual realm. Much of what a healer achieves in his or her career is, in a sense, accomplished through the *vimbuza* dance, and much of what he or she becomes as an *nchimi* is a direct result of being able to control the spiritual energy generated in the music of the spirits.

Kuvina/*To Dance*

How is an *nchimi*'s dancing different from mine? The answer is obvious, for we are worlds apart. More importantly, from a Tumbuka viewpoint, how is the dancing of a healer different from the dancing of ordinary Tumbuka who are afflicted by the *vimbuza* spirits?

After living in the compounds of healers for extended periods of time and observing *nchimi*, novices, and laymen dancing *vimbuza*, I was struck by the divergent possibilities inherent in the musical experience of trance. The same basic music would sometimes elicit a wild and potentially violent spirit possession in a novice or layman and at other times the controlled, remembered divinatory trance of an *nchimi*. Furthermore, depending on the circumstances of a particular trance episode, a novice or layman might have a relatively tame but still amnesic encounter with the *vimbuza* spirits, and under special circumstances an *nchimi*'s trance might verge toward the chaotic.

Because music seems to be a constant—some quantitative changes accompany the divinatory trance, which I will discuss later, but they do not affect the point being made here—the locus for the change in the trance process must be in the healer's experience of the music. Locating the change within the healer's experience does not seem to be saying much more than the obvious: there is no different kind of music for the divination trance, and therefore the change is in the healer's relationship to the music. This, in fact, is one of Rouget's (1985) main points, since for him it is evidence of the mistaken views of Neher (1961, 1962) and other supporters (e.g., Needham 1967; Walker 1972) of a physiological interpretation of music's effect on the phenomenon of trance.[20] What is more important, I believe, is that locating the changing nature of the trance within the experience of the *nchimi* turns the investigation into a phenomenological one, rather than a simple objective analysis. It emphatically does not become an analytic of subjective states, an investigation of a healer's internal psychology, but rather a phenomenological inquiry into that which is given. In the temple of a Tumbuka healer, that which is given first is musical experience.

When I asked Tumbuka who were not healers about their dancing, most replied that they didn't remember when they danced. They clearly made the point that it is not the person who dances, it is the *vimbuza* spirits. People don't dance to become possessed by the *vimbuza*, they dance because they *are* possessed.

Most *nchimi*, on the other hand, say that when they dance, not only do they recall the experience but they *must* remember, for if they didn't, how would they know what was wrong with their patients, or how to heal them? Most *nchimi*, however, during their initiatory sickness, become possessed by the spirits, and like ordinary Tumbuka afflicted by *vimbuza*, they dance but do not remember. As the special illness of the *nchimi* matures (*kudankha*), the way a fruit becomes ripe, the *vimbuza* dance is transformed from a trance of spirit possession, with its accompanying memory loss, into the divinatory trance of "seeing," which is characterized by the conscious remembering of the dance experience.[21] During divination, the *vimbuza* spirits are still activated—that is, "heated" through drumming and singing—but their role in the trance changes from that of possessing spirit to that of numinous source of energy.

This maturation of the disease, which in essence is the transformation from patient to healer, relates to the change in an adept's relationship to musical phenomena. When novices are first brought before the drums, *vimbuza* spirits fully absorb the psychic space; the experience is amnesic. But as adepts learn to focus their dancing style, a "lucid form of possession" occurs (Oesterreich 1966), a kind of consciousness-doubling, which involves the co-presence of both person and spirit.

Nchimi healers are not just mouthpieces for the spirits. They are not mediums in the sense of being merely conduits for the spirits, as is the case, for example, with Korekore mediums in Zimbabwe, who are believed "to speak when possessed with the voices of long-dead spirits" (Garbett 1969: 105). In divination, *nchimi* healers speak to patients as themselves, but this is a self that has been transformed through contact with the realm of the spirits. This transformation involves an expansion of an *nchimi*'s being, for in this case, contact with the spirits involves an incorporation of spirit into the psychical body of the healer. There is no question that it is the *nchimi*, as an individual, who proclaims during divination, but it is an individual who is both himself and more than himself at the same time. The *nchimi*'s trance is not a loss of self—as these kinds of trances are so often described—but an expansion of self.

Consciousness-doubling in Tumbuka divination also entails a doubling of spirit type. The *vimbuza* spirits, by themselves, are not sufficient to enact the divination trance. Diviner-healers need also to incorporate the ancestral *mizimu* spirits in order to "see." The ancestors do not possess a healer during the divination trance but communicate within the trance. Ancestors may convey knowledge through dreams and visions, but they cannot physically possess someone. The foreign *vimbuza* are the only category of spirits who can possess, who can physically enter a person's body. For the Tumbuka, the crossing of the boundaries of the physical body is not a symbolic gesture but an existential reality.

This transformation of the *vimbuza* from possessing spirit to divinatory trance parallels the healer's transformation from novice to *nchimi*. In order for an *nchimi* such as Lußemba to "see," which is the sine qua non of being a healer, she must bring the *mizimu* and *vimbuza* spirits into the correct alignment. As Lußemba replied in response to my question about how this was accomplished: "Right in the dancing is where the vimbuza and mizimu mix." The desired configuration is brought about through the music and dance of *vimbuza*, which also involves a phenomenon of rhythmic doubling, something I deal with in chapter 5.

So long as the *vimbuza* spirits fully possess the novice during the dance, people consider them to be too "hot," and the *mizimu*, as it were, are shut out of the process. An important part of an adept's training to become a healer involves cooling the *vimbuza* (see chapter 3) just enough to allow the *mizimu*, as the Tumbuka put it, "to go on top," so that instead of possessing the dancer, the *vimbuza* act as a source of energy that "pushes" the *mizimu* "up," thus creating the necessary conditions for "seeing." This intricate dance of spiritual energy is configured within musical experience.

To understand musical experience in this case, we need first to investigate trance dancing as essentially a clinical praxis. In the Tumbuka health care system, therapeutic intervention is determined by etiology, which in turn is determined through the divinatory trance of *nchimi* healers. Therefore, trance dancing is essential to an *nchimi*'s medical practice. It is during the public enactment of this divination trance—when healers dance their disease—that the disvalued states of patients are transformed into meaningful cultural forms of illness. Loss of appetite and shooting pains in the chest and legs are no longer just symptoms but part of a witchcraft-induced illness known as *chilaso*, and fast heartbeats, chills, and splitting headaches turn out not to be symptoms of malaria, as they were diagnosed by the medical assistant at the hospital in Rumphi, but affliction by the *vimbuza* spirits.

In the terms of medical anthropologist Arthur Kleinman (1980), divination turns disease into illness—that is, it turns dysfunctional physical states into culturally shaped experiences. Although this view seems to give disease (at least so far as Western medicine is concerned) a preferential position, as physically "real," over the more socially structured concept of illness, Kleinman's point, as I take it, is that from a phenomenological perspective the cultural shaping of experience becomes part of the tissue of reality—specifically, a clinical reality— when issues of sickness and health are concerned. The "cultural construction of clinical reality" (ibid.: 360) has physiological effects both in the presentation of physical symptoms and in the healing process, something Daniel Moerman (1979: 59) calls the "enacting [of] cultural physiology." In Tumbuka healing, cultural physiology includes an embodied music, a musical experience that shapes clinical processes. Musical experience in the temple of an *nchimi* is first and foremost part of an indigenous medical technology.

Mizimu *Radio*

It seems strange to call music a technology. Music may be many things in the Western world—aesthetic object, entertainment, or commercial product, to name a few—but it is rarely, if ever, thought of as a technology.[22] Of course there is technology associated with music—for example, the making of musical instruments or the encoding of musical data on compact disks—but we don't associate the acoustic properties of music with the control and practical application of energy.

Though we do not relate expressive aspects of culture, such as music and dance, with technology, let alone with medical technology, this is exactly how Tumbuka healers speak of dancing prophets and drummed spirits. When the Tumbuka speak of spirits, trance, and music, they tend to use metaphors that reveal this relationship to technological processes.

For the moment, I want to concentrate on one particular metaphor that I encountered from many different sources and that I believe is telling. It is a kind of linguistic opening for the outsider into the way *nchimi* conceptualize and experience this technological musical process. Although the metaphor came in slightly different versions, it was put succinctly by Nchimi Mulaula—the dreamer of doves and white robes—who seemed to have a knack for stating things clearly. When I asked him how *vimbuza* music helped him to "see," he replied, "Vimbuza is the battery for the mizimu radio." This metaphor, framed in technological terms, reveals a conceptual structure, what Lakoff and Johnson (1980: 235) call an "imaginative rationality." Metaphors are always abstractions; this one is part of an indigenous theory about the relations between music, trance, and healing.

At first, the radio metaphor seemed to me to be an unusual choice to explain the workings of *vimbuza* in the divination trance. What does it mean to equate music with batteries and divination with a radio? Why choose a piece of Western hardware technology to explain the workings of music and spirits? Batteries and radios, as metaphorical concepts, are definitely more "experience-distant" (Geertz 1983: 57) for Mulaula than are *vimbuza* and "seeing." Simply put, *vimbuza* has been a part of Tumbuka culture much longer than radios have. But as I heard other *nchimi* use almost identical metaphors, and as I began to connect them with other metaphors people used to discuss divination, the battery metaphor not only emerged as a logical choice but also revealed itself as a core concept in a conceptual structure.

People construct their metaphors from what is at hand. In 1983 there were 1.06 million radio sets in use in Malawi (Government of Malawi 1987: 654); by 1987, the time of my research, there undoubtedly were considerably more. This averages out to be about one radio for every six people, with probably a much higher ratio in urban centers than in rural areas. This ratio is nowhere close, of course, to that in industrialized countries, where the question would be not whether someone had a radio but how many. Still, there are enough radios in Malawi that no matter where one travels, they are a prominent feature of the "soundscape," to borrow Murray Schafer's (1977: 3) term.

One of my first encounters with this aspect of the Tumbuka soundscape occurred shortly after I had arrived in the North. I had heard of an old *nchimi* who lived in a remote village and decided to pay him a visit. As I approached the village, after hiking for two hours into the bush, the sound that filtered through the trees wasn't that of women singing as they pounded their maize, or of men passing the time playing the *bango* or *kalimba,* or even of children playing. It was the distorted sound of a radio playing at full blast the latest hit from South Africa.

Virtually every village (and healer's compound) has at least one radio, which, by necessity, is battery powered, since rural areas are not on the national electrical grid. The radio is the main link with a wider world, the only form of mass communication readily available to rural Tumbuka. For many Tumbuka, radios have taken on more the aspect of a communal necessity than of an entertaining diversion. As a result, C- and D-cell batteries are prized commodities among the rural population. Indeed, the alkaline battery is probably the single most visible— and I should include audible, given its almost exclusive use in radios— sign of Western hardware technology in the rural areas of Malawi.

Batteries are relatively expensive items for the Tumbuka, and great care is taken to get the most use out of them. In that sense, I was a walking gold mine of battery power. My portable tape recorder, which used three D-cell batteries for power, was good for three hours of recording. After that the batteries failed to maintain a constant recording speed, but they were still usable for powering portable radios. Those used batteries became much-desired items because of the cost (and poor quality) of local Malawian batteries. To get more life out of the batteries, Tumbuka would put them in the sun "to heat up" because, according to both Malawian popular belief and some Western technical experts, this gives them longer life. Tumbuka heat *vimbuza* spirits *and* D-cell batteries.

Because of batteries' association with radios, most Tumbuka make a direct connection between battery power and sound.[23] Batteries provide the energy that allows one to "open" a radio. Tumbuka don't "turn on" radios, they "open" them, and when one opens a radio one hears music, the news, commercials, presidential speeches, and the usual panoply of broadcast programs. Nowadays one can, strangely enough, even hear programs of *vimbuza* music on MBC (Malawi Broadcast Corporation),[24] the only radio station in Malawi, which puts a kind of doubled mirror twist to the metaphor that "vimbuza is the battery for the mizimu radio."

Actually, two sets of metaphors are embedded in Mulaula's statement: battery/*vimbuza* and radio/divination. "Mizimu radio" is not the *mizimu* themselves but the divination trance. There is an internal relationship within each set—*vimbuza* is a battery, and divination is a radio—and also a correlation between the two sets—batteries are to radios as *vimbuza* is to divination.

The first metaphor, battery/*vimbuza*, is about energy technology. Mulaula is making a correlation between two sources of energy—one produces electricity through chemical reactions, the other produces energy through music and dance. That Mulaula, like most Tumbuka *and* most Westerners, does not fully understand how batteries work does not affect the analogy in the least. Both are technologies in the sense that they are cultural means—batteries with their characteristic chemical reactions are as much a cultural artifact as are music and dance—of controlling energy for utilitarian purposes.

Music and dance in the context of *vimbuza* are not for entertainment (though they may entertain), but for purposes of healing. Kapferer (1983: 178) makes a similar point in regard to Sinhalese exorcisms: "Sinhalese exorcisms are artistic forms. But their art is turned to the practical purpose of acting upon the problems which affect the lives of human beings in a mundane world." In both cases, music and dance are part of an indigenous healing praxis.

The second metaphor, which in Mulaula's statement is not as explicit as the first, for it is embedded in the phrase "mizimu radio," is about communication technology. Radios and divination transmit information, whether it be in the form of pop music on the radio or the revealing of who is a witch through divination. These communication technologies, for radios as well as divination, give "voice" to the invisible. Radios give sound to invisible radio waves; the divination trance gives sound substance to the invisible spirits. The invisibility of the spirits has important ontological and existential significance in Tumbuka culture, the implications of which I will deal with later.

Finally, Mulaula is saying something about the relationship between two different categories of spirits in Tumbuka culture. The spiritual realm is classified by the Tumbuka into two overarching categories based on a binary opposition that revolves around the origin of the spirit entity and its relationship to Tumbuka society. Any spirit that is not ancestral to the Tumbuka is classified as a foreign *vimbuza* spirit. *Vimbuza* are the quintessential spiritual embodiment of the "other." Significantly, during the divination trance, it is not the *vimbuza* who "see," it is the *mizimu*, the ancestors of the Tumbuka. *Nchimi* never talk about "heating" their *mizimu* spirits. The *vimbuza* are the source of energy, the "battery," for the *mizimu*, who, in a sense, "transmit" through the *nchimi*.

What emerges from these metaphoric associations—in essence,

what *nchimi* are saying when they say spirits are batteries and divination a radio—is that trance is part of an indigenous medical technology. For the Tumbuka, the music and dance of *vimbuza* are the essential means by which to initialize and control this diagnostic procedure.

Music's status as part of a medical technology frames its phenomenological presence. This does not mean that healers and their patients do not experience an aesthetic dimension in *vimbuza* dancing, drumming, and singing, but rather that it is precisely within the dimension of performance that music becomes a numinously charged process designed to call forth and shape spiritual energy. In doing so, it becomes not merely a technology in terms of an instrumentality of means and ends, but a technology in Heidegger's (1977) sense: a technology that reveals a world. The world that *vimbuza* music reveals, however, is quite different from the one revealed by battery-powered radios and other modern Western technology.

The Technology of Trance

What is revealed through modern Western technology, according to Heidegger (1977: 3–35), is a world that is seen as a "standing-reserve" of energy waiting to be tapped. To say that this technological lens has not only revealed a particular kind of world but also helped to shape it is an understatement. It is an aggressive stance that surveys and orders all it sees as a-waiting-to-be-used.

Modern technology approaches the world as a repository of energy waiting to be released, and when it is set free from its binding force in things, it is transformed and utilized in the production of goods. Thus the mountain is no longer part of a chain that arises from the earth but a storehouse of mineral resources. The river no longer is free to meander through the countryside but is a source of hydroelectric power. Even the arts become transformed into products waiting to be produced solely for their commercial potential to be used up.

There is an extreme danger in all of this, Heidegger warns us. The "revealing" of modern technology, of world as standing-energy-reserve, threatens to drive out all other kinds of revealing: "As soon as what is unconcealed no longer concerns man even as object, but does so, rather, exclusively as standing-reserve, and man in the midst of objectlessness is nothing but the orderer of the standing-reserve, then he comes to the very brink of a precipitous fall; that is, he comes to the point where he himself will have to be taken as standing reserve" (1977: 26–27). It is no accident that we now speak of work forces, manpower, labor resources, and, not incidentally for this study, supplies of patients for hospitals. In this kind of unabated attenuation of presence, which is a "challenging" of the world, the possibility exists "that man will lose his true relation to himself and to all else" (Lovitt 1977: xxxiv). Everywhere everything will be brought under the ruling gaze of order and control. The Cartesian subject will reach its ultimate destination by relating all it surveys to itself as the constituting subject. The world will then become "enframed," and thus out of control. Human beings will become invisible as the pure relationship—the standing-reserve—between subjects and objects.

Was there a time in Western culture, Heidegger asks, when technology revealed a different possibility? Was there a way of technology that was a different mode of being-in-the-world? The answer for Heidegger, not surprisingly, lies with the pre-Socratic Greeks, for whom art and technology were one: "In Greece, at the outset of the destining of the West, arts soared to the supreme height of the revealing granted them. They brought the presence of the Gods, brought the dialogue of divine and human destinings, to radiance. And art was simply called *technē*" (1977: 34). *Technē*, the etymological root of our word technology, was on a different order of revealing from that of standing-reserve, and art was more than aesthetic experience. The early Greeks participated in the very act of the revealing of Being—that is, technology was for them an art.

So it is for the Tumbuka, who, in their healing arts, bring the radiance of the gods through a music that is *technē*. The world that is revealed through the technology of *vimbuza* music is a bringing-forth that is not a challenging but a letting be, which results in a revealing that is, to use Heidegger's terminology, a "bursting-forth." What bursts-forth for trance dancers are the *vimbuza* spirits; it is an unconcealing of the numinous in the everyday—the sacred revealed through the profane, as Eliade (1963) puts it. Through music, the Tumbuka encounter their world in a primary reality that establishes, to paraphrase William Lovitt (1977: xxxiv), true relations to themselves and to all else, including, most importantly, the *vimbuza* spirits.

In Tumbuka divination, medical technology is part of musical experience, and musical experience a mode of being-in-the-world for both spirit and human. This is not merely the eccentricity of a specific cultural style informed by a system of religious beliefs—a medical practice grounded in free-floating concepts—all to be explained away as differences typically uncovered by ethnographers or ethnomusicologists. Musical experience, as a technological mode of being-in-the-world, takes on ontological significance as an authentic mode of existence. Authentic existence is not to be found in some kind of mystical experience but in the everyday, where possibilities unfold, where existential choices are made. For the Tumbuka, music, spirits, and trance penetrate the very fabric of everyday existence, an everyday where worlds are moved by spirits and spirits are moved by music.

The first night I saw a diviner-healer dance, I turned to the man next to me and asked him what the *nchimi* was doing. "He's X-raying the patients" was his reply. This brings up another metaphor, explicitly technological and medical in its associations. The divination trance is part of the health care system of the Tumbuka, just as X rays are part of Western medical praxis: they both serve in diagnosis. They both "see," but in different ways, revealing different worlds. The Westerner plugs in the machine; the Tumbuka plays music.

God, Humans, and Spirits

The week before I danced at Lußemba's I had a recurrence of the head-aches that had struck me the previous year when I first came north. I was on the express bus headed for Mzuzu, the capital of the Northern Region, to begin my research when I started getting strange headaches, unlike any I had previously experienced. They had a kind of rhythm to them: they would come in cycles about every thirty minutes, last for an intense five minutes or so, and then go away, only to return in half an hour. The headaches started as soon as we crossed the border into the North and didn't stop until about a week later. At the time, it didn't seem like a very auspicious beginning to my research; now it seems to me that perhaps it was.

When the headaches started again at Lußemba's, I thought I was having another bout of malaria, for malaria had been the diagnosis the doctor at the mission hospital in Mzuzu had made of my headaches the year before. He concluded that I had a chloroquine-resistant strain, even though my blood test was inconclusive, and he prescribed a quinine-based drug different from the one I had been taking as a prophy-lactic. Resistant strains of malaria are endemic in the North, but as I was to find out, a diagnosis of malaria didn't mean all that much since doctors applied it to virtually any symptom. The drug seemed to have little effect, and curiously, it wasn't until after attending my first few sessions of *vimbuza* that my headaches finally started to subside.

It wasn't so much that I began feeling better right away but that, surprisingly, I didn't feel any worse given the considerable decibel lev-els inside a healer's temple. Having the sound of the drums literally pound against my head—good *vimbuza* drumming moves a consider-able amount of air—did not seem particularly conducive to recovery.

"The louder the better," according to healers. The bodily sensations induced by drums sounding the rhythmic modes of the *vimbuza* spirits, the dynamic power of call and response singing, the intensity of clapping augmented by concussion sticks, and the sound of trance dancing itself are more than acoustical phenomena; for healers and their patients they are physically felt, substantial sources of energy.

Initially, I seriously considered not even going to see *vimbuza* until I started to get at least some relief from the headaches. I couldn't imagine sitting inside the temple without feeling as if my head was, as the Tumbuka put it, going to "blow its top." But after attending several sessions of *vimbuza*—research opportunities presented themselves which I could not turn down—I found that instead of getting worse, the rhythm of the headaches in fact began to slow down, and they did not come with quite the same frequency or intensity. By the end of the week, my symptoms had pretty much disappeared.

At the time, I didn't think too much about what had transpired. I decided that I had indeed contracted a mild case of malaria (I had myself convinced that I could almost feel the parasites invading my bloodstream every thirty minutes or so), and that it was a coincidence that the new quinine-based drug I was taking eventually started to work about the same time I was attending *vimbuza*. All this may well have been the case (except, of course, for *really* feeling the parasites). At least one doctor trained in tropical diseases, however, to whom I talked after my return to the United States, stated that my symptoms didn't sound like any kind of malaria he had ever heard of.

What I didn't realize at the time was that if I had sought the help of a traditional healer and told him about my headaches, I would have been describing one of the classic symptoms of *vimbuza* possession. Although the *vimbuza* spirits can cause any manner of sickness, from ulcers to problems with menstruation, severe headaches are almost always an accompanying symptom. The standard procedure for relief of these headaches is, as the Tumbuka say, to "dance the disease" (*kuvina nthenda*). It wasn't until a year later at Lußemba's, however, that I joined the Tumbuka in that form of therapy.

It is only now, when I look back on these episodes from a distance, that there seems to be some kind of relationship between my symptoms and the circumstances of my work—a resonance between my internal state and external actions, and the dynamics of *vimbuza* affliction.[1] A weak reading of this relationship would posit an interesting series of coincidences; a strong reading would come down on the side of a meaningful set of equivalences.

Regardless of what I told myself at the time, from a Tumbuka perspective there would have been little doubt about what was going on. Whether Chewa, Yao, or Mzungu, if you are in the North, have severe headaches, and then dance *vimbuza*, it is fairly obvious that you are troubled by the *vimbuza* spirits, whether you know it or not. For me, the sequence of events was a series of conscious decisions made in the context of my fieldwork. For the Tumbuka, my actions were a chain of events no doubt directed by the spirits.

Most Tumbuka I met did believe that I was afflicted by the *vimbuza* spirits, even though Mzungu don't get "African diseases." White men don't get *vimbuza*, yet why would I be living with *nchimi* and attending all those sessions of *vimbuza* dancing if I weren't sick? The only precedent for what I was doing was an intriguing story that I heard from several different sources about an Mzungu who, in the 1940s, got *vimbuza* and starting running wild in the bush. As the story was told to me, this white man eventually became an *nchimi* and started a "business" of his own, but, of course, finally ended up going crazy, *chifusi*.[2]

I was unable to follow this story up to find out how much of it was fact and how much fiction, which really isn't that important. The point is, people were using this story to help explain me and my circumstances at the time. I also believe that this story was, in part, a cautionary tale—white men shouldn't mess with African things. I often had the feeling people were waiting around to see when I would start showing the first signs of mental instability.

My illness had in fact mirrored, at least on the surface, a typical scenario of a spirit-caused disease. Many of the patients I met at the compounds of *nchimi* went first to a Western-style hospital for treatment, as I did, and many of them, like myself, were diagnosed as having malaria. For most of these people, if treatment with a quinine-based drug proved to be effective, then the particular episode of illness was considered closed. When symptoms persisted, however, other etiologies were suspected, and these patients usually turned to the traditional health care sector, as did I—although at the time I thought it was for research and not medical purposes.

A Tumbuka Theory of Illness

Spirits are only one of three possible causes of disease[3] (*nthenda*) in the Tumbuka theory of illness. God and witches (*ßafwiti*, plural of *mfwiti*) are the other etiologic agents. Any one of these agents may cause identical symptoms in a person who is ill. Since the same set of symptoms may be caused by different sources, illness is not classified, nor is therapeutic intervention initiated, according to symptomatology, but rather according to which agent is responsible for the illness.

Treating someone for malarial symptoms is of little value when the real cause may not be a mosquito bite but the machinations of a witch or the capriciousness of a spirit. It is these last two etiologies that are responsible for what the Tumbuka call "African diseases," and in these cases Western medicine can offer at best marginal help. Only traditional healers can provide effective therapy when spirits or witches are involved in an episode of illness.

Of course, Tumbuka do quite often get malaria, even though they have developed a certain amount of natural immunity to it.[4] They are well aware that malaria is caused by the bite of a mosquito and that quinine-based drugs are effective in its treatment. This information, however, was not bestowed on them by the medical missionaries of Livingstonia who first introduced Western medicine to northern Malawi but was something handed down for generations, a long-standing part of local knowledge. Indeed, concerning malaria, Tumbuka medical insights were way ahead of the understandings of the Scottish medical missionaries.

In early accounts from the missionary newspaper *The Aurora*, one can read of the rather quaint notion held by the local population that malaria was caused by mosquitoes—obviously an example of their primitive thinking. Doctors, on the other hand, had known for some time that malaria resulted from breathing bad air (mal-aira), "the noxious vapours of the swamps and low-lying parts of land," and "that the only way to prevent fever was to erect European dwellings on as high a ground as possible" (Gelfand 1964a: 232, citing the prevailing opinion in the late nineteenth century). For treatment, the Tumbuka traditionally extracted quinine from the bark of the *chinchocho* tree. The missionaries followed the dictates of Western medical science and built tall beds to avoid breathing the infectious miasma. Nowadays, both use antimalarial drugs readily available at government and missionary hospitals and clinics.

Occasionally, despite precautions such as taking chloroquine regularly and using industrial strength "jungle juice" to keep the mosquitoes away, researchers also get malaria. Besides the two bouts with headaches, the only other time I suffered anything more than minor ailments while I was in the field was when I contracted another case of malaria, and unlike the other episodes, there was no doubt as to the diagnosis. When I finally got myself to the government hospital in Rumphi—after strong suggestions by the healer I was staying with, who didn't want a dead Mzungu on his hands—my temperature was 104 degrees and rising, and I was verging on having hallucinations. This time the blood test was conclusive, and this time the antimalarial drug I was given started working within twenty-four hours. This case of malaria had little resemblance to my other so-called malarial episodes.

Malaria is a prime example of what the Tumbuka classify as a God-caused illness. It is not *sent by God*—who, as I have said, for the Tumbuka is a *deus otiosus* (see chapter 1, note 19)—to punish some transgression, but it is merely part of the existential reality of the world. God, Chiuta, created the world, and included in this world are naturally occurring illnesses such as malaria.

I did not encounter explanations like those expressed in Turner's research on the Ndembu (1968) and Evans-Pritchard's on the Azande (1937) that involved why I got malaria this time and not others, since being bitten by mosquitoes can be a daily occurrence. According to these authors, the Ndembu and the Azande believe all illness and misfortune have a supernatural component.

Although this lack of a natural causation theory has been taken by researchers as a common feature in most African societies, it may not be as widespread as previously believed. According to Gillies (1976: 358), "the conclusion drawn by ethnographers in their accounts of ideas of disease causation have tended to be rather too sweeping, and have not taken sufficient note of discriminations made by the actors, both between different kinds of illness and between the levels of etiology and pathogenesis." Using evidence from Turner's and Evans-Pritchard's own material, Gillies makes a case that the Ndembu and the Azande do, in fact, classify some diseases as natural.

Gillies's mapping of this cognitive space, overlooked in much of the literature on healing systems in Africa, has a direct relevance to *ng'oma*-type institutions found throughout southeastern and southern Africa. Junod ([1927] 1962: 475) reports for the Thonga that the fourth, "less common cause" for disease is Heaven, which approximates the Tumbuka classification of God. In the same vein, Tew (1950: 18) cites "the hand of God" as a Yao disease classification. And Ngubane (1976: 321–22), in discussing Zulu notions of disease causality, mentions an indigenous category of "physical ailments which are believed to 'just happen' without association with any personal malice." She goes on to state that Zulus are aware of the contagious and infectious nature of some of the diseases of this class. In each of these cases, illness is perceived as a naturally occurring part of the world.

When a Tumbuka says that an illness came from God, he or she does so in this context of natural causation. In Tumbuka medical theory, God-caused illnesses are probably closest to the Western medical conception of disease, and it is only in cases of these naturally occurring illnesses that Western medicine can offer any help.

Missionaries and Medicine

Throughout Africa there is a dualistic system of medical care. Every country in Africa has Western-style hospitals that, in varying ways shaped by local conditions, deliver health care in the Western mode: antibiotics are dispensed, X rays taken, babies immunized, broken bones set, and operations performed. But everywhere we find Western medicine in Africa, we also find older and more widespread, parallel, indigenous systems of health care. Contrary to the expectations of Western medical practitioners, the "miracles" of modern medicine have not supplanted traditional health practices in Africa. Indigenous healers and the medical systems they represent are flourishing in most African countries.[5]

The Tumbuka of northern Malawi are no exception, having access to both traditional and Western health care systems. These two systems are not mutually exclusive but interact with each other on various levels. The Tumbuka choose which system to utilize according to the types of symptoms they manifest, the etiology of their illness, its nosology, and the reputation and effectiveness of each health care system in relationship to specific diseases. A patient may even shift back and forth between the two systems during the course of a single episode of illness, depending on the progression of the illness and the efficacy of the medical procedures applied to it.

Not only does patronage shift between the two health care systems, but a certain amount of syncretism has also taken place between the two. For the most part, this syncretism has been engendered on the traditional side, although recently the more enlightened of the Western-trained doctors have begun to take account of certain aspects of indigenous health care in their own practices. Later I will deal with the syncretism between Western and traditional healing; for now I mention it only to bring out the fact that there are not simply two entirely separate systems coexisting side by side in Malawi. Western health care, in fact, may not have been as foreign and "other" as some accounts have made it seem.

Whereas traditional healing, with its use of music and trance, has a long Tumbuka history,[6] Western medical practice is a rather recent import to northern Malawi, introduced in the late nineteenth century by the missionaries of the Free Church of Scotland. Following David Livingstone's example, these "men of God" came to Malawi as medical missionaries. They believed that the quickest way to win the hearts of Africans was through the miracles of modern medicine.

The ideology behind this work of men trained in both medicine and religion was put concisely by Bishop Smythies of the Universities Mission to Central Africa (UMCA):

> What is meant strictly by a medical missionary is I suppose neither a medical man who gives simply his services as a doctor to missionary work, nor a priest who is also a doctor but a doctor who uses all his medical knowledge for a missionary end; whose aim is to use the great influence which his profession gives him to draw his patients to the love of God; who longs not only for the healing of bodies but for the salvation of their souls. . . . It seems as if only through medical work, which is sure in the long run to be welcomed, that an opening to the hearts of these people can be found. (quoted in Gelfand 1964a: 8)

Western medicine was first introduced to the Tumbuka within this context of religious evangelism. The power to heal was inexorably linked by the missionaries to the power of a Christian God.

Dr. Laws, the head of the Livingstonia Mission, had been qualified in medicine and divinity at the University of Aberdeen. As Gelfand states (ibid.: 40), "at first, very wisely, in order to win their confidence in the white man's 'magic,' Laws confined his surgery to minor procedures which were likely to be successful." News of these successes spread quickly through the North, drawing many people to the mission station to be healed by this powerful new "magic."

Commenting on Laws's use of chloroform during surgery, the Reverend James Jack, writing at the turn of the century, related the missionaries' view of how Africans perceived this new "magic":

> Occasionally there were severe cases requiring the use of chloroform. This "sleep medicine," as the natives called it, was a

never-failing wonder to them. If in the early Christian church there was the power of working miracles, there was something almost equivalent in Nyasaland in the modern science of surgery with its chloroforming operations. To the simple natives the cases were apparently miraculous. So far as they could see, the white man first killed the patient, and then, when [the patient was] quite dead, he cut the trouble out; then he bound up the wound and made it better; and then, finally, he brought the patient back to life again. Every cure, too, was like a nail in the coffin of superstition and witchcraft. Patients went back to their homes cured, taking with them the praises of the white man's skill and kindness, and, better still, carrying in their hearts some message of the Gospel of God's grace. (Jack 1900: 130)

What Jack failed to appreciate—besides the hint offered by the term "sleep medicine" that the natives did not believe the patient had been truly killed—was that although Africans might have taken back the gospel and proclaimed the wonders of the white man's healing, they still interpreted the process from a traditional standpoint.

This points to an important issue that has been largely ignored in African scholarship. We know from the writings of these early missionaries (Elmslie 1899; Fraser 1914; Laws 1934) what they thought of Africans and what they believed Africans thought of them, but we know little of how Africans perceived these foreign newcomers who claimed to be both healers and religious experts. Although there are no written records from this time by the Africans who experienced it, certain logical inferences may be made. It seems probable that the Tumbuka assimilated Laws into their category of "healer," for their healers were also, in a sense, religious men. Both Tumbuka healers and medical missionaries used powerful medicines in their medical practice, both claimed special access to the spiritual world—Tumbuka healers attributed their power to the spirits, missionaries attributed theirs to Jesus—and both used music. While for medical missionaries, the singing of Christian hymns never impinged directly on medical procedures, as did the drumming and singing of *vimbuza*, this fact may not have been self-evident to African patients. After all, it must have been obvious to the Tumbuka that this was one way these Mzungu healers paid respects to their God. It is likely that for the Tumbuka these early missionaries represented not a new social category but rather a different manifestation of an already existing social niche.[7]

We can see a parallel process at work when missionaries first introduced the Bible into the North. The Bible has a unique history and place in the culture of the Tumbuka-speaking peoples of Malawi. It was the first book translated into chiTumbuka, and because of the restrictive language policies of the central government at the time of my research, it was the only book that could be legally published in that language.[8]

The Bible was fitted by the Tumbuka, as were the missionaries, into a preexisting cultural category, in this case, divination. The "Book" was perceived as a powerful instrument that allowed the missionaries to "see." According to Elmslie (1899: 169), one of the first missionaries in the North, "at this time, of course, a book was in their eyes nothing but an instrument of divination, and . . . they believed that it told us what was in their minds. They spoke about 'The Book,' as the Bible was so often referred to by us, and they thought there was only one book." From the Tumbuka point of view, given the "white fathers'" daily pronouncement that the Bible was the Word of God, it was a logical connection that the Bible was the way missionaries made contact with the spirit world in order to divine.

Today, some *nchimi* have retained this sense of divinatory power connected to the Bible and have incorporated it into their healing. As I mentioned in chapter 1, Lußemba sometimes augmented her divination by holding a Bible and randomly turning to a page, reading a passage, and interpreting it in the context of the patient's problems. Chikanje, her first husband, often quoted the Bible from memory during divination sessions.

The Bible can also show up in the initiatory dreams of *nchimi* as a symbol of God's call to become a healer. We have already come upon this in Chikanga's dream in which the prophets gave him a Bible along with his new *nchimi* name, a song, and a staff. Chikanje had a similar dream shortly before he became an *nchimi*. In it, his grandfather handed him covered white plates in which were put ritual offerings: a fly whisk—the symbol of *nchimi* and chiefly authority—and a Bible, with the verse, "My son, if thou wilt receive my words, and hide my commandments with thee" (Proverbs 2:1). He took this to mean that he should obey and stay true to the words of the ancestors.

Chikanje, in fact, incorporated the Bible into his healing practice more than any other *nchimi* with whom I worked. During divination, he often made reference to some verse from the Bible—among his favorites were verses from the Book of Daniel, particularly the parts concerning dreams and prophecy. He also relied on the Bible as a justification for what he did as an *nchimi*, and he sometimes went beyond this, as we shall see, using the Bible as a virtual instruction manual.

A Biblical Sacrifice

One of Chikanje's most striking uses of the Bible that I encountered was during an animal sacrifice he conducted for two young male *nchimi*. He had trained both of these healers, who were now out on their own trying to establish their own "businesses." They had come to Chikanje for help because they had been having trouble "seeing." It is common for new *nchimi*, during the first years of their practice, to return frequently to the healer who trained them to receive guidance and help. Chikanje slept on the matter—that is, dreamed—and decided that their *mizimu* (ancestors) were unhappy. In order to appease them they should pay respects by sacrificing white doves and a chicken at the Njakwa Gorge, a sacred site for the *mizimu*.

A few days later, at about noon, the two *nchimi* and I, along with Chikanje and his ten current apprentices, made the short trip to Njakwa, roughly half of us walking and the other half crammed into my old Peugeot. The gorge is about 5 kilometers from Chikanje's compound in Bwengu, where the South Rukuru River turns northeast to enter the Henga Valley. When everyone finally arrived at the site, we sang a few Christian hymns, and Chikanje gave a prayer praising the Lord and asking the *mizimu* ancestors to accept the chicken and doves the two young *nchimi* had brought, for they were "doing a sacrifice like they did in the times of Moses and Jesus."

After some preliminaries at the gorge, we walked along the riverbank and headed upstream, where the main part of the sacrifice began. A fire was built, and we stood in a semicircle as one of the male assistants took out a Bible in chiTumbuka and announced, "Leviticus one, verse fourteen." He proceeded to read aloud (the following is an English translation from the King James Version):

14 And if the burnt sacrifice of his offering to the LORD *be* of fowls, then he shall bring his offering of turtledoves, or young pigeons.

As this was read, a pigeon—for sacrificial purposes, the Tumbuka consider pigeons and doves to be the same thing—was handed to Chikanje. The reader continued:

> 15 And the priest shall bring it unto the altar, and wring off his head

and Chikanje twisted off the pigeon's head;

> and burn *it* on the altar; and the blood thereof shall be wrung out at the side of the altar:

and then he poured the blood from the body of the pigeon next to the fire.

> 16 And he shall pluck away his crop with his feathers, and cast it beside the altar on the east part, by the place for ashes:

This was not done.

> 17 And he shall cleave it with the wings thereof, *but* shall not divide *it* asunder:

Chikanje took each wing of the pigeon and broke it in two, but without severing it.

> and the priest shall burn it on the altar, upon the wood that *is* upon the fire:

When this was read, one of Chikanje's assistants took a knife and opened up the bird. Chikanje reached in and pulled out its heart, and threw it upon the fire.

> it *is* a burnt sacrifice, an offering made by fire, of a sweet savour unto the LORD.

With the reading of these words, the main part of the ceremony was concluded. The chicken was then killed in the usual way, by cutting off its head. All three birds were cooked over the fire, and we sat down for an afternoon meal. In Leviticus, God gives Moses explicit instructions on how animal sacrifices should be conducted. Chikanje takes this as a literal prescription for action.

Doctors and Prophets

From the viewpoint of Malawians and Europeans involved in delivering Western-style health care, there is an opposition between the empirically based biomedical approach of Western medicine and "superstition riddled" indigenous healing practices. The majority of Tumbuka, however, still see Western medicine from the perspective of traditional medical praxis. They do not make an ideological distinction between Western and indigenous health care.

When a Tumbuka utilizes Western medical facilities, he or she does so within a traditional framework. X rays are conceived of as a kind of divination, and drugs such as penicillin and chloroquine are thought of qualitatively in the same terms as *mankwhala*, indigenous medicines. This conceptual framework has also engendered an interesting kind of appropriation of certain aspects and symbols of Western medicine by traditional healers—religion is not the only element of Western culture that is syncretized in traditional healing. One *nchimi* I knew, for example, would don a white doctor's frock he had somehow procured from the government hospital in Rumphi, and at 2:00 P.M. every day would make the "rounds" of his patients. Other *nchimi* had collections of vitamins and antibiotics that they used as part of their pharmacopoeia. Nchimi Mulaula even claimed to be in touch with the spirits of Mzungu doctors who helped advise him on cases that were caused by God. Tumbuka healers and their patients see Western and traditional medicine not in opposition to each other but rather as forming a continuum.

It would be misleading, however, to imply that all Tumbuka believe in and utilize the traditional sector of the health care system. Staunch members of the Church of Central Africa Presbyterian (CCAP), the current designation of the edifice created by the Livingstonia missionaries, tend to view the traditional health sector as backward and based on superstition. The church actively dissuades people from going to traditional healers, mainly because of their associations with witchcraft and spirits. One may even be excommunicated from the CCAP if found to be patronizing these healers.

Although some people accept the church's position on this matter, most people still believe in the power of witchcraft and spirits. It is the rare Tumbuka who will categorically state that there is no foundation to these beliefs. All around them they see evidence of people suffering from illnesses caused by witches and spirits. I have talked to many Tumbuka who are CCAP members but who have been afflicted with what they believe to be spirit-based or witchcraft-based illnesses. This creates a serious dilemma for them, because indigenous healers are believed to be the only health care providers able to help with these kinds of illnesses. People often feel they must choose between the church and getting well.

Typically, though, a Tumbuka—for example, someone with malarial symptoms of chills and fever—will go first to a Western medical facility such as the government hospital in Rumphi. If the treatment that is prescribed fails to alleviate those symptoms, then a consensus usually begins to coalesce among the patient and his or her relatives that forces other than God are involved in the illness. At this point, the help of a traditional healer is usually sought.

As in many indigenous health care systems, there are two kinds of traditional Tumbuka healers: *sing'anga*, who are basically herbalists providing primary health care for their kinsmen and neighbors on a part-time basis, and *nchimi*, who are full-time medical professionals.[9] An *nchimi*'s practice includes not only an extensive pharmacopoeia but also divination, which makes them the diagnosticians—and dancers—nonpareil in Tumbuka society.

Although some *sing'anga* use limited forms of divination, for the most part they are not concerned with the etiology of an illness.[10] They prescribe treatment according to the symptoms that an episode of illness presents. If you are sick and go to a *sing'anga* for help, *you* describe what is wrong, and the *sing'anga* prescribes appropriate *mankwhala* from his or her store of medicinal compounds. In this sense, *sing'anga* are actually situated more toward the Western medical end of the continuum, for this is how Western-trained doctors approach health care in Malawi—through the treatment of symptoms.

When a patient comes to an *nchimi* for medical help, he or she, significantly, says nothing. The silence is filled with musical sound as the drums call forth the *vimbuza* spirits. It is up to the *nchimi*, while entranced, to discover the history and symptoms of the disease and, most importantly, to determine the cause. An *nchimi*'s reputation, and hence his or her business, is built upon the perceived accuracy of this divinatory information.

Robin Horton (1967: 155–87), one of the few scholars to deal with the theoretical relationship between divination and diagnostics, makes a clear distinction between the two. One method operates in "closed" traditional healing systems, the other, in the "open" scientism of Western medical thought. Although Horton makes much out of this difference—converging causal sequences versus direct one-to-one relationships—he does acknowledge that divination and diagnosis are basically two differing techniques for what in the final analysis is the naming of disease. Both are theoretical—Westerners use germ theory, the Tumbuka use spirits—and logical within their respective systems.

If an illness fails to respond to treatment, whether it be home remedies, Western drugs, or *mankwhala* prescribed by a *sing'anga*, most Tumbuka usually suspect that either witchcraft or spirits are involved. Witches are by far the most common cause of illness in the North, according to the Tumbuka. Since there is no one-to-one relationship between witchcraft-caused illnesses—that is, those disvalued states caused by human beings—and the symptoms these illnesses produce, determining what type of witchcraft is involved and who is doing the bewitching is crucial for successful treatment. This is precisely where *nchimi* play such an important role in the Tumbuka health care system, for they name not only the disease but also the witch. And this is precisely why music is crucial to clinical efficacy, for it is music's ability to heat the spirits that fuels the divination trance.

It is useless to treat malarial symptoms with chloroquine or a *sing'anga's mankwhala* if the illness is actually caused by witchcraft. Attacking the problem through the treatment of symptoms will be of no benefit, because it is the witchcraft that must be neutralized. And it will ultimately serve little purpose to neutralize the witchcraft if the witch is not found and prevented from carrying out his or her evil intentions. Thus, when witchcraft is suspected, people usually turn to *nchimi* for help, for their powers of divination make them the witchfinders par excellence.[11]

An African Disease

Tumbuka with whom I associated may have thought I was afflicted by the *vimbuza* spirits, and they knew I had *mizimu*, for everyone does, but they never, at least openly, suspected I had been bewitched. Witchcraft is believed to be most effective against one's own kin, particularly blood relations, which for the most part left me out of the equation since none of my relatives were around. In addition, there was a general belief that witchcraft didn't work on Mzungu, it being an "African disease," although everyone seemed to have at least one story about a white man who had in fact been "witched." A favorite—people would tell this story with particular relish—was about a missionary at Livingstonia who didn't believe in witches and ridiculed those who did. He woke up one morning to find himself in bed. The bed, however, wasn't in his bedroom but in the middle of the road—obviously the work of a powerful *mfwiti.*

Moving beds was not the only thing witches could do. I was struck by the numerous and diverse acts the Tumbuka attributed to these purveyors of evil. They could make themselves invisible, fly through the air, covering great distances in a short amount of time, travel underground (an *mfwiti* once tried to invade Chikanga's compound in this way and kill him), change themselves into hyenas or other wereanimals, raise the dead from their graves to become slaves, or carry out more mundane matters such as causing someone's crops to fail or a person to lose his job. But what witches could do best, and what they did most frequently, was to make people sick, often with the intention of killing them.

Before I discuss how witches accomplish their nefarious deeds, however, I want to deal briefly with why, according to the Tumbuka, men and women set about to harm their fellow human beings. Why do brothers bewitch brothers, sons bewitch fathers, aunts and uncles bewitch nieces and nephews, grandfathers bewitch granddaughters, cowives bewitch each other and occasionally their husband, and sometimes—though theoretically it shouldn't work if they are not kin—neighbors bewitch neighbors? The Tumbuka, for the most part, have one answer—jealousy. A man is jealous of the cattle his brother will inherit, a co-wife of the gifts and attention her husband gives his new bride, a neighbor of his neighbor's success in growing a small cash crop of tobacco. Many Tumbuka bemoaned to me the fact that Africans are "not like Europeans, who don't care if people have things and get ahead." In their view, Africans do not want their fellow Africans to have what they do not.

This situation has been exacerbated by the introduction of a capitalist economy in the North that has fueled a desire for consumer products beyond the reach of most Tumbuka. Often called the "dead North" because of its lack of economic development, this region has not shared in even the modest economic gains Malawi has achieved since gaining independence in 1964. Most Tumbuka attribute this state of affairs to a conscious program carried out by the government of then president-for-life, Hastings Kamuzu Banda.

As a result, the Tumbuka—who are the most politically significant ethnic minority in Malawi, who before independence held many of the mid-level administrative positions in the colonial government, and who in essence constituted an educated elite as a result of the Livingstonia Mission—have occupied a peripheral position in the political economy that has developed in Malawi since 1964. The central government viewed the Tumbuka as a threat, and a concerted effort was made to diminish their influence after independence (Vail and White 1989). Opportunities for bettering one's position are now few in this economic and political environment, which creates intense competition for the few opportunities that do exist, and jealousy of those who succeed.

The overwhelming majority of Tumbuka are subsistence farmers, dependent on seasonal rains to grow enough food to feed their families. Traditionally, the Tumbuka have had a decentralized society based on the autonomy of heterogeneous clans. A system of village headmen, subchiefs, and chiefs (native authorities)—a vestige of British colonial rule—is still in place, but on a day-to-day basis, the clan group remains the functional sector of society.[12] People live in extended-family compounds, which usually house brothers and other patrilineally related kin. Each man owns a garden, from which he feeds his family and in which he sometimes grows surplus produce to raise funds for school fees and for what people now consider necessities: processed sugar, salt, and soap. In a country that has one of the lowest per capita incomes in Africa and one of the densest populations, the Tumbuka are now the poor among the poor.

Under these conditions, there was a general consensus in the North that witchcraft had reached epidemic proportions and was getting worse by the day. Accusations of witchcraft, although technically illegal, were so numerous that they were taken as a common part of everyday life.[13] But they were a side of everyday life that was associated with darkness and hidden forces, with things that were unseen, concealed, and thus evil.

A moral battle is taking place in Malawi between the forces of good and evil. In Tumbuka society, this battle is being played out through the roles of *nchimi* and witch. People see *nchimi*, and *nchimi* see themselves, as the front line in the war against witches. Through their divinatory powers, *nchimi* expose witches and take measures to counteract their evil doings. Witches, on the other hand, are continually trying to cause "confusion" and to "cloud" the "seeing" of *nchimi*.

βafwiti (witches) constitute a parallel world that is in direct opposition to that of *nchimi*. In a way, each defines the other: healers carry their deeds in the metaphoric light of the public arena; witches ᴊe their actions under the cover of darkness. *Nchimi* use *mankwhala* ᴨedicine) to relieve suffering and make manifest that which is hidden; *ßafwiti* use *nyanga* (potions) to cause suffering and misfortune and to conceal their evil deeds. *Nchimi* are prophet healers who work through God's graces; witches are the evil messengers of Satani (Satan). And significantly, given the focus of this study, both *nchimi* and witches use music and dance, but *nchimi* dance in their *thempli* in order to help people, while witches dance on the graves of their victims.

This logic of parallel opposition extends even into the realm of musical sound itself. I once asked Mulaula if witches had their own music. "Of course they do," he replied, "only you can't hear it." In the temple of an *nchimi* healer, music making is a public event, a musical experience that reveals a world. Witches, on the other hand, play their silent whistles under the solitary cover of night, wearing helter-skelter the broken possessions from the graves of their victims. They construct an oppositional musical reality, one that does not reveal a world but covers and conceals it.

Electric Nyanga

The practice of witchcraft is a moral choice made by individual Tumbuka. In general, Tumbuka do not hold an Azande-like (Evans-Pritchard 1937) belief in born witches who are unaware of their own acts.[14] Witches effect their evil deeds through the conscious manipulation of specially prepared medicines called *nyanga*. These "bad" medicines have the power to act over long distances and need not be in actual contact with the victim to be effective.[15] Tumbuka maintain a clear distinction between poison such as the bile from a crocodile, which can kill a person but is not produced through witchcraft, and *nyanga*, which is made lethal only through a witch's manipulation of certain materials that are inert in their natural state.

All adults in Tumbuka society have the potential for using witchcraft against their enemies. If one does not know how to make witchcraft substances, then they may be purchased from people who do. *Nchimi*, in fact, are sometimes suspected of dealing in these goods, the rationale being that since these healers know how to fight witchcraft, then they must know how to make it. This puts *nchimi* in an ambiguous position in Tumbuka society—they are respected but also feared and, to a certain degree, morally suspect.

Nyanga, or the knowledge necessary to make it, may also be passed down from father to son. There is a certain covert sentiment among the Tumbuka that to be a full adult male, one should have some kind of access to the power of witchcraft (*ulowa*), if for no other reason than protection against the *nyanga* of one's fellow man. In other words, you are not so likely to be a victim of witchcraft if you are known to have (or at least are suspected of having) the means to retaliate.

This handing down of esoteric knowledge may even extend to the *mizimu* ancestors. Although on the whole the *mizimu* are considered moral spirits in the sense that they are concerned with upholding the traditional values of Tumbuka society, some *mizimu* have the potential for doing evil. If a person is bad during his or her life—for example, if he or she is an *mfwiti*—then this evil character will carry over into the afterlife. In fact, witches may call on their own ancestors, if they, too, were witches, to help them in their nefarious dealings.

According to Nchimi Chikanje, such was the case with a Mr. Shaba, who was instructed by his grandfather on how to make a particular kind of witchcraft: "His paternal grandfather was an mfwiti who had died some time ago. One night this mzimu came to Mr. Shaba in a dream and told him how to make the following nyanga: Take a newborn pup and bury it on top of a grave. Put nyanga made from roots in with the pup, add more soil, and then plant beans. When the beans are ready, swallow them whole without chewing. This nyanga will help you to be invisible." A bad *mzimu,* however, is considered fairly rare, and once enough time has elapsed and the *mizimu* is incorporated into the ancestral group, its evilness is, in a sense, cleansed.[16]

Tumbuka consider *nyanga* to be a living thing. It has a substantiality to it that can be seen and touched. Witches combine various substances into compounds, much in the same way *nchimi* prepare *mankwhala.* But *nyanga* contains something more, a witchcraft base called *chizimba,* which gives the *nyanga* its efficacy. This base is usually made from animal parts, including such things as lion claws, porcupine quills, hyena brains, or, in the case of Mr. Shaba, a puppy, and it may include such esoteric items as pubic hair from an Mzungu—as was pointed out to me by more than one Tumbuka. In the most potent form of *chizimba,* human flesh is said to be used: many a murder in Malawi is attributed to witches looking for human flesh to use in making a particularly powerful *chizimba.* Incantations called *nthembo* may also be said over the resultant mixture, further increasing its potency. Once activated, *nyanga* has inherent power; it is something alive. Just being near it, even if it was intended for someone else, can make one sick. A not uncommon diagnosis by an *nchimi* would be that a husband had *nyanga* hidden in his hut, and it was making his whole family sick. In a sense, *nyanga* is a kind of overdetermined matter.

For Tumbuka, *nyanga* is the physical evidence that witchcraft exists. Not only can you see and touch it, but you can also get sick from it, even die from its effects. There are virtually hundreds of different kinds of *nyanga*, all virulent in their intended purposes. A form called *chilaso*, a mixture of vegetable matter and animal parts in which needles are inserted, causes sharp pains in the body. One form of *supa*, the generic term for *nyanga* put in a gourd container, can cause fainting spells that eventually may lead to a coma. When Mulaula first became sick with the healer's disease, it was this form of witchcraft that attacked him. Another form of *supa* may make a woman infertile, one of the most serious afflictions to befall a woman in a patrilineal society such as the Tumbuka's. There is even a type of "electric" *nyanga* made from the chemicals found in batteries, which causes people to have pains that are like electric shocks.

During a divination one night, Mulaula accused a man of having this kind of witchcraft. As always, the *ng'oma* drum was sounding the rhythmic mode of one of Mulaula's Zambian spirits, and on this night the choir was singing one of the "deeper" *vimbuza* songs, "Sanda Iyo," a song about dying. As he danced to heat his *vimbuza*, Mulaula called the person forward, signaled for the music to stop, and began to question him:

Mulaula   You have mixed battery chemicals in a Vaseline jar.
          What is this medicine used for?
Accused   It is for my children to rub on their face for protection
          against witches.
Mulaula   How come you use this medicine alone? Your wife refuses knowledge of this bottle. She has only seen a
          Coke bottle.

Mulaula then began to sing "Sanda Iyo," and the choir responded:

solo   *Ahe para nafwa, muzamudaßila.*
       When I die, you will admire.

chorus   *Sanda iyo Sanda iyo.*
         Sanda (white burial cloth) there.

solo   *Ahe para nafwa, muzamucheketa.*

> When I die, you will cut. [Cutting refers to cutting either a coffin or a dead body to administer medicine so as to protect it from witches.]

Mulaula once again signaled for the music to stop:

Mulaula   What sort of medicine is for you only? If it kills people, who will be to blame? If you say it is for defense, how come defense for you only?

   Now I suggest you go get it, but your wife will remain here. The wife sits away because she is menstruating.

Accused   The medicine was given to me by my late uncle.

Mulaula   What chizimba [witchcraft base] is battery chemicals for?

   The two men are going to go with you to collect the bottle with a letter to the village headman,[17] but the rest are staying here.

   The medicine is an electric shocking nyanga.

Obviously, some types of *nyanga* operate on principles of sympathetic magic: *nyanga* that uses needles causes sharp pains, and ones containing battery acid cause electric shocks. There are other ingredients, however, based on the principle of contagion—for example, dirt collected from the footprint of an intended victim to use in a potion. Often, in actual practice, elements of both types are found in the same concoction.

Most *nyanga*, regardless of its kind, has a black, tarlike appearance; the stuff looks evil (fig. 2). When *nchimi* "pluck" these medicines from witches—in other words, when they find this "witchcraft stuff" through divination—they first neutralize it by dipping it in a specially prepared medicine called *mbozgha*. Then it is usually left on drying racks to die. People who are caught by *nchimi* with *nyanga* are also neutralized with *mbozgha* medicine, which is rubbed into small incisions made with a razor on the forehead and arms.[18] If a person who has gone through this neutralization process uses *nyanga* again, according to *nchimi*, the witchcraft substance will come back on them, causing death or, at the very least, serious illness.

Nyanga not only is responsible for diseases of all kinds but also can cause misfortunes such as financial disasters, problems in love, and poor harvests. This clearly takes us out of the realm of what Western medicine considers illness. Our theory of illness is, for the most part,

Fig. 2. *Nyanga* (witch medicines) that have been put on an *nchimi's* drying rack to die

bounded by the physical body. Social misfortunes such as failing in business or losing a lover are not considered the province of the medical profession. It is true that psychotherapies deal with certain social problems, but these are considered to be "illnesses" only in cases where social dysfunction is a result of pathological states. If one goes bankrupt, for example, because of bad financial decisions or unforeseen changes in the economy, the bankruptcy is not construed in Western culture as an illness or anything remotely related to our conception of a medically disvalued state. But if bankruptcy is a result of compulsive gambling or alcoholism, then financial ruin may be considered symptomatic of an underlying neurosis.

The Tumbuka, however, in the case of witchcraft, do not make a sharp distinction between illness of the body and social misfortunes. Social and bodily afflictions are part of a continuum. Causation in both cases may be the deliberate use of *nyanga*. Treatment for infertility caused by witchcraft is ultimately no different from the treatment received for bad luck in business that is the result of the evil effects of *nyanga*. In both instances, therapy is directed at the cause, which involves neutralization of *nyanga* and the witch who is causing the problem. And the only people who can effectively deal with these kinds of problems are *nchimi*, dancing prophets who can ferret out these evil-doers. *Nchimi*, however, cannot do this alone: they must have the help of the *mizimu* spirits who give healers the gift of divinatory sight, enabling them to identify and thus stop those who partake in this dark practice.

Paying Respects

While for the most part the ancestors are helpful, they can be demanding, and if their demands are not met they can be troubling. If dissatisfied with the actions of their descendants, they may bring disease upon those who do not obey their bidding, as was the case with Lußemba, who became ill when she refused her ancestors' wishes that she move to her uncle's land.

The three most commonly cited reasons for *mizimu*'s sending illness or allowing it to happen are someone's failure to obey their wishes, transgression of some taboo, and failure to carry out certain obligatory rituals. All three are usually subsumed under the general category of "not paying proper respects." It is not always the offending party, however, who gets sick. Often it is a relative who suffers the consequences.

An example of this kind of displaced punishment is the case of a divorced woman who came to see Nchimi Chikanje because her son was sick and was not responding to treatment given both by a local healer and by doctors at the mission hospital in Mzuzu. Chikanje "danced the question" and divined the cause to be an illness sent by the boy's dead paternal grandfather. This *mizimu* was upset because the boy's father would not allow him to live in his paternal village. The boy had dreamed that his grandfather told him to leave his mother and go live with his father. The mother took him to his father's village, but the father refused to accept the child. Chikanje stated that if the father did not relent and take the boy, then the child would die and the death would be on the father's head. The *mizimu* was upholding the moral standards of the community, since in the patrilineal society of the Tumbuka, children from a divorce belong to the father's lineage.

A similar example can be seen in the following incident, told to me by Lußemba. In this case, it was not Lußemba who disobeyed the *mizimu* but her second husband. In a dream, the *mizimu* told Lußemba to go to a certain road where she would find some money. She should use this money only to help patients. Lußemba did what she was told and found two kwacha (U.S. $1.00 [exchange rate in 1987]). Her husband found out about the money and demanded that they divide it. She gave her portion to a patient who got well; the husband kept his. Because her husband disobeyed the *mizimu*, Lußemba says, shortly after this she got sick, and the *mizimu* told her they would "cut some of her seeing." The *mizimu* are exacting, and so long as their request is not fully respected, especially when it is directed at a healer, then it is the *nchimi* who will suffer.

Healers, in particular, must be careful to maintain a correct relationship to the *mizimu*, for they rely on the ancestors for the ability to divine. If the *mizimu* are angered, they may hinder an *nchimi*'s "seeing," causing a loss of business and sometimes much more, as Mulaula was to find out.

Cement Tombs and Dirt Graves

I had been searching for Mulaula for a week when I finally found him in a one-room shack behind the only paved road in town. The road ran through the small municipality of Rumphi, where you could buy petrol, if there was petrol to be pumped (there could be a two-week wait), purchase manufactured goods at the local PTC (the People's Trading Company; ironically named, given President Banda's personal financial stake), or sip a beer while listening to the latest hit from South Africa on one of the ever-present radios housed in one of the many one-room bars just off the main road. I was surprised to find Mulaula living so near all this "city" stuff, for he had a decided disliking for all that the town of Rumphi symbolized.

This is not to say that Mulaula didn't embrace the "Commerce and Christianity" that came to this part of Africa on the heels of David Livingstone. Mulaula, like all healers, was a professed Christian, and he certainly had the entrepreneurial spirit. He was relatively young, only thirty-six, but already was a healer of some renown, particularly noted for his witch-finding abilities.

His *chipatala* (hospital) is located in the Vongo Hills behind Rumphi, about a forty-five-minute walk from town. The *mphepo*, "spirit-wind,"[19] is strong in these hills, and Mulaula's *chipatala* had grown to be one of the largest healing compounds in this part of Africa. It was an impressive site, with over seventy-five huts for live-in patients, its own small market, and a general store. This kind of concentration of dwellings—other than in townships like Rumphi or the city of Mzuzu—was unusual for the Tumbuka. For the most part they were still settled in traditional small compounds made up of extended families, usually consisting of no more than ten huts or so. Large or even moderate-size villages were simply not part of the landscape in the Rumphi District.

At the *chipatala* there was a constant coming and going of patients and their relatives, and always the odd assortment of government officials and other personages seeking various kinds of protection and "good luck" medicines. Mulaula started out with virtually nothing—a dream from his *mizimu* brought him to this place in the bush in 1979—but by the time I met him in 1987 he had a flourishing practice. However, this was before he took sick and could no longer perform his duties as an *nchimi*—which was what brought me to Rumphi.

Several people had told me that they had heard Mulaula was seriously ill and had stopped his "business." But rumors were rampant in the North, especially about prominent healers, and therefore I wasn't very concerned initially. However, when the two British doctors at the government hospital, a husband and wife volunteer team, told me they had seen Mulaula the week before and his prognosis was not good, I took the rumors more seriously.

A few months before, with Mulaula's consent, I had invited the doctors to come visit his compound. Unlike most of their colleagues, they were interested in traditional medicine and wanted to establish contacts with the local healers. In their view—and at the time, the official view of the World Health Organization—there needed to be, instead of an adversarial relationship, a more cooperative venture between traditional healers and Western medical practitioners. With their limited resources, the doctors knew that it was impossible to deliver effective health care to a majority of the population, and so they believed it was essential that traditional healers be incorporated within the overall strategy. The doctors could offer help, for example, by providing Mulaula with such things as rehydration salts, analgesics, antimalaria tablets, antibiotics, and vitamins for his patients. Mulaula could definitely help them in cases of "African diseases" such as spirit possession and witchcraft. Mulaula was receptive to what they had to say, and the doctors invited him to come visit them in town. But when he finally took them up on their offer, it was not a matter of reciprocity but to seek medical help.

It was not unusual for healers to go to the government hospital if they were sick from a bout of malaria, for example, or had an injury such as a bad cut or a broken bone. And they often referred patients to the hospital who were too ill for them to treat. *Nchimi* knew that dying patients were bad for business, and so they usually sent their worst cases to Rumphi. The British doctors were not particularly thrilled with this arrangement, because the hospital was beginning to get a reputation as a "house of death," and people were becoming reluctant to go to the hospital themselves or bring their seriously ill relatives there. One of the reasons the doctors wanted to visit Mulaula was to convince him to send these patients to them earlier, when they might have a better chance of saving their lives.

According to the doctors, when Mulaula finally decided to seek their help, he also had waited too long, and it seemed as if there was little they could now do for him. Judging from a preliminary examination and the pathology of his symptoms, the doctors told me, it was a distinct possibility that Mulaula had cancer of the esophagus, and they thought he might not last the year. He couldn't keep anything down and he was deteriorating rapidly. They needed to do some follow-up tests, but Mulaula hadn't kept his return appointment. They wanted to know if I knew where he was, or if I had seen him. This all came as quite a surprise, for the last time I had seen Mulaula, only a month before, he seemed to be doing fine.

After talking with the doctors, I immediately made the trek to Mulaula's hospital in the Vongo Hills behind town. When I arrived at the compound, it was unusually quiet. There wasn't the usual bustle of activity associated with the arrival of new patients and their relatives, the preparation of medicinal compounds, and the other numerous activities associated with the thriving business Mulaula had established. Mr. Chilwa—a former government civil servant and now Mulaula's main assistant, secretary, and majordomo—came out to greet me and confirmed that Mulaula was indeed extremely ill and staying with a cousin in Rumphi, a woman whose husband was a tinsmith with a small shop in the local market. He wasn't quite sure where the cousin lived, but said that if I asked around Rumphi I was sure to find him. Mr. Chilwa was clearly troubled, for Mulaula hadn't been at his *chipatala* for the previous two weeks, and the place was barely hanging together.

Of all the healers I stayed with in northern Malawi, Mulaula was the one with whom I stayed the longest. How many nights had I spent in his temple watching him dance *vimbuza*, and how many nights had we sat around the fire discussing the world of spirits and witches? I felt particularly close to him and was very concerned about his well-being, a concern that wasn't alleviated in the least when I finally found him in town, living amid a cluster of small workers' cabins.

When he came out of the one-room shack where he was staying, Mulaula seemed listless and obviously had lost quite a bit of weight. He still had that intensity in his eyes and the charismatic bearing that I always thought would have made him an excellent candidate for rock-and-roll stardom had a different life trajectory found him growing up in an American city. But now he seemed truly troubled by his circumstances. We sat down to talk and I asked him what was wrong.

About a month ago, he said, he began having an upset stomach, and whenever he ate, he would vomit. This was not so unusual for Mulaula, who had a long history of stomach trouble, which over the years came and went in frequency and severity. After all, this was one of the initial presentations of symptoms when he first got sick with *nthenda ya uchimi*, the disease of the prophets. But this present episode of illness was particularly severe. It had lasted longer than ever before and had been resistant to all his attempts to treat it. Never before had the illness progressed to the stage where he could no longer do his business. He felt he couldn't stay at his compound because of all the demands put on him there, and that was why he had come into Rumphi to stay. Not only was Mulaula worried, but so were his three wives and the twelve assistants who were in training with him at the time.

I mentioned to him that the British doctors were concerned about his health and wanted to see him again to conduct some tests. But he informed me that going back to them was useless, for he had already found out the cause of his malady, and they couldn't help. That night after seeing the "Brits," he had had a dream from his *mizimu*. In the dream they asked him why he had gone to see the British doctors when it was they who were withdrawing their protection and allowing a witch to attack him because they were upset about the state of their grave. Had they not asked him the year before to build a concrete tomb, and had he not so far failed to do so? Until the tomb was built and the proper respects paid at their gravesite, they informed him, he would remain ill and perhaps even die.

His failure to provide the tomb was not for lack of trying. Mulaula was in the unenviable position of having the financial resources yet nowhere to spend the money. There simply were no bags of cement to be had for the past year in the Rumphi District. After all, this was the "dead North," economically undeveloped, with little infrastructure. He had even tried to procure the cement from his brother-in-law in Lilongwe, the nation's capital, but transportation could not be arranged. The ancestors don't accept excuses, however, and it was either a cement tomb for themselves or a dirt grave for Mulaula.

He asked if there was any way I could help secure the cement. I said I would try, but I thought there was little chance that I could do any better and asked him if there was anything else I could get for him. He said no, but not to worry, something would turn up. I didn't feel it was my place to tell him what the doctors had told me, but encouraged him to go back for at least a short visit, though at the time I didn't think it would do much good. We talked for a while longer, but I could tell he was tired and wanted to get back to his room. When we said our good-byes, I had the distinct impression I might never see him again.

I haven't seen him since that day, but it has now been some time since Mulaula finally got his bags of cement from his brother-in-law in Lilongwe, built the tombs for his grandparents, and resumed his practice. I heard that after Chikanga died—it was rumored that some witch finally got to him—Mulaula assumed the mantle of *nchimi ya uchimi*, the prophet of prophets.

Vimbuza *Medicine*

Not only do witches have to contend with *nchimi* healers and *mizimu* spirits who are continually trying to thwart their power, but they also must deal with the *vimbuza*. The *vimbuza* contribute to the fight against witchcraft through the divination process: drumming, dancing, and singing heat the *vimbuza*, providing the energy that fuels the trance state. But the *vimbuza* are more than "batteries" for the "*mizimu* radio"; when witchcraft is involved, they also work directly on the patient's body like a medicine.

When *nyanga* attacks a bewitched person, it often attracts the *vimbuza* spirits, who, acting as a kind of antibody, enter the person's body in an attempt to neutralize the witchcraft. In such cases, spirit possession, even though the Tumbuka consider it a disease, is nevertheless a desirable condition. More than one Tumbuka has told me that *vimbuza* spirits saved his or her life.

These spirits, who both help and afflict, are a kind of catch-all category that includes any spiritual entity not directly descended from the Tumbuka. It is the distinctive feature of foreignness, the status of being the "other," that groups the many different kinds of *vimbuza* spirits into one category. In this sense, they stand in categorical opposition to the ancestors. Unlike the ancestral *mizimu*, *vimbuza* is an open-ended category of spirits. Although the *mizimu* are, in theory, infinitely expandable, this expansion is vertical and so is limited to the actual number of Tumbuka themselves. All Tumbuka will eventually die and attain the status of *mzimu,* but all *mizimu* are of one basic type—ancestor. They are a closed category of spirit entities. No foreigner or animal will ever be able to become a Tumbuka *mzimu.*

The *vimbuza* category, however, is infinitely expandable in a horizontal sense. Any new phenomenon encountered by the Tumbuka has the potential, theoretically, to be transformed into the spiritual energy of *vimbuza.* Although I did not encounter unusual manifestations such as the possession by airplane and guitar that Elizabeth Colson (1969: 71) reports finding among the Tonga of Zambia, during my research I did collect the names of more than twenty-five different kinds of *vimbuza* (see appendix A). Some, such as *vyanusi,* were spirits that had a wide currency; others, such as *Geremani,* the spirits of German soldiers who died in Tanzania (then called German East Africa) during World War I, were restricted to possessing only one or two individuals. What they all had in common, other than their distinctive feature of foreignness—their status of "otherness"—was their ability to physically possess their human hosts, thus causing affliction.

This is an ontological distinction, a question of being, that delimits *mizimu* and *vimbuza* spirits. *Mizimu* cannot enter into the physical world of human beings as the *vimbuza* can. *Vyanusi* and *Geremani* are spirits who can physically enter your body as a presence; deceased grandfathers and great-uncles cannot possess you in this sense. They may visit you in dreams and visions, but they cannot cross the physical barrier of corporeality. *Mizimu* are marked in this way ontologically, a marking that has ramifications in Tumbuka medical theory. The ancestors, significantly, are not the symptomagenic agents of illness, as are the *vimbuza.* Rather, they merely send an illness or allow one to happen by withdrawing their protection, as was the case with Mulaula.

By far the majority of *vimbuza* spirits are those from foreign peoples who, for various reasons, have come into contact with the Tumbuka. With only a few exceptions, they are not the spirits of individual persons but rather the spiritual energy of entire peoples.[20] These spirits are, in many respects, a living history of the Tumbuka-speaking peoples of northern Malawi. The coming of ivory traders across Lake Malawi in the eighteenth century, the invasion by the Ngoni in the mid-nineteenth century, and the arrival of Europeans in the latter part of that century have all been incorporated into the pantheon of *vimbuza* spirits.

The translation of these foreign groups into *vimbuza* spiritual energy, with the resultant affliction and its musical therapy, can be seen as one mechanism by which the Tumbuka coped with sometimes abrupt and jarring cultural change. Events often beyond the control of the Tumbuka became pacified, at least spiritually, through the *vimbuza* complex. The spirit of the Ngoni comes out in the *vimbuza* dance of *vyanusi,* and the wind (*mphepo*) of the Balowoka (the first group of traders from the east) is manifested through the spirits of *ßaMwera.*[21] Interestingly, one of the only spirits not to manifest itself in dance is the *Mzungu* (European) *vimbuza*—perhaps because dancing is not part of the Tumbuka's perception of Scottish missionaries and British government officials.

In a discussion of the "enlargement of scale" with which people in central African societies had to deal, Terence Ranger and John Weller (1975: 7) reach a similar conclusion concerning spirit possession: "People had to deal with a wide variety of aliens—as raiders, or caravan porters, or trading partners. A first step to dealing with them seems often to have been the creation of a dramatic stereotype, expressing what were held to be the essential qualities of the alien group, and acted out through rituals of spirit possession." The *vimbuza* spirits are much more than a coping mechanism, but for a full understanding of the phenomenon, scholars cannot ignore their historical implications. Virtually every people with whom the Tumbuka have come into sustained contact has left its imprint on Tumbuka society through spirit possession, including the autochthonous population the Tumbuka first encountered in northern Malawi. These are possibly the original *vimbuza* spirits, although the Tumbuka I worked with were not clear on this point.

Vimbuza may be the spirits not only of foreign peoples but also of animals. These spirits are never attributed to domestic animals such as goats or chickens but are always animals of the bush, and in that sense they also fit into the category of foreignness. In comparison with the multitude of human *vimbuza* spirits, animal spirits play a decidedly minor role. The lion, however, is considered one of the most powerful of the *vimbuza: nkharamu,* as it is called, plays an important part in the divination trances of some healers. During episodes of possession, it is one of the few spirits that can become seriously violent, wanting to kill people.

The spirit matrix of the lion also contains many historical connections. Most healers consider *nkharamu* to be under the *vimbuza fumu za pasi* (lit. "chiefs of the ground"). These spirits come from central Zambia, and are generally identified with the Bemba and Biza peoples.

The Bemba, indeed, call the spirits of dead chiefs *mipashi* (Richards 1951: 184), a direct linguistic connection of which the Tumbuka are unaware. Included in the *mipashi* is Chitimukuru, the spirit of the Bemba hereditary paramount chief (see Vansina 1966: 88–89; Wills 1985: 55–57). The same spirit is found under the *vimbuza* category of *fumu za pasi*. For the Tumbuka, Chitimukuru lives on in spirit and song:

> solo/chorus *Chitimukuru wawera timunwalike mangenjeza*
> Chitimukuru has come; let us dress him with *mangenjeza*.

(*Mangenjeza* is the chiBemba word for the *mang'wanda*-like belts of tin worn by Bemba diviner-healers known as *ngulu* [Richards 1951: 185].) Chitimukuru, according to the Bemba, was possessed by the spirit of the lion, and this is what gave him his power. For the Tumbuka, these connections between *fumu za pasi*, *nkharamu*, and *Chitimukuru* are further expressed musically in the close relationship between the rhythmic modes specific to these spirits (see chapter 5).

All of the foregoing *vimbuza* relate to specific groups, whether they be foreign peoples or animals. There are also a few *vimbuza* that are spirits of a more generic nature. For example, *kachekuru* is the *vimbuza* of old people who have stiff joints, a kind of *vimbuza* of arthritis. Another example, the *vimbuza ßachota*, are spirits that like to eat fire. These types of *vimbuza* are defined according to specific traits they display.

Whether ethnic group, bush animal, or stylized attribute, *vimbuza* cause illness through the state of possession itself. The Tumbuka believe that health results, in part, from a balance in the body between hot and cold. When a *vimbuza* spirit enters a person's body, it can upset this balance, causing an excess of heat. It is this excess of heat that causes illness. The affliction may take virtually any form, ranging from splitting headaches to infertility in women, from general body malaise to, in extreme cases, death. So long as the *vimbuza* are embedded in the physical body in a heated state and do not "come out," they cause suffering.

I will deal with possession in detail later, but it is important to mention here that most illnesses resulting from possession by *vimbuza* spirits are not *caused* by what Bourguignon (1973: 13) calls the "radical discontinuity of personal identity." The spirits do enter the afflicted person, and he or she is considered "possessed," but not possessed in the sense of entering a trance in which the conscious will is taken over by the spirit.

This kind of spirit-possession trance usually occurs during the treatment phase, when the particular drum modes are sounded. Following homeopathic principles, the drum modes resonate with the particular mode of the *vimbuza* spirit (see chapter 5), heating it past a critical threshold into the world of the living. It is during this musical treatment that the *vimbuza* take over the personality of the patient and "come out," expressing themselves through the *vimbuza* dance. The illness itself is caused precisely by the fact that the *vimbuza* are physically in the patient in a heated state but have not been heated sufficiently to "come out" and "cool down" through the process of trance dancing.

While spirit possession is the cause most people attribute to *vimbuza* illness, many healers offer a somewhat different theory of how the *vimbuza* operate as etiologic agents. In this view, *vimbuza* is both the name of a class of spirits and the name of a substance that is part of the physiological makeup of all human beings.[22] As this theory goes, everyone is born with this *vimbuza* substance inside him or her. Although there is no unanimity on this point, most healers seem to think the substance is in the bloodstream—many cited the fact that it doesn't show up on X rays as evidence for this assertion. In its inert state, this *vimbuza* substance is benign, but when activated or, in Tumbuka terminology, "heated," it can cause symptoms of varying degrees of intensity, including death if it is left untreated.

The initial activation or heating of this *vimbuza* substance occurs as a result of the intrusion of a foreign entity into the body. This activation may happen in one of two ways: foreign spirits may enter a person's body, which causes the *vimbuza* to heat up, creating the imbalance previously mentioned; or, if someone has been "witched," then the *nyanga* in the body, which is also a foreign substance, causes the *vimbuza* to heat. But in this case, the *vimbuza* heat also attracts the *vimbuza* spirits, which results in possession.

Whether *vimbuza* is understood as both bodily substance and spirit or merely as possessing spirit, the actual state of possession, as I mentioned before, is considered a positive force when witchcraft is involved, even though the possession can cause illness. Indeed, the most common reason given for occurrences of *vimbuza*-related illnesses is that the *vimbuza* have entered a person to help counteract the deleterious effects of *nyanga*. When questioned about how and why the *vimbuza* spirits fight witchcraft, patients and healers stated that they did not know the answer. All were adamant, however, that the *vimbuza* spirits helped to save lives.

Although people could not offer explanations of how and why the *vimbuza* spirits fight witchcraft, they did offer two explanations for why people become sick when the *vimbuza* spirits help in cases of witchcraft. The first explanation centers on the fight between the spirits and the *nyanga*. The Túmbuka refer to this fight as a "warring" between the two sides. It is this actual war inside the body that causes sickness. When pressed on this point, the Tumbuka would often refer to the following proverb to explain what they meant:

> *Usange nkhuzi zibiri zikutimbana*
> When two bulls are fighting
> *Utheka niwo uku fukutika*
> it is the grass that suffers.

The second explanation is a logical continuation of the first. Once the *vimbuza* have helped to neutralize the effects of the *nyanga*—whether by drawing attention to the witchcraft or actively fighting it or both—they are still in the body in a heated state, creating an imbalance that can cause illness. In other words, the *vimbuza* act as a kind of medicine, but a medicine that has a certain undesirable side effect: an excess of heat. Healers were quick to point out, however, that this side effect was much easier to deal with from a medical standpoint than was illness caused by witchcraft.

One qualifier must be mentioned concerning the role of *vimbuza* in fighting witchcraft. Although the *vimbuza* can help in this fight, they cannot win the battle by themselves. A person afflicted by witchcraft also needs the help of an *nchimi* healer who can administer special antiwitchcraft medicines and identify who is doing the "witching." Therefore, it is imperative for a person who is bewitched to seek the help of a qualified healer.

In this matter, the *vimbuza* are considered to be of great benefit not only because of their ability actively to fight the witchcraft but also because this fight causes the person to become ill. *Nyanga* may remain hidden in the body without causing outward symptoms until the person is beyond help. Tumbuka would often relate this action of the *nyanga* to the way army ants attack. An ant does not crawl up its victim's leg and start biting immediately, but waits until many ants have gathered, when all begin to bite at once. The same is true of witchcraft, which will hide in the person's body, working its evil but

without producing symptoms serious enough to require medical attention. When the victim finally does get sick, it is usually too late to save
him.

If *vimbuza* come to fight the *nyanga*, then the fight often causes
an illness severe enough that the person will seek the help of a healer.
It is usually during the diagnosis of the symptoms caused by the *vimbuza* that a healer will discover the involvement of witchcraft and will
begin to take appropriate measures to cure the patient. More than once
patients told me that *vimbuza* had saved their lives by causing them
to be sick enough to go to a healer for treatment, and as a result, *nyanga*
that was trying to kill them was discovered.

This brings us to an interesting aspect of the Tumbuka theory of
illness that is quite different from the conception of illness in the West.
In Western medical theory, illness is judged negatively, but for the
Tumbuka some illnesses have a positive value attached to them. Not
only is *vimbuza* an illness that can save lives, but it is also a necessary
component in the creation of the prophet healers known as *nchimi*,
extremely valuable and highly regarded members of their society. These
healers are called to their vocation through the spirit affliction of *vimbuza*, and as we shall see, *vimbuza* becomes an important element in
the diagnostic procedures these healers employ in their medical practice.

How this scenario of witchcraft-*vimbuza-nchimi* is played out in
the lives of individual Tumbuka is illustrated in the following story,
which was told to me by a woman who, at the time, was an apprentice
under Nchimi Chikanje. Meras was in her mid-thirties and had been
living at Chikanje's compound for the previous two years. I asked her
to tell me the history of her disease (*nthenda*).

Wife of the Wind

"One night, while asleep, I dreamt that I was sitting around a fire with
six other people who all had their hands spread over the fire. One old
woman had her hands under the other hands. That hand went up to
my neck and she tried to strangle me. Then I felt my heart being pulled
as well. The other people said, you don't have to kill this one because
she is a quiet lady. The old woman protested, saying, she is the most
liked person around here so she has to go. The other people pulled the
old woman's hands away. All the people were ßafwiti [witches].

"When I awoke from the dream, I ran to my mother-in-law's house and banged on the door with my head. The door opened and I fainted. When I woke up from fainting, that is when the illness started. I felt like my heart was growing smaller and that paralysis was coming from my toes. I couldn't sleep or work, and my internal organs felt upset. This lasted for three days, when relatives came to take me home to Mphrembe [a small town in southern Mzimba District].

"While I was there, I visited several nchimi who confirmed that I had been 'witched.' The mufwiti were relatives from my husband's side; my husband's brother's wife (who was the woman who had tried to strangle me), his father's elder brother, his younger brother, and my husband's grandfather.

"I was mainly helped by my mother's younger sister, who had been an nchimi. She first took me to other nchimi, but decided to dig her own roots to help me. She also told me that I had vimbuza who had come to fight the witchcraft.

"The vimbuza came with a message from God. They told me that the name of my disease will be Nyamphepo [lit. "wife of the wind"]. To fulfill the use of this name, I was told to sacrifice a goat, a white cock, and a white dove. I was also told that from that day I would be able to sleep again.

"I started to work a little bit after this, and one day when I had finished with the pounding I decided to sit at an open ground near my house. When sitting there, I saw a vision of two people dressed in white gowns. They said they had come with a message from God. They would be staying inside of me, and that they had come with three commandments: I should never engage in witchcraft, I should never steal, and I should never commit adultery.

"After this vision, I started getting ill again. My stomach felt like it was going up into my chest. Then my mother and younger sister took me to an nchimi at Ekwendeni. He said, 'this daughter of ours is suffering from vimbuza.' My mother wanted to prove that I had nthenda, so she found three patients and brought them in front of me. My vimbuza heated up, and I 'saw' each patient's troubles. The following day I gave them medicine, and they got better. In the morning, when I was giving the medicine, my stomach was back in its place. I used nthenda Nyamphepo to 'see' people.

"That night I dreamt that I should leave for Mzimba south to see Nchimi Euthini. When I went there the nchimi tried but failed to do the necessary things. I was supposed to go with the nchimi to the place where I was born with a white cloth to pay respects to my mizimu. Then we were to go back to the nchimi's place and ask my husband to buy me an outfit, a red uniform with white crosses and a white hem.

"The nchimi didn't do any of this, and the nthenda got frustrated. The mizimu decided to look for a suitable place for me. They told me to go to Nkhamanga, and if I didn't get help there to go to Bwengu. I decided not to go to Nkhamanga but to come straight to Nchimi Chi-kanje's at Bwengu. That was two years ago.

"I told Chikanje why I had come, and that we should pay respects to my mizimu with a white cloth. When we were to go to my home to pay respects, I said that we were also expected to carry a few patients with us, and that once there, we should beat drums to tell the vimbuza that we had come.

"A couple of months later, we went to my home and did as we were directed. After doing those things, that night I dreamt that my grandfather, grandmother, and young father [father's brother] came to my door with the white cloth, which they were putting on their heads. They entered my house and told me:

> You have been sick for a long time because you haven't pleased us. We have seen what you've done [presenting a white cloth], now go to Chikanje and buy another piece of white cloth. With the white cloth, you and Chikanje and a few patients should go to the graveyard where we are sleeping. When giving the white cloth to the vißanda [ghosts], start with your grand-mother's grave. Bow from the position of her head, then the middle. Do the same thing with the other two graves. Then put twenty-five tambala [U.S. thirteen cents] on top of your grandmother's grave. It will be at the graveyard that you should be given the uniform, and put it on right there. Stand for a while there, then you will see what will be bestowed in you by the vißanda.

In the dream I was told that half the way to 'seeing' was complete, but to complete the 'seeing' I need to go to the graveyard and do these things. So far I have not done these things, and I will still be sick until I go to the graveyard."

The Disease of the Prophets

From her initial crisis to her still-unsettled outcome, Meras's life took on the quality of a drama played out in a world of cabalistic witches, dancing prophets, and drummed spirits.[23] It is evident from her story that her illness displayed all the features of *nthenda ya uchimi*, the disease of the prophets. Not only was she possessed by the *vimbuza* spirits who came to fight witchcraft, which happens to many people, but she also was visited by the *mizimu* in dreams (the named ancestors, her grandparents and uncle who asked for a white cloth) and in visions (unnamed ancestors in white robes who brought commandments from God), a much rarer occurrence. The initiatory aspect of her disease can also be read in her description of getting better after she first treated someone—that is, her stomach settled down—and in her remark that she will remain sick until she starts fully "seeing" patients. As with other healers worldwide, if the spirits' call goes unheeded, dire consequences will result.

Although Meras's disease began with witchcraft, it quickly took on the profile of an election by the spirits to become a healer. The witchcraft in her case acted as a kind of triggering mechanism that set this election in motion.[24] There seems to be a kind of irony at work here in which witchcraft begins a process that culminates in the creation of an *nchimi* who will fight the evilness of witches. Meras's personification of her disease as the *nthenda* Nyamphepo (wife of the wind), which will also become her *nchimi* name, is indicative of much more than just a disease: it represents a complex interaction between witches, spirits, and the one afflicted, an interaction that has the potential of producing an *nchimi*, a highly valued member of Tumbuka society.

But before Meras can begin to "see" as Nchimi Nyamphepo, she must first achieve the correct alignment of spiritual energy. Part of this process is paying respects to the ancestors, which she will do at the gravesite of her paternal grandparents and uncle. But the *vimbuza* spirits must be cooled to allow the *mizimu* "to go on top," and there is only one way to achieve this configuration—the *chilopa* blood sacrifice. And central to the *chilopa* is the music and dance of *vimbuza*.

three

Blood and Spirit

The *Chilopa* Sacrifice

My first encounter with a *chilopa* sacrifice was entirely unexpected.[1] Before I witnessed this event, I had no idea that animal sacrifices were a part of *vimbuza* healing, for no one had spoken of it to me in Malawi before I started my research.

The encounter occurred shortly after my arrival in the capital of the Northern Region, Mzuzu, a city of about sixty thousand. While I was teaching at the University of Malawi, I had made the acquaintance of a magistrate for the North who lived there. We discussed my research, and he suggested that he might be able to help me in my efforts and that I should contact him when I came north.

Taking him up on his offer, I called on the judge, and he put me in touch with two of his court messengers who seemed to know quite a bit about local healers. It is not surprising that people associated with the court would know about local healers, given the fact that most *nchimi* have had several run-ins with the law. *Nchimi* are witchfinders, and witchcraft accusations are technically illegal (see chapter 2, note 13). Most have spent some time in jail, though once they have established a reputation as an effective diviner-healer they are usually left alone by the local authorities. The court messengers suggested that we visit a well-known *nchimi* by the name of Mzimu who lived on the outskirts of town. All *nchimi* adopt a new name when they start their practice, usually symbolizing some special attribute of their power. Mzimu was supposed to have an unusually close and powerful relationship with his ancestral spirits.

Although somewhat reluctant to begin my research right away, given my continuing bout with cyclical headaches (see chapter 2), I decided that for fifty minutes out of every hour I could at least get something done. That afternoon we borrowed the judge's car and drove a few miles outside of town to the small airport that services the Northern Region. Directly across from the airport's only runway, on the other side of the highway, was a small cluster of mud huts that was the compound of Nchimi Mzimu. I was looking forward to meeting my first healer, even though my enthusiasm was dampened a bit by my physical condition and because I was not—as I had envisioned I would be—out in the bush, but directly in the landing approach path of Malawi Airlines.

When we pulled into the compound, people rushed around the car to see who this Mzungu was and what he wanted. One of the court messengers explained to a young man who approached the car that I was a teacher from the University of Malawi and that I wanted to meet with Mzimu to talk with him about what kinds of things he did as an *nchimi*.

The young man disappeared into the largest hut in the compound, which, I was to find out, was Mzimu's *thempli* (temple), the place where he diagnosed patients and caught witches. After a few minutes, he came back outside and escorted us into the hut. Inside was seated Mzimu, a portly, middle-aged man dressed in the typical assortment of secondhand clothes imported into Malawi from the United States, including a pair of checkered polyester pants and a V-neck sweater. (The interesting combinations of clothes the Tumbuka put together never ceased to amaze me. I was particularly fond of the T-shirt Nchimi Mulaula often wore when divining, which had "DISC JOCKEY" displayed in bold letters across the front. This seemed to fit well with his identification of radios with divination [see chapter 1].) The only item that identified Mzimu as an *nchimi* were the numerous strands of *mboni* ("witness") beads that he wore around his neck and wrists. When we walked in, he was in the process of seeing several patients who had come seeking his advice.

He welcomed us to his compound and invited us to sit down next to him as he finished seeing the remaining patients. Along with the patients, there were six women in the *thempli* who served as a chorus. They sang songs and shook rattles made from old oil cans. One of the messengers explained to me that the singing helped Mzimu divine the patients' troubles.[2]

From what I could make out over the singing and rattles, which were quite loud—the louder the better for divining, I was told—several of the patients were women suffering from *vimbuza* because of witchcraft. At the time I thought this meant that witches had sent the *vimbuza* spirits. Mzimu also pronounced that someone had *nyanga* of a black mambo, and commanded the culprit to bring this witchcraft stuff to him so he could neutralize it. The young man who had brought us into the *thempli* pulled out an object made of several small pieces of wood or possibly roots that had been smeared with a black substance, in order to show us what "this witchcraft stuff" looked like. It was explained to us that this object, which Mzimu had "plucked" from a witch, could be changed into a black mambo (it wasn't clear whether this meant a "real" snake or the "shadow" of a snake) for the purposes of attacking someone.

After about an hour, Mzimu finally turned to me and asked if I had any questions. Because this was my first interview with an *nchimi*, and because my chiTumbuka at the time was minimal, Mzimu's English nonexistent, and the court messenger's translations somewhat confusing, I didn't even get the difference between real snakes and shadows cleared up. Little substance emerged from this first interview, which was cut short by the growing darkness and our need to return the judge's car. Before we left, however, Mzimu invited us back the next day. He said something was going on that he was sure I would be interested in seeing. This sounded intriguing, and I made arrangements with one of the messengers to accompany me.

We were to meet at 1:00 P.M., but the next day, when the messenger still hadn't arrived by 2:00, I decided to go to Mzimu's by myself. With the airstrip as a convenient marker, I didn't have too much trouble locating his compound. When I arrived, Mzimu came out to greet me, and when he realized that I was alone, he seemed surprised but pleased. He called for one of his assistants to bring out some chairs, and we sat down in front of the *thempli*. Because of our mutual lack of interlinguistic competence, Mzimu didn't offer any explanations about what was to transpire, and neither of us said much beyond formal greetings. As I sat there, wondering what was going to happen, two drums were brought out of the hut and a crowd began to gather. One of the women in the crowd raised a song, and the drummers began to play. When no one around me offered to explain what was going on, I decided to sit back, put on my observer's hat, and watch the proceedings.

Finally some "real" music. Until now I had been very frustrated in my attempts to hear performances of indigenous music in Malawi. While teaching at the university, I had made forays into the surrounding villages to try to remedy the situation. But I soon discovered that Africans, contrary to popular beliefs, did not sing all the time, and music was far from being a functional part of all activities, as one sometimes supposes it is when reading the literature on African music. Up to this point, the main feature of musical culture in Malawi for me had been MBC, the only Malawian radio station.

Shortly, a woman around nineteen years old was brought out of the *thempli* and sat down in front of the drums. As she sat there she seemed almost to be in a stupor, remaining motionless except for leaning her head right next to the *ng'oma* master drum, which at the time was playing full blast one of the *vimbuza* modes. Accompanying the *ng'oma*, adding to its energy, was the *mphiningu* drum, sounding a repeating pattern that reminded me of the *kagan* part in a West African Ewe percussion ensemble.[3] Different songs in typical call and response form were being sung mostly by the women and young girls in the crowd, while the majority of the men and boys looked on. After about fifteen minutes of this, as a new song was raised and the drums began a different rhythmic mode, the young woman began to tremble. As soon as she showed signs of responding to the music, the drummers intensified their playing and the women sang with renewed force. Abruptly she began to roll on the ground in front of the drums.

This lasted for only a few minutes until she stopped, crawled over to the drums, and bowed before them in the traditional Tumbuka manner of paying respect by lying on one side and then the other (fig. 3). Then she stood and began to dance (fig. 4). Attached to her waist were the *mang'wanda* belt of tin and the *mazamba* skirt, and around her legs she wore the *nyisi* jingles. Her dance consisted mainly of short bursts of intense energy that shook the *mang'wanda* in time with the six-pulse figurations of the drums. As she danced, Nchimi Mzimu, who by now was watching the proceedings from behind the drums, walked over and put some kind of dry brown powder in her mouth. She rolled this around her mouth and over her gums while she continued to dance.

Suddenly she stopped dancing, and I gathered from the actions of the *nchimi* and one of his assistants that something wasn't going right with the dance. They called for someone to get ashes from one of the cooking fires, which they smeared on the woman's legs and the heads of the drums. As I found out later, this was an act of purification done because one of the women singers was having her period and shouldn't have been there, since this was upsetting the spirits.[4]

With the ashes cooling the effects of menstrual blood, the woman renewed her dancing with vigor. After about fifteen minutes of her intense dancing, Mzimu and one of his assistants pulled the woman to

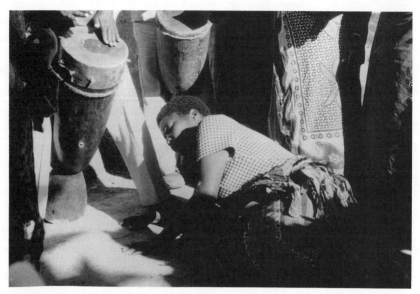

Fig. 3. Patient ritually bowing to the drums

Fig. 4. Patient dancing *vimbuza* to heat her spirits for the *chilopa* sacrifice

Fig. 5. Nchimi Mzimu passing the dove over the patient's head

the ground, and with the help of the women in the chorus began the slow *nkufi* clapping, the traditional way to address the spirits.

After the *nkufi*, the drumming and singing resumed, and the woman stood up and began to dance again. Someone in the crowd handed Mzimu a tin plate covered by another tin plate that had a red cross painted on the top. Inside the plates was a live white dove, which Mzimu took out and began passing over the patient's head while she danced (fig. 5). After a few passes, he handed the dove to one of his assistants, who held the dove's neck up to the woman's mouth. To my complete surprise, she bit into the dove's throat and began to suck its blood (fig. 6). It so happened that from where I was seated, I could look directly into the dove's eyes. Strangely, the dove didn't struggle at all, and as its eyes began to lose their light, the whole ritual took on a kind of serenity that transcended my initial shock. I sat and watched as the dove slowly sank into death.

In the final act of the sacrifice, the dove's breast was split open and the woman was given its heart to eat. She then staggered from the dance circle and collapsed. I wasn't sure what I had just witnessed, but I realized that this ritual was of an extraordinary character and must have a deep significance in the world of *vimbuza*.

Over the next year, I had the good fortune of attending ten other

Fig. 6. Patient sucking blood from the throat of the dove

performances of *chilopa*,[5] which is a significant number considering that most Tumbuka will see only a few *chilopa* in a lifetime, and some, none at all. I witnessed every kind of *chilopa*, from the sacrifice of doves and chickens to that of goats and, as it turned out, on my last day in the field, the *chilopa* of a cow, a very rare occurrence. But I don't think any of them had the impact of this first *chilopa* across from the Mzuzu airport at the compound of Mzimu.

The Sacrificial Axis

Chilopa is serious and dangerous business. The *vimbuza* spirits want fresh blood, and if this desire is not satisfied through the drinking of blood from an animal sacrifice, then the *vimbuza* will start feasting on the blood of the afflicted. If the *chilopa* is not done correctly, the patient's stomach will swell from the blood. In both cases, the result could be death.

The blood sacrifice of *chilopa* is the axial point of *vimbuza* affliction. Its outcome often decides whether those afflicted will return to their everyday life or enter the world of witchfinder, prophet, and healer. If, after a *chilopa* is performed, a patient's *vimbuza* "cools" to the point that the patient becomes asymptomatic, then this is considered to be the end of the treatment, at least for the foreseeable future, and the person returns to his or her normal life.

This does not mean that the patient is cured—cures are nonexistent—for *vimbuza* is an ongoing reality in the lives of those who are afflicted. Periodically the *vimbuza* may heat up, which will cause symptoms of disease. This might happen every other week, every other month, or every other year. There is no identifiable, set pattern for occurrences of *vimbuza;* it varies with the individual. But when it does occur, the person will dance the *nthenda* (disease) to relieve the symptoms. In this way, *vimbuza* dancing takes on the form of a maintenance therapy.

If, on the other hand, the *vimbuza,* although cooler, still remain sufficiently heated to produce symptoms, and the special dreams of the ancestors intensify, then this is a sure sign that the patient has the healer's disease *(nthenda ya uchimi).*[6] For the "elect," one *chilopa* is rarely enough to appease the *nthenda.* Therefore, as in Tembo's case, more blood must flow before the *vimbuza* are satisfied.

Tembo's Chilopa

Tembo's illness had started while he was studying for his end-of-year school exams.[7] One day while coming home from school, he began to get a severe headache that made the top of his head feel as if it were going to "blow its top," a typical description by *vimbuza* sufferers of the intensity of these kinds of headaches. What was atypical about Tembo's symptoms was that he didn't want to be around people because he felt that his fingernails were like lion claws, and he was afraid that he would kill someone. He also began having a recurring dream that caused him great anxiety. In the dream, someone is calling his name. He knows that this person has come to strangle him, but when he turns to see who it is, he cannot see the person's face.

At the time of his illness, Tembo was in his early twenties, unmarried and living with his parents in his home village. After several weeks, his *mizimu* came in a dream and told him to go to Nchimi Chikanje for help. When I first met Tembo, it had been eleven months since he had followed his ancestors' advice and come to live at Chikanje's compound.

During those eleven months, Chikanje had been treating Tembo for his troubles, which, according to Chikanje, showed strong signs of

being *nthenda ya uchimi*. Not only was Tembo being troubled by the
vimbuza, but also the ancestors were coming to him in his dreams,
the classic presentation of an initiatory illness within the *vimbuza*
complex.

Treatment for Tembo consisted of taking medicines and dancing
vimbuza in order to cool (*kuzizimiska*) and stabilize the disease. After
several weeks of this, as the *vimbuza* spirits began to cool down and
become more stable, he started having dreams about "things past and
future that were true." According to Tembo:

> I dreamt that Chikanje's daughter would have a baby girl, and
> she did.
>
> I dreamt that Chikanje's sister's son would pass away, and
> he did.
>
> I dreamt that my brother's son would die, and the following
> day it happened.
>
> I dreamt that a flying bed came from Mzuzu to Bwengu to
> give me a gift. The next day a lorry stopped in Bwengu and a
> friend gave me bananas which I sold for two kwacha.

Chikanje confirmed that what Tembo dreamt came to pass. He also
remarked that the intensity and accuracy of prediction in Tembo's
dreaming was unusual and pointed to the fact that Tembo's *nthenda*
must be strong.

During this period of intense dreaming, Tembo's *mizimu* once
again came to him in a dream and told him what needed to be done in
order to please them and satisfy the *vimbuza*. First he must pay respects
to them (the *mizimu*) at his home village by presenting a circular white
cloth embroidered with crosses. After this he should do three *vilopa*
(plural of *chilopa*). During one *chilopa* he should suck the blood of a
white cock and a white she-dove, during another, the blood of a brown
she-goat with a white patch on its forehead, and finally, for the last
chilopa, the blood of a female cow spotted red and white. There is a
relationship between the size of the *chilopa* and the intensity of the
disease. Strong healers have strong *nthenda* that require much blood.
Tembo had the potential, if he completed the prescribed course of action, to become an important healer.

Four days after I met Tembo, he did the first of the *chilopa*, the
cock and the dove, which in its main outlines followed the *chilopa* I
had witnessed at Nchimi Mzimu's. Some six months later he performed

the second *chilopa*, killing a goat and sucking its blood. It is this *chilopa* that I want to focus on now.

In the six months between the first and second *vilopa*, Tembo had experienced quite a bit of trouble. After the first *chilopa*, we went to Tembo's village and he presented to the *mizimu* the white cloth they had asked for. That night he and Chikanje danced *vimbuza* together and divined the troubles of several patients. First Tembo would "see" a person and diagnose his or her problem; then Chikanje would "see" the same patient to check whether their diagnoses matched. Neither one could hear the other, for they talked directly into the ear of the patient, and the drumming, singing, and clapping continued throughout the divination. If the diagnoses matched, which for the most part, according to Chikanje, they did, then Tembo would be well on his way to becoming an *nchimi*.

Within a month, however, Tembo's *mizimu* became upset and blocked his "seeing." I had a hard time finding out the reason, but it seems that it had to do with Tembo's breaking some rules regarding sexual conduct. Whatever the reason, unfortunately for Tembo, at about the same time this was going on, Chikanje left for an extended trip to the southern part of Mzimba District. For the next few months Tembo was left pretty much on his own. His *nthenda*, which had become more stable as a result of the first *chilopa*, heated up and began to cause him trouble again. Things got to the point where Tembo even sought the help of Nchimi Mulaula, who, however, refused to help without Chikanje's permission. There is a professional ethic between healers not to interfere with each other's patients.

Chikanje finally returned from Mzimba in late July, and Tembo was put back on a regime of medicine and dancing to help cool and stabilize his *nthenda* once again. By October, Chikanje decided that it was time for Tembo to do another *chilopa*, which set in motion a series of events that activated a wider social field around Tembo.

The first in a series of preliminary steps taken prior to the *chilopa* is the procurement of the animal to be sacrificed. This is an important choice because the animal must satisfy the *vimbuza* spirits. The spirits' designation of which animal to use in a *chilopa* is usually much more detailed than merely whether it should be a chicken or a goat. They often specify sex, color, and markings, as can be seen in Tembo's choice of a reddish brown female goat with a white patch on its forehead.

If the *chilopa* is to be a dove or a chicken, procurement is fairly easy. But obtaining larger animals for sacrifice can entail a heavy financial burden on the patient's family, which is probably one of the main reasons why the *chilopa* of a cow is rare. Goats, however, were used in many of the *vilopa* I witnessed, and with goats costing up to 45 kwacha (U.S. $23), this could be a considerable expense in a country where per capita income is only $180 a year.

To pay for the *chilopa* of a goat, one usually needs assistance not only from one's immediate relatives but also from one's extended family. There is social pressure on all relatives to contribute, since a failure to help may be interpreted as malice toward the patient, and malice is often a sign of intended witchcraft. It is important that the animal to be sacrificed is given with "one heart"—in other words, without resentment or animosity on the part of those who contributed toward procuring the animal.

Chilopa activates the social field of the patient's family both through financial commitments and in more direct ways. On the day of the *chilopa*, the immediate family assembles at the *nchimi*'s compound. All family disputes should be publicly stated and resolved, or else the *chilopa* could go wrong and the patient be killed from the effects of the blood. Hostility within the family is seen as a destructive force, and unless it is resolved the spirits will become offended and will reject the healing properties of the *chilopa*.[8] This is a vivid example of the importance the Tumbuka place on social and familial harmony in the promotion of health, and its role in sickness when lacking.

In Tembo's case, everything was taken care of with relatively little trouble. His mother's brother supplied the goat, and the *chilopa* took place on October 4, 1987, in the early morning hours after a night of divination by Chikanje and *vimbuza* dancing by several patients. Everyone who lived at the compound attended the *chilopa*, including Chikanje's wives, children, relatives, in-patients and their relatives who were staying to help with their care, and all assistants in training. People from the surrounding areas came as onlookers. At around 5:30 A.M., Tembo walked into the *thempli* in full *vimbuza* attire and wearing his *nchimi* outfit, which had been requested by the spirits in a dream. It consisted of red shorts and a shirt embroidered with crosses. Around his head he wore a long strip of red cloth (*mraza*), which traditionally symbolizes mourning.

After entering the temple, Tembo sat down in front of the drums in order to heat his *vimbuza*. The women apprentices, who always make up the core of the choir (*kwaya*) at any healer's compound, raised a song that they knew Tembo's *vimbuza* would respond to, since by now they had had many experiences in the temple with his spirits. As the song took shape and the *kwaya* responded to the soloist's call, and as the drumming synchronized with the women's clapping, Tembo's arms and legs began the fine tremolo shaking characteristic of the heated *vimbuza*. After a few minutes, the *vimbuza* spirits inside of Tembo rose to dance.

At this point in the proceedings, Chikanje, who had been sleeping for the past few hours in order to dream about what medicines he should give Tembo during the *chilopa*,[9] came into the temple dressed in his blue satin choir robe to watch Tembo dance. It was crucial for Chikanje to monitor the dance during this stage in the ritual in order to gauge the status of the *vimbuza*. The spirits needed to be heated enough to be strong when they took the *chilopa*, but not overheated so that they would begin to cool down by the time the blood was taken. Chikanje also needed to decide the appropriate moment to perform the *nkufi* clapping to "officially" inform the spirits of what was going to take place.

After about a half hour of dancing, upon a signal from Chikanje, two of the senior women adepts pulled Tembo to the ground and, with the other women in the chorus, began the *nkufi* clapping. Tembo's father and Chikanje talked to the spirits inside Tembo:

Chikanje Now you will be happy. Your father is here. Be happy! My child should eat.

Father I am happy to be coming here for the first time to Chikanje's. You were a dead child. Now that we can talk to each other, we pray to God that he should continue helping.

All your mizimu, of your aunt or whomsoever, must forgive you. With me, I'm happy Chikanje should work. Even Chikanje's vißanda [lit. "ghosts," but in this context meaning ancestors] should be okay.

I pray hard, my child.

Chikanje The parents have come. I'm only adding to what he said at first that the mizimu were giving you problems. We are going to the mountains to take you back home, just because you were a sick man. That is why I was leaving you. Now your parents are saying I have looked after you well. That is pleasing to know. The mizimu should come in a good way. Not that it should be disturbing people, or even yourself.

Come with good dreams!

Now your parents have come with a chilopa of a

red she-goat with a white patch on the forehead that
the mzimu told you about. That is what has been
found. Your parents have come to kneel in front of
you. Chilopa should be given to mphepo zinai [the four
winds] and mizimu so everything should go on well.

The nthenda got you when you were at school.
You had to leave the school, just like me. The nthenda
is continuing up to now. Like this it is not pleasant to
parents. So it is the same problem on your part. First
Corinthians nine.[10]

We stand outside so that it is wider.

Following the *nkufi,* Tembo danced for a short time and then was
led outside. Chikanje told me that the actual *chilopa* is always done
outside so that the spirits do not in any way feel confined, so that the
assistants can see better when cutting out the parts of the animal that
are used for ritual purposes, and for the pragmatic purpose—there always seemed to be a pragmatic side to what *nchimi* did—of "not getting
all that blood all over the floor and having to clean it up."

Once outside, Tembo resumed his dancing. As he danced, Chikanje
gave him a brown powdered medicine to prevent him, as Chikanje
explained, from getting sick from the blood. The medicine was also—
once again the pragmatic factor—to hide the taste of the blood because
"that blood tastes *too* bad." At a signal from Chikanje, two men
brought the goat into the dancing area, a circular space defined by the
drummers, *kwaya,* and others who were in attendance. The men held
onto the goat's legs and turned it on its back. Tembo danced closer to
the goat with an increased intensity.

Suddenly, he fell upon the goat, grabbing its mouth with his hands,
and while holding it tightly so that the goat could not open its mouth,
he put his mouth over the goat's mouth and nose. At first the goat
struggled, but the men held on to its legs, and once it realized that it
could not escape, it gave up the fight. Slowly Tembo suffocated the
goat with his mouth.

As the goat slipped into death, one of the men holding it continually checked its eye reflexes to determine exactly when death finally
overcame the animal. At the moment of death, Tembo was pulled away
from the goat's mouth and held back as its throat was slit. Chikanje
poured more of the brown medicine on the wound, and then Tembo
was released. He buried his mouth in the goat's throat and began to
suck the fresh-flowing blood. He was allowed to drink the blood for

only a few seconds before the goat was pulled away from him and taken out of his sight. This small quantity of fresh blood is enough, if the *chilopa* has been done correctly, to cool the *vimbuza* spirits.[11]

Throughout the sacrifice, the singing and drumming never ceased. Even as Tembo lay prostrate on the ground suffocating the goat, as the animal neared death he began shaking the *mang'wanda* belt of tin worn around his hips, in effect dancing while lying down. After the blood was taken, he stood up, and each of the *vimbuza* inside him came out, one after another, to dance.

While Tembo danced, the goat was cut open, and a piece of the heart was cut out and given to him to eat. Then the gallbladder (*nyongo*) was removed,[12] and Chikanje took it and squeezed the bile over Tembo's head. As the bile ran down Tembo's face, he was not supposed to blink if it got into his eyes or spit if it went into his mouth. If he had done so—Tembo did neither one—then it would have meant that he was not ready for the *chilopa*. According to Chikanje, the bile would make his *nthenda* bitter, that is, strong, so that he would not be afraid of finding witches and denouncing them no matter who they were, even a high government official or one of his parents.

After the pouring of the bile, the distinctive rhythm of *vyanusi* was sounded on the drums, and Tembo began to dance the *vimbuza* of the Ngoni with a spear that someone handed him. Unlike most of the other *vimbuza* rhythmic modes, that of *vyanusi* covers the span of twelve pulses that cannot be divided into separable halves for purposes of variation, and the dance does not utilize the hip-shaking of the *mang'wanda* tin belts, but rather involves a crossing of the feet that precisely matches the motional configuration of the drum figure (see chapter 5).

A special connection exists between this *vimbuza* and *nchimi*. Most healers consider it the strongest *vimbuza*, and some attribute to this spirit their ability to smell witches—*vyanusi* is derived from the Ngoni word *izanusi*, which means "those who smell"—and to find certain medicines—that is, roots—in the bush. *Izanusi* were Ngoni diviners who were also witchsmellers (see Read 1956), and there is strong evidence that *nchimi* appropriated many of the practices of the *izanusi* into their own, but it would take us too far afield to deal with this syncretism here.

In the final part of the ritual, a halter (*machowa*) was fashioned from the skin of the goat and placed around Tembo's chest. Once the halter was put on, the gallbladder was blown up like a small balloon and affixed to the goat skin. From this point on, the halter acts, in part, as a sign to others that Tembo has recently performed a *chilopa*. So long as he wears the halter he must refrain from sexual intercourse, and no one may speak to him unless they first give him a silver coin. After the first time a person gives a coin, he need not repeat the act on subsequent occasions. Tembo must wear this halter for the next month or so, until Chikanje decides through his spirits that it is time to remove it.

With the halter in place, and while Tembo was still dancing, all of the other apprentices walked up to him and offered congratulations by shaking his hand. He danced different *vimbuza* for about thirty minutes after this, and then finally walked away from the dance area. The rest of the people dispersed, and the only remaining thing to do was to divide up the goat among the participants. Everyone involved got a share of the meat, with Chikanje getting a sizable amount for being "master" of the *chilopa*.

A portion of the meat, a piece from each of the major internal organs of the goat, however, was specifically kept out for the *mizimu*. In the final act of the *chilopa*, Tembo returned to his hut and this meat was cooked and given to him to eat.

The Raw and the Cooked

"The vimbuza want blood; the cooked meat is for the mizimu." This explanation, offered by Chikanje, with its binary, contrasting categories of raw and cooked foods, evokes comparisons with the ideas of Claude Lévi-Strauss at more than a superficial level. When Chikanje states the obvious, that the ancestors are Tumbuka and of course they eat their food cooked, he is intimating much more than a gastronomical preference, for these are manifestations of a deeper structural level that expresses not only transitions from nature to culture but ultimately a "transcendent unity of man and nature" (De George and De George 1972: xxix). For Tumbuka during *chilopa*, as for the neighbors of the Bororo Indians of South America, "culinary operations [are] mediatory activities between heaven and earth, life and death, nature and society" (Lévi-Strauss 1969: 65).

Chilopa is infused with binary oppositions, the raw and the cooked being only one of many that inform the sacrifice. In many ways, *chilopa* is mythic in its content, and therefore it is not surprising to find such oppositions bubbling to the surface. Its themes are ultimately about life and death, which, in the action of the sacrifice, are given an immediacy unparalleled in the ritual lives of *nchimi* and their followers.

Although the *chilopa* sacrifice is amenable to structural analysis, it is not reducible to it. The concrete reality of particular people sacrificing particular animals and eating those animals, in one mode raw, in the other, cooked, is played out through the structure of the performance. Binary oppositions in the ritual of *chilopa* are not static emblems but part of a dynamic process. It is this aspect of performance—that which Kapferer (1986: 202) terms the "structuring of structure"—that I am most interested in here, for this is what imparts meaning to the lived experience of *chilopa*.

Much of what is expressed in *chilopa*, the explicit and implicit "meaning" of the ritual acts of the sacrifice, is on the phenomenological surface of the ritual: in the most overt features of *chilopa* can be found its deepest significances. To get at this kind of saying—to move from distant perspectives to ones that are near—requires a description that tracks the various oppositions as they naturally issue forth from the phenomenon of *chilopa* itself.

Animal Sacrifices

Of all the things I experienced in the world of Tumbuka prophet healers, *chilopa* was, perhaps, the most "experience-distant" (Geertz 1983: 57). I come from a culture where people don't have to kill what they eat but can buy it in sanitized packages in grocery stores. For me, seeing an animal killed for food was definitely a distant experience. An animal sacrifice was even more distant, and the drinking of blood directly from an animal's throat was so distant that it was beyond my horizon of possibilities.

For the Tumbuka, the majority of whom live on what they can grow and raise, killing an animal for food is part of everyday life. If you want to eat chicken, you get one of your children to catch a hen or cock, cut off its head, clean it, and then cook it. The Tumbuka were much more connected to the "reality" of eating meat—you have to kill it in order to eat it—than I was.

Although killing a chicken is part of everyday life for the Tumbuka, that doesn't mean it happens every day. Meat is a luxury in the Tumbuka diet, and chicken is usually eaten only for occasions such as the visit of a relative or a person of importance. But it happens often enough that when a chicken is killed, nobody thinks anything about it, except for the occasional researcher, who nevertheless learned very quickly to enjoy the chicken and got over feeling sorry for it.

The same holds true for goats and cows, even though eating their meat is even more uncommon in the Tumbuka diet. Goat meat is part of a meal only on special occasions such as weddings, visits by in-laws during the dry season, or a man's celebrating some good fortune that has come his way by sponsoring a *pwano* (feast). Cows are rarely slaughtered, for they are a sign of a man's wealth, and men are reluctant to reduce their herds. Cows are used mainly for the payment of *lobola* (bride price), a practice adopted from the Ngoni.[13]

This kind of hierarchy of domestic animals—goats are worth more than chickens and are used as food on more special occasions—carries over into *chilopa*. Virtually all *nchimi* perform multiple *vilopa*, as in Tembo's case, which invariably begin with smaller domestic fowl and move on to larger and more important animals such as goats and, on rare occasions, cows.[14] In *chilopa*, the bigger the animal, the stronger the *nthenda* (disease), and the stronger the *nthenda*, the more powerful the healer.

The Tumbuka have no particular emotional charge or sentimentality toward animals in general. For the most part, they don't keep pets; the occasional dog or cat that lives around a compound has to fend for itself. Feeding a pet animal verges on immorality in an environment where families will go hungry if the rains come late, or even starve if they don't come at all. When an animal is killed, for whatever reason, there is no malice involved; it is done solely for practical reasons. This includes the killing of an animal in the *chilopa* ritual, although this is not any ordinary killing but a sacrificial act charged with spiritual energy.

But what exactly are the Tumbuka doing when they ritually drink the blood of doves and goats? When I first saw *chilopa* at Nchimi Mzimu's, I had little knowledge or understanding of the complexities of *vimbuza* affliction and how it related to the wider social and cultural field of traditional healing in northern Malawi. But even without this knowledge or understanding, I found that the events of the sacrifice seemed to have a logical structure that made sense to me, even if, at the time, I couldn't articulate exactly what kind of sense it made.

A Phenomenology of Blood

To begin to answer the question of what the Tumbuka are doing in (and through) *chilopa*, we must take a look at the ritual as a whole, as a "performance" in Kapferer's (1986: 192) sense of the term: "a unity

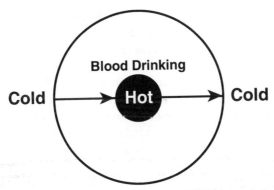

Fig. 7. The directional structure of *chilopa* represented as a field phenomenon

of text and enactment, neither being reducible to the other." Performances such as the Sinhalese exorcisms that Kapferer describes and Tumbuka sacrifices such as Tembo's *chilopa* have a directionality that informs both text and enactment. In Sinhalese exorcism, this is a shift from the demonic possession of the midnight watch to the comic drama of the morning hours, when the masked exorcists appear. In *chilopa*, the movement of spiritual energy from a heated to a cooled state—hot and cold being the most overarching of many binary oppositions in *chilopa*—informs the structure of the performance and imparts meaning to the ritual. Musical experience is the means through which this process unfolds.

The raison d'être for *chilopa* is to cool the *vimbuza* spirits by satisfying their thirst for fresh blood. This cooling of the *vimbuza* reestablishes an equilibrium between hot and cold forces in the person's body that had been thrown out of balance by the heated condition of the *vimbuza*. In the Tumbuka theory of illness, the *vimbuza* spirits heat up and afflict people for various reasons, and sometimes for no reason at all. This affliction can manifest itself in many different symptoms of illness, but the root cause of all *vimbuza* illness is this overheated state, and hence an imbalance of hot and cold.

The movement to and away from spiritual heat is the directionality that gives structure to the ritual of *chilopa*. Central to this movement, the element that informs its directionality, is the act of drinking the fresh blood of the sacrificial animal. The structure of the entire performance radiates from this focal point: all processual movement in the ritual is toward this act, and all subsequent events move away from it.

A diagram best illustrates the directional structure of the *chilopa* ritual as it relates to the binary opposition of hot and cold (fig. 7). The circumference of the circle represents the boundaries of the ritual, the area of spiritual cold; the center represents its hottest point. The horizontal axis represents the temporal flow of the sacrifice, with time moving from left to right. As ritual acts move along the horizontal axis toward the center, they increase in heat until the hottest part of the *chilopa* is reached, the drinking of fresh blood. After the drinking of blood, ritual acts continue to move along the axis, but now the direction is toward the circumference of the circle, where spiritual energy is cool. I will take my cue from the logic of *chilopa* and turn, first, not to the beginning of the ritual but to its focal point, the concentration of greatest heat, and then work my way outward to the boundaries of the performance.

The drinking of blood from the throat of an animal is an intense and dramatic act. It is as if a magnifying lens has been put over the entire ritual, collecting metaphoric rays from the different events of the *chilopa* and focusing them on this one act, creating a hot center. Dancer, singer, drummer, and *nchimi* all contribute to this focused attention on what is, in the logic of the *chilopa* sacrifice, not so much a killing as a drinking of life. Significantly, blood is not drunk from a cup or a bowl, as it is in many other sacrifices in Africa, but is taken directly from the throat of the animal. It is blood that is still flowing through veins and arteries; it is more than raw, it is still warm with life.

This kind of "eating" of life by the *vimbuza* spirits is likewise applicable to animals that are suffocated during *chilopa*. Goats are always sacrificed in this way, but sometimes doves and chickens may also be suffocated; it is entirely up to the spirits. Suffocation, perhaps, is a poor term for what takes place, for it is not merely a matter of blocking the intake of air, but it also involves the active sucking or drinking in of the air of the animal. Considering that spirits are often referred to as *mphepo* (wind) and that the Tumbuka associate the breath of life with both wind and spirit, the drinking of an animal's breath is akin to taking in or incorporating its life essence. This is not, of course, a substitute for the drinking of blood, which, regardless of the method of sacrifice, is still the central act of the ritual, but is isomorphic with it.

A particular tenor is cast over the entire ritual by the unusual methods of sacrificing used for *chilopa*. Death for the animal is not sudden, as it is, for example, in the initiatory rituals of Ndembu diviners (Turner 1968: 301), where a goat and a cock are beheaded at dawn and death is quick and immediate. The killing in *chilopa*, in comparison, is relatively slow, whether it is done by suffocation or the sucking of blood. Although the time rarely exceeds a few minutes, it is enough to impart a feeling of process to the sacrificial act, which is something not found in sacrifices where death is sudden. In the case of *chilopa,* instead of a taking of life, there is a taking *in* of life—a significant ontological difference.

When a patient bites into the neck of a dove or drinks blood from the throat of a goat, it is the *vimbuza* spirits, acting through the physical body of the patient, who perform the sacrifice. This is unlike most sacrifices in West African and Afro-Caribbean religious practices that involve spirit possession (see Besmer 1983; Deren 1953; Herskovits 1937, 1938; Métraux 1972), where the animal is sacrificed by a priest *for* the spirits, instead of by the person who is possessed. In other words, during *chilopa* the *vimbuza* are directly feeding on the animal's blood, and hence, in a very real sense, its life energy. This is precisely why the actual sacrifice is a killing that takes time.

If the *vimbuza*'s desire for blood is not satisfied with animal blood, then the *vimbuza* will begin feeding on the blood of the afflicted person. The person, in effect, is offering the blood of the animal as a substitute for his or her own.[15] But what is the *vimbuza's* intense desire for fresh blood all about?

In the spiritual realm of the Tumbuka world, the *vimbuza* are spirits who are strongly attracted to the world of the living in its full existential reality. They are the only spirits who can physically possess a person and thus participate in the world through the body and senses of the one possessed. The *mizimu,* the ancestors of the Tumbuka, may visit people in their dreams or come to them in visions, but they never possess the physical body of a person as the *vimbuza* do.

The complete possession of a person, when that person's personality and will are supplanted by the *vimbuza* spirits, occurs only through the medium of music. Drumming, singing, and clapping generate musical energy which, according to Tumbuka theory on the subject, heats the *vimbuza* spirits past a critical threshold, resulting in their actualization in the world. This actualization is in the form of the trance possession dance of *vimbuza,* which the Tumbuka equate with "play." As was expressed to me during my dancing, the *vimbuza* are invited to "come play with their children." In *chilopa,* this "play" is not for amusement, nor is it the "deep play" of Balinese cockfights (Geertz 1973: 443) where *"no one's status really changes"* (italics in the original). *Chilopa* is play that is serious business with certain irreversible results for both the sacrificer and the sacrificed.

Blood, Heat, and Music

Immediately before and after the drinking of blood—and sometimes during, as was the case with Tembo—*vimbuza* dancing is the main ritual activity. Typically, possession happens sequentially, as each spirit—multiple spirits are always involved in *vimbuza* possession—comes out to dance when its particular music is played.[16] The tendency, however—very significantly—is for more spirits to come out and dance after the drinking of blood than before.

Moving toward the drinking of blood (in the diagram, moving from left to right toward the center), the purpose of music, and by extension the *vimbuza* dance, is to heat the *vimbuza* spirits and to keep them heated so that at the moment of drinking blood they are at their hottest point. At this stage in the ritual, music is like the convex glass in our metaphor of a magnifying lens, focusing the various *vimbuza* to a point of intense heat.

The Tumbuka ascribe a precise physical reality to *vimbuza:* they are located in different areas of the patient's body simultaneously. Some may be in the feet, some in the head, the arms, virtually anywhere in the body. For the *chilopa* to have its full effect, all these *vimbuza* should come together as one for the drinking of the blood. It is music that has the ability to focus the different *vimbuza*—as Nchimi Mulaula put it, "to search around the body and bring all the *vimbuza* to the heart."

As soon as the proceedings move from inside the temple to outside, which again is a move toward the center of the diagram and thus heat, the drummers and the *kwaya* tend to restrict the musical repertoire. At most, only a few different kinds of *vimbuza* spirits are invoked through the singing and drumming at this point. The closer the ritual moves toward the center, the more the music concentrates on one *vimbuza* style. Usually this is *vimbuza waka* (lit. "just *vimbuza*"), which, with its six-pulse motional patterning (see chapter 5), is a style that in many ways contains the essence of *vimbuza* dance and music. Ritual intentions seem to be concentrating all of the *vimbuza* inside the patient through this one style. There is a kind of compression of spiritual energy, generating heat toward the denouement—the drinking of blood.

After the blood has been taken by the patient, the animal is immediately removed from the dance area, and a small piece of the heart is cut out and given to the patient to eat. According to Chikanje, this should be done as quickly as possible so that the "heart is still warm." Besides the blood, it is the only part of the animal that is ingested raw.

The connections between blood and heart are unmistakable, and eating a piece of the heart gives a kind of closure to the blood stage of the *chilopa*.

As the ritual enters its cooling-down phase, which is a movement away from the drinking of blood (that is, to the right of center along the horizontal axis of the diagram), any remaining signs of blood on the ground are quickly covered up with dirt, and the patient's blood-smeared face is washed by one of the adepts. The reason the blood is quickly cleaned up, *nchimi* explain, is so as not to excite the *vimbuza*.

In this cooling-down phase, all the *vimbuza* spirits inside the patient are given free reign and allowed to dance for as long as they want. What music brought together as one for the drinking of blood, it now individuates back into the plural. The music for each kind of *vimbuza* that is afflicting the patient is played so that each spirit can possess the patient and come out to dance. But now the purpose of the dancing is to dissipate the energy of the heated *vimbuza* spirits and thus cool them down.

While the patient dances, a series of ritual acts is performed using parts of the sacrificial animal. Since these acts are most fully developed in the sacrifice of a goat, I will concentrate on this type of *chilopa*.

In the first of these acts, the gallbladder of the animal is removed and the bile is poured over the patient's head, a kind of baptism in bile. This clear liquid is the only bodily fluid of the animal used in the ritual besides blood, and it is symbolic, at least in part, of the *mizimu*, in opposition to the blood associated with the *vimbuza*.

For patients who have the disease of the prophets, the bile is supposed to make the *nthenda* bitter and strong. But this is also done for ordinary patients. When I asked Chikanje why the bile was poured over patients who were not training to become *nchimi* and would not need a strong *nthenda* to "see," he replied, "We open the door to the *mizimu* for everyone. Maybe things will change in the future and the *mizimu* will come to this person."

In this "opening of the doors for the mizimu," bile is explicitly associated with the ancestor spirits. And the association is reinforced in the way *nchimi* read the ritual: they watch to see whether the person blinks as the bile runs down the face and into the eyes, or whether he spits if it goes into the mouth, neither of which should happen. *Nchimi* "see" with the help of the *mizimu*; their eyes must be strong. *Nchimi* must be able publicly to condemn witches and their evil deeds with their words (that is, mouth), which must be bitter. There is also a color symbolism that reinforces the association of bile with *mizimu*.

Whereas red, the color of blood, symbolizes the *vimbuza* spirits, the color always associated with the *mizimu* is white—which, in the context of *chilopa*, metaphorically becomes colorless, or clear. With the pouring of the bile on the patient, the *chilopa* begins to shift its ritual concerns from the *vimbuza* to the *mizimu* spirits.

After the bile is poured, the *machowa* (skin halter) is prepared and put on the patient, and the gallbladder is blown up and affixed to it. (Here I treat the *machowa* and the affixed gallbladder as one thing.) This ritual act is usually carried out while the patient is still dancing, but in one *chilopa* I attended, the *machowa* was put on in the hut later while the patient was eating the cooked meat. Beyond attributing to it the obvious sign function of identifying persons who have recently performed a *chilopa*, *nchimi* did not have much to say about the *machowa* other than that it was something that had always been done. As Chikanje would usually say when I asked him questions about the meaning of ritual acts for which he had no explanation, "It is a following of tradition as in the Bible, Proverbs two, verse one."[17]

A similar kind of halter is pictured in S. G. Lee's account of a Zulu ancestor spirit cult (1969: 138, plate 8). He states that the goatskin strips "indicate the presence of the ancestors." In fact, the *chilopa* has much in common with other sacrifices found in southeastern and southern Africa. This seems to be further evidence of an identifiable southern/southeastern-African–style healing complex.[18]

Moving away from the drinking of blood, in either direction from the center or focal point on the diagram, the ritual becomes increasingly cooler. To the right of center, this cooling follows a natural progression forward in time, but for the sake of this discussion, I now want to move backward in time—back inside the temple and thus, in the context of the diagram, again from a hotter to a cooler condition.

Inside and outside are spatial orientations that provide a context for ritual events in *chilopa*. A move from inside to outside constitutes an increase in ritual heat, and a move from outside to inside is a movement to lessen that heat. This is relatively obvious in the final act of the *chilopa*, where we can oppose the inside eating of cooked meat to the outside drinking of blood. It is less clear why the initial move from inside the temple to outside is an increase in heat, since continuity is maintained with the performance inside the temple and there are no sudden increases in the intensity of the music or dance, other than what has just been described in the way of restricting the repertoire.

A clue can be found, however, in what *nchimi* have to say about the matter. As I mentioned earlier, one of the reasons that the *chilopa* is held outside, according to Chikanje, is so that "the vimbuza spirits should feel free." Implicit in this statement is that the *vimbuza* spirits are more contained inside the temple—in a sense, they are under more cultural control. *Vimbuza,* it should be remembered, are foreign spirits, relatively wild and untamed compared with the *mizimu,* the ancestors and upholders of Tumbuka culture. In the logic of the *chilopa* ritual, outside can be equated with nature and inside with culture, and therefore a move outside is a movement toward the wildness and foreignness of the *vimbuza* spirits (and therefore toward heat).

Maintaining our retrograde movement in time—that is, working outward toward the periphery of the circle in figure 7—before the context shifts to outside, the *nkufi* clapping is performed inside the temple in order officially to inform the *vimbuza* spirits about what is to take place. *Nkufi* is a kind of paramusical phenomenon, to use Ellingson's (1987: 165) term. This speaking to the spirits is not sung, but neither is it spoken in a normal, everyday voice. Instead, it is intoned to the slow, rhythmical clapping of the adepts. *Nkufi* is explicitly designed to pay respects to the *vimbuza* spirits; in a sense, it is to appease them and thus to assert a certain amount of cultural control over their actions. In other words, although ritual events are aimed at heating the *vimbuza* spirits for the purpose of performing the animal sacrifice, the *nkufi* clapping helps ensure that they will not become wild and out of control. Again, inside acts tend to be more cultural in their orientation.

This retrograde movement from outside to inside (left of center on the diagram) is mirrored in the events that occur later, in actual time, when the patient retires to his or her hut to eat the cooked meat. While the focus of the *chilopa* is clearly on the drinking of blood, the eating of the cooked meat is structurally just as important. Drinking blood is only one pole of a dyad. It takes both poles to illuminate the structure of the ritual.

Virtually everything about the eating of the *chilopa* meat is opposite that of drinking blood. The blood is drunk outside, where animals eat; the meat is eaten inside, where Tumbuka normally eat. Singing, drumming, and dancing are integral components of the emotionally charged atmosphere surrounding the drinking of blood; eating meat is done in a relaxed and casual manner, as if taking a normal meal. The *vimbuza* spirits do the drinking of blood; the patient symbolically eats the meat for the *mizimu* spirits (because the *mizimu* do not possess people, this act must be symbolic). Blood is ingested raw; meat from the sacrificial animal is thoroughly boiled so that there is absolutely no trace of blood. The *vimbuza,* as foreign spirits exemplifying the

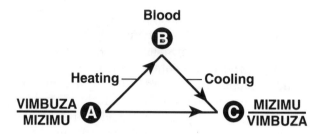

Fig. 8. The relational transformation that the spirits undergo during *chilopa*. A to C represents the temporal flow of the ritual; A to B, the heating-up stage; B, the drinking of blood; B to C, the cooling-down stage; C, the eating of cooked meat. At the beginning of the ritual, the *vimbuza* are on top and the *mizimu* are on bottom; by the end of the ritual, their positions are reversed.

"other," represent nature in the paradigmatic structure of the *chilopa* sacrifice—they eat their food raw. The *mizimu*, the ancestors of the Tumbuka, upholders of traditional culture and society, eat their food cooked.

Within this binary structure of raw and cooked food, we also find a transformational process at work that is responsible for bringing spiritual energy into the correct alignment for purposes of divination. In order to be able to "see," *nchimi* must have the *mizimu* "on top," with the *vimbuza* spirits supplying the energy from below.

During the initial phases of the prophet's disease (*nthenda ya uchimi*), the *vimbuza* are heated to such a degree that they are often uncontrollable. A typical symptom associated with this illness is running wild in the bush. Music and dance slowly cool the spirits, bringing them under social and cultural control, but this is deemed by the Tumbuka to be insufficient to push the *mizimu* spirits on top. In order for this to occur, a *chilopa* must be performed.

At the beginning of the *chilopa*, the configuration of spiritual energy has the *vimbuza* "on top" (fig. 8). As the ritual moves toward the central act of sacrifice, the ascendant position of the *vimbuza* is reinforced through ritual acts that increase the spiritual heat of the *vimbuza*. Once they have drunk the blood, the ritual shifts gears: the *vimbuza* are cooled further through their actualization in the dance, and the *mizimu* begin to take the ascendant position. Ritual concerns turn toward the process of "seeing" (e.g., the pouring of bile), which culminates in the final act of the ritual when the *mizimu* symbolically eat the cooked meat of the sacrificial animal, claiming, in a sense, their ascendant position. It is at this point that the adept is considered a *mutwasa* (lit. "new moon") and has the potential eventually to become a full member of the society of prophet healers.

The spirits are now in their correct alignment: the *mizimu*, read culture, on top; the *vimbuza*, read nature, on bottom. In structuralist terms, *vimbuza* is to *mizimu* as nature is to culture and as raw is to cooked. Nature should serve culture, not the other way around. Before the drinking of blood, the *vimbuza* are, in a sense, overdetermined nature—in Tumbuka terms, they are overheated. This is perhaps why the Tumbuka see *vimbuza* affliction as a counterforce against witchcraft, which, in a sense, is overdetermined culture, for witchcraft is man-made.

By fulfilling the *vimbuza*'s natural desire for blood within the culturally determined ritual of *chilopa*, a beneficial source of energy is brought under the cultural control of the *nchimi*—it now fuels the divination trance. *Nchimi*, however, do not have to drink blood every time they "see." Instead, the performance of *vimbuza* music recreates the necessary conditions for divination. But how does music work in this structuralist scheme?

Music, of course, is a cultural artifact, yet according to the Tumbuka, the music of *vimbuza* comes not from humans, at least not from humans in the flesh, but from the *vimbuza* spirits through the dreams of those who are afflicted. Most *nchimi* report that in the first months of their initiatory illness, dreams are often filled with *vimbuza* songs. These songs usually form an important part of an *nchimi*'s musical repertoire. In other words, music is a priori connected explicitly with the realm of nature through the *vimbuza* spirits. The seemingly incongruous position of music as emanating from both culture and nature is exactly what gives music such power in the *chilopa* ritual. It is the prime mediator between nature and culture—it partakes of both human and spirit. Transformations and transactions between *vimbuza, mizimu*, and Tumbuka occur not *through* music but *in* the music.

It is in the music of *vimbuza* that the *chilopa* sacrifice constructs the paradigmatic structure that is reenacted every time an *nchimi* "sees." When an *nchimi* dances, music heats the *vimbuza* spirits, which supplies the energy for the *mizimu* to "see"—it pushes the *mizimu* on top. Music transforms the natural energy of the *vimbuza* into a culturally useful form. It becomes a technology that is the locus of a sacred clinical reality.

The Musical Construction of Clinical Reality

Music makes translucent the boundary between human and spirit. Within this musical opening to the realm of the spirits, transactions between *nchimi* healer and *vimbuza* and *mizimu* spirits are effected. This opening is where the special "seeing" of divination is enacted, where spirits are encountered directly, and where the battle against witchcraft enjoined. In sum, it is where clinical reality is constructed.

Clinical reality, according to Arthur Kleinman (1980: 42), is a complex of interrelated features including "the beliefs, expectations, norms, behaviors, and communicative transactions associated with sickness, health care seeking, practitioner-patient relationships, therapeutic activities, and evaluation of outcomes." By broadening the evaluation of clinical efficacy from the biomedical paradigm held by Western medicine to include these sociocultural components, Kleinman seeks a "comparative science of healing." Through comparative studies we may indeed find universal aspects of health care, but in the final analysis, all healing is local because it is personal.

Chinese shamans (*tang-ki*), Kleinman tells us (ibid.: 218–19), who diagnose the ills of their patients by becoming possessed by a particular god, who see their patients in a shrine house, and who use treatments such as writing charms in their own blood, construct a clinical reality far different from that of Western-style doctors in Taiwan, who have all the high-tech trappings of professional clinics and offices. In order to understand and accurately assess the efficacy of health care systems such as those practiced by Chinese shamans or Tumbuka prophet healers, one must expand the analytical focus beyond the confines of the Western biomedical model.

Tumbuka patients and practitioners construct a very different clinical reality from the narrowly focused "mechanistic view of bodily dysfunction" (Kleinman 1980: 303) found in Western-style medical practice. The distinction between Tumbuka clinical reality and that of the Western health care system, however—and probably that of the Chinese shaman as well—is more than a variation in specific content, regardless of how radical that variation is. A world of difference exists between walking into a doctor's office and entering the compound of an *nchimi*.

When a patient seeks Western-style health care, whether it is in the United States, Taiwan, or northern Malawi, he or she is treated as a passive element in the secular clinical reality that is encountered in the offices of doctors, clinics, and hospitals. The biomedical approach to healing focuses on the body as a physical object to which medical procedures are applied. X rays are taken, operations performed, and medicines dispensed on the basis of depersonalized, symptomatic diagnoses.

When a Tumbuka enters the compound of an *nchimi*, on the other hand, he or she enters a clinical reality that is not only sacred in its dimensions but also a reality that can be experienced and expressed directly and actively through music. Musical performance in this context is not a Geertzian (1973: 93–94) model "of" or "for" anything—in Tumbuka healing, musical performance *is* clinical reality.

Vimbuza *Nights*

Only a few miles from Lußemba's compound is the *chipatala* (hospital) of Chikanje, her first husband and the *nchimi* who introduced me to the clinical reality of the prophet healers of northern Malawi. In my first days at Chikanje's, a number of these healers, including Lußemba, came to his compound to see this strange Mzungu who, as rumor had it, was afflicted by the spirits. According to local gossip, I was staying with Chikanje in order to learn to become a healer and start my own "business" back in the United States.

Although Chikanje knew that I was there doing research, he nevertheless was convinced that more than research was involved in my stay, even if I didn't know it yet. A few weeks after I had settled in at the compound, he told me one day that he had actually been expecting me for some time. It seems that for the past several years he had had an unusual recurring dream about an Mzungu who came to his compound

carrying a bright blue light. He told me that he could never quite figure out what this dream meant—that is, until I arrived with the 300-candle-watt gas lamp that I used for filming at night. It had not only a bluish cast to its flame but also a bright blue gas canister for a base. Chikanje decided that I had not come to his compound by chance but had been directed there by the spirits to learn the ways of an *nchimi*.

A few nights later, as I was sitting outside, Chikanje came up to me and pulled out a folded piece of paper that contained a fine brown powder. He told me that it was dream medicine, to dream the dreams of the ancestors. I should take it just before going to sleep, inhaling it like snuff through my nose.

I was looking for opportunities to move closer to the *vimbuza* experience in any way I could, so that night, with more than a bit of apprehension, I took the medicine, having no idea what might happen. I expected the drug would have psychoactive properties and I would have some kind of hallucinogenic experience. I inhaled the medicine, and, as if it were snuff, proceeded to sneeze, but I continued to sneeze every thirty seconds or so for the next ten minutes—not exactly the mystical experience I was planning on having. When I finally went to sleep, however, I had the first in a series of dreams that, by the end, had me thoroughly shaken.

Although many different things happened in these dreams, they all had a common thread. There was always a point at which I would dream that I was awake. This in itself was not so unusual. Like many people, I had had dreams like this before. What was unusual was that over a period of about a week, each dream that contained this element became more convoluted. By the end of the week I was dreaming that I was awake, but then awoke from my dream and realized that I was dreaming that I was awake only to realize that in fact I was dreaming that I had awakened from my dream that was about being awake. If this sounds confusing, let me assure you that it was. My sense of boundary between dreams and waking reality was becoming decidedly confused. When I look back on these dreams, it now seems to me that I was entering the clinical reality of the compounds on both a conscious *and* an unconscious level. Dreams, in effect, began to take on a new sense of reality for me.

Dreams were not the only phenomena to take on a new kind of reality. When I was having this series of dreams, I was also regularly staying up through the night watching the spirits dance, while listening to the singing and drumming of *vimbuza*. During these all-night ses-

sions, music, too, began to take on a tangible, physically felt real
that I had never experienced before.

At Chikanje's, as in most healers' compounds, a normal village
routine of retiring shortly after sundown and rising at dawn is super-
seded by a schedule that regularly requires wakeful periods of twenty-
four hours or more. Every Wednesday and Saturday, all-night divination
sessions are held in the temple, and on Sunday or Monday there is
usually an all-night dancing session for patients afflicted with *vimbuza*.
Everyone in the compound is expected to attend these sessions and
contribute to the proceedings through music making. And since music
is a constant throughout the entire night, musical performance takes
up a fair percentage of a person's total waking hours. We have, in postindustrial Western culture, nothing comparable to this communal level
of music making on a day-to-day basis.

After a few months, I began to realize that *vimbuza was* the musical culture of the people living in the compound. Contrary to my expectations, women and young girls did not sing when they pounded maize
(when I asked them why not, they replied simply that it was something
their mothers had done, and they just didn't do it anymore). Men did
not sing while working, elders did not sit around the fire at night telling
story songs, and no one sat around in the shade absentmindedly playing
the *bango* (a small board zither) or *kalimba* (a lamellaphone). Indeed,
playing these instruments was becoming a dying art. Mr. Hunga, the
old man who lived across from Chikanje's compound and who often
drummed for him, was the only person I knew who had a *bango* and
knew how to play it—but more about him later, as he figures promi-
nently in what takes place. Of course there is other music: during dry
season, when in-laws come to visit, a social music is performed, and
music is an important part of weddings and funerals. But on a day-to-
day basis, the music of *vimbuza* forms the vast majority of performed
music—and I stress "performed," for there was always the ubiquitous
radio.

These weekly healing events structured around music making im-
posed a rhythm on the daily life of the compound. Most of the research
on indigenous healing has virtually ignored this aspect of performance.
Not only are normal sleep patterns disrupted for people living in a
healing compound, but also the emotional tenor of the compound is
altered from day to day. *Vimbuza* nights are emotionally charged, with
a large expenditure of energy for everyone involved. The day after one
of these all-night sessions, the compound is usually tranquil and re-

laxed. In a very tangible way, the enactment of *vimbuza* controls the ebb and flow of everyday life in the compound. And in a very real and immediate way, music controls the ebb and flow of *vimbuza*. In this sense, musical performance gives a macro-rhythmic structure to the outer form of clinical reality constructed within the compound.

If this is true of the compound as a whole, it is even more pronounced for an *nchimi* like Chikanje. Patients will eventually leave the compound and return to their home villages, but an *nchimi*'s life revolves around his practice. All the healers that I lived with had an amazing ability to function on limited amounts of sleep.

Throughout the night, *nchimi* "dance their disease," a musical experience that transforms consciousness. Turner (1986: 43) refers to a "*meta*-power" that is released in such trance states: "This is akin to what I have often seen in Africa, where thin, ill-nourished old ladies, with only occasional naps, dance, sing, and perform ritual activities for two or three days and nights on end. I believe that an increase in the level of social arousal, however produced, is capable of unlocking energy sources in individual participants." Similarly, an *nchimi* seems to get stronger as the night wears on and the people in the temple focus on music making.

After a night of divination, which involves long periods of intense dancing by Chikanje, most of the next day is taken up with preparing and dispensing medicine to the patients who had been divined the night before. Sleep is usually relegated to a few hours at odd intervals during the day, and even this sleep time is often a part of healing work, for dreaming is another way of making contact with the spirits. In dreams the *mizimu* might communicate a new recipe for a herbal medicine, where to find the appropriate ingredients, who might be a witch, which medicine to use for a certain patient, and myriad other things that relate to an *nchimi*'s day-to-day medical practice.

In the Temple

Quiet days and musical nights occupied most of my time at the compound. On nights when there was no *vimbuza* dancing in the *thempli*, I would often take Chikanje's dream medicine—sneezing, although still part of the process, was becoming a relatively minor affair—and the next morning I would tell him any unusual dreams that had come to me. Well-established healers are often associated with particular outstanding abilities: Chikanga is the witchfinder nonpareil, Mseka is

Fig. 9. Nchimi Chikanje at the grave of his grandfather

well-known for his powerful *mankwhala* to cure infertility, and Chikanje is famous not only for his power to dream but also for his ability
to interpret the dreams of others. I dreamt about a *chilopa* sacrifice one
night, and Chikanje's interpretation of this dream resulted in my first
experience as a focus of the ritual proceedings inside the *thempli.*

In the dream, a goat is killed as part of a *chilopa* sacrifice. The
animal is skinned and a white fur wristband is fashioned and put on
my wrist. As soon as it is put on, the band starts to glow a brilliant
white. The dream had an emotional weight to it, and dreams like this
I always told to Chikanje. He interpreted the dream as coming from
the *mizimu* and having special import. Its importance was intensified
for him because the previous day he had taken me to his grandfather's
grave to pay respects to his ancestors.

That day everyone from the compound walked in single file to the
gravesite a few miles away. The adepts wore their official dress, the
women all in white with red crosses embroidered on their skirts, and
Chikanje dressed in his blue satin choir robe. When we reached the
grave, which was covered in concrete and topped with a concrete headstone (fig. 9), a sign of prestige few Tumbuka could afford, Chikanje said
a prayer and the group sang Christian hymns. Following the hymns, he
handed me covered plates and instructed me to sprinkle the food inside

them in front of the headstone. Chikanje asked his *asekuru* (grandfather) on my behalf to accept this gift as a show of respect. After singing a few more hymns, we returned to the compound. It was the next night that I dreamt about *chilopa* and the glowing white wristband.

White being the color associated with the ancestors, Chikanje took the fact that the wristband was glowing as a sign that his *mizimu* had accepted my offering. More importantly for what followed, he told me that the dream was also from my *mizimu* and that the wristband meant that the spirits wanted *mboni* beads, the "telephone to the spirits." On Saturday, he would honor the request of my spirits and officially present the *mboni* to them inside the temple.

All people, whether healer, farmer, second wife, or tailor (which was Chikanje's profession before he became an *nchimi*), who are afflicted by *vimbuza* wear *mboni* beads.[1] They are strands of small store-bought beads worn around the wrist or neck. Most people wear only the white beads symbolic of the ancestors; other "*vimbuza* people," however, especially healers, also wear red or blue ones. The different colors relate to different types or categories of spirits. For example, blue is often associated with *ßaMwera* (lit. "wind from the lake"), who are variously said to be the spirits of people who crossed the lake, that is, Balowoka traders (see Vail 1972), or sometimes the spirits of the lakeshore Tonga. Occasionally blue beads are said to be those of the *vimbuza mulaula*, although exactly who these are the spirits of was never made entirely clear. Red beads are usually a sign of the *vyanusi*, the spirits of the Ngoni invaders from South Africa.

Mboni beads, however, are much more than merely signs and symbols of the spirits. They are a functional part of the communication technology that links human and spirit. When someone close to a "*vimbuza* person" dies, another strand of *mboni* is added in order to appease both *vimbuza* and *mizimu* spirits and to maintain the lines of communication. If this is not done, the *vimbuza* may heat up, causing sickness. In the case of healers, it may "bind the legs" of an *nchimi* and "cloud" his or her "seeing." In order to use *mboni* as a "telephone to the spirits," healers often sleep with their head lying on the beads worn around their wrist, which, according to them, gives direct access to the spirit world. This access occurs through dreams, the realm where the *mboni* are functionally most active.

The next Saturday, the day I was to receive my *mboni*, Chikanje, his younger father (his father's brother), and his paternal aunt gathered in my room to clap *nkufi* for my spirits. My *mphepo* (spiritwind) was officially informed of what was going to take place that night and was beseeched to accept what they had asked for in a good way. A long strand of white beads was pulled from a tin-covered plate filled with *ufu*, white maize flour. Chikanje showed me the beads and requested that I put a silver coin in the *ufu*. The beads were put back in the plate and, along with the coin, were once again covered, which signaled the end of the ceremony.

Saturday night was for divination, and people had been arriving at Chikanje's compound all day. Some had come from nearby villages, but others had walked for days to get to his *chipatala* at Bwengu. People had come for different reasons—minor but persistent ailments, life-threatening diseases, bad luck in business or love, to clear up accusations of witchcraft—and on this night, some came to see the Mzungu get his *mboni*, which was a kind of public and official confirmation that the rumors of my *vimbuza* were true.

At sunset the drums, which are kept in the temple, were brought outside and their heads heated over an open fire. They are heated and then played and then heated and played again until the animal skin is tightened sufficiently to give the drum a clear, ringing sound. Drummers and especially *nchimi* are very particular about the sound of the drums. In *vimbuza* music, timbre has structural implications essential to the realization of the various *vimbuza* drumming modes, an issue I deal with in the next chapter.[2] With the tuning and playing of the drums outside acting as a kind of signal that divination was soon to begin, people started entering the temple.

Chikanje's *thempli*, the largest building in the compound, held about fifty people, but on divination nights many more were packed inside. Some nights there were so many people that one could barely move, and this was such a night. I was always amazed at the Tumbuka's ability to cram more people than seemed possible into buses, and to do the same thing in a *thempli*. Just when I thought it would be impossible to fit one more person inside either of these situations, ten more would somehow be accommodated.

Once everyone was more or less settled inside, Muhone, one of the female adepts who led the singing calls for *vimbuza* songs (she eventually became Chikanje's fifth wife), raised "Charo Nchinonono," a well-known Tumbuka/Christian hymn:

> *Charo nchinonono muzimu wane pulika iwe*
> This world is difficult, my ancestors hear me.
> *Charo nchavitima muzimu wane pulika iwe*
> This world is full of sorrows, my ancestors hear me.

Para tikupenja tipenjere mwa Yeso iwe
If we are seeking we should seek in you, Jesus.
Ati Yeso fumu yane mundivimba tirenge imwe
They say, Jesus my Lord you protect me.
Ati para tikulera tilirie mwa Yeso imwe
They say if we cry, we should cry through you, Jesus.
Ati para tikugona tigonere mwa Yeso imwe
They say if we sleep we should sleep through you, Jesus.
Ati para tikupenja tipenjere mwa Yeso imwe
They say if we are seeking, we should seek in you, Jesus.

Divination sessions in the temple always commence with the singing of Christian hymns in the missionary-taught, four-part harmonic style, and "Charo Nchinonono" was often chosen. It always seemed a good fit for the activities at hand, given the focus on suffering and misfortune of those gathered in the temple.

Hymns are a genre unto themselves. Although certain aspects of hymn-style singing have been syncretized with the more traditional sounds of *vimbuza* songs,[3] hymns are conspicuous in their homophonic style of singing, complete with simple chorale-type voice leadings, relatively slow tempo, and the absence of any instrumental (percussion) accompaniment, including clapping. People sing soprano, alto, tenor, and bass parts, and in fact use these terms to describe their own singing. When I asked people what made a good singer, I was often told that it was someone who could easily change parts—for example, between the soprano and tenor parts—while singing.

I always found it an interesting juxtaposition that Christian hymns were being sung inside a "temple" that was the functional center of a traditional "hospital." At Chikanje's, the hospital surrounds the temple, which is an inversion of the situation at the mission-run hospital at Livingstonia, where the hospital is, in a sense, surrounded by the temple. When a Tumbuka is treated at Livingstonia, hymns are not sung in a doctor's office or while X rays are taken, and never are medical procedures of any kind performed inside the very Scottish looking brick church located high on the Livingstonia escarpment. Music is reserved for religious services and never impinges on the world of Western medicine practiced in the hospital. Paralleling the difference in Western and Tumbuka healing between a sacred and a secular clinical reality is the fact that for the Tumbuka, music and healing are intimately connected, whereas for the medical missionaries of Livingstonia, music and healing are totally separate phenomena.

After a few more hymns were sung, Chikanje entered th
Dressed in his full *vimbuza* attire, he sat in his chair in fr
drums. Sitting next to him, also in chairs—everyone else either stanas
or sits on the floor—were his main assistants: those adepts who had
been with him the longest and who were now *mutwasa*, new moons,
who were beginning to "see." He joined along in singing a hymn, then
raised his hands and stopped the singing in order to pray (*kulombe*),
asking God and Jesus for their blessings for what was about to take
place. When the prayer was finished, Chikanje rested his chin in the
palm of his hand, as he always did, and waited for his *vimbuza* to heat
up. What until now had been Christian in content—hymns and prayers
that could be heard in any church in the North—quickly changed its
focus as the drums began to call forth the *vimbuza*.

Mr. Hunga, the old man I mentioned who lived across the road from
Chikanje's compound, was the *ng'oma* master drummer that night. He
often played for Chikanje and knew his dance style well. Most *nchimi*
have a special drummer who plays specifically for divination. These
drummers are the closest thing in the temple to musical specialists.
They do not drum for a living, but if an *nchimi* does not take care of
his drummer, as in providing gifts of food and things such as soap or
tobacco, a loose economic reciprocity, then that drummer might be
hard to find on divination nights. Often, the drummer is related to the
nchimi, which helps to increase stability in what could at best be
termed a semiprofessional relationship. For example, Nchimi Mulaula's
younger brother, Saza, whom I discuss in more detail in chapter 5, lives
at Mulaula's compound with his wives and children and drums almost
exclusively for his brother. At Chikanje's, Mr. Hunga, the father of
Chikanje's third wife, has been playing for him for twenty years.

Hunga first sounded the rhythmic mode of *fumu za pasi* (lit. "the
chiefs of the ground") (see appendix B). Each type of *vimbuza* spirit has
its own rhythmic mode to which it responds. Rouget (1985: 67) uses
the term "motto" for roughly the same musical phenomenon, but I
believe that "mode" imparts much more of the improvisatorial and
variational nature of the drumming, and hence of its reality, but more
about this later. For *fumu za pasi*, as with many other *vimbuza* modes,
the rhythmic structure is built around a combination of two six-pulse
phrases that are articulated through timbral changes and structural gaps
(see chapter 5).

Fumu za pasi is a class of *vimbuza* that includes the spirits of dead
chiefs and one of the most dangerous *vimbuza*, *nkharamu*, the lion
spirit. *Nkharamu* is a powerful *vimbuza* spirit that is often used by

nchimi for divination, but it also can be one of the most difficult *vim-buza* to control. Stories abound about this spirit's attacking people in the temple and how it sometimes wants to eat young children or babies. I have seen more than one temple emptied of people who became frightened and fled when *nkharamu* appeared in a fierce way.[4]

While Hunga established the basic rhythmic configuration of *fumu za pasi* and the other drums synchronized their parts with the *ng'oma*, Muhone began to sing about the lion:

> *Kumusoro kumusoro kumusoro*
> At the *musoro* tree
> *Nkharamu zalira kumusoro.*
> the lion cries.

And in the standard call and response form of virtually all *vimbuza* songs, the *kwaya*, composed mainly of patients, relatives, and adepts, answered her:

> *Nkharamu zalira kumusoro.*
> The lion cries at the *musoro* tree.

The lion is said to mark this tree (*Pseudolachnostylis mamprouneifolia*) with his scent glands and, according to the Tumbuka, often to hide a kill in the tree or bury it close by; that is why it roars at the *musoro*.[5] The song, of course, is not just about roaring lions but, more importantly, about crying spirits.

The *kwaya* that responds to Muhone is an expression of the maximum number of people involved in music making during the proceedings in the *thempli*. At any one time there are never more than three drummers playing and two lead vocalists singing the calls. Therefore, it is in the choral responses and the accompanying clapping—a word that does not do justice to the phenomenon—that people most fully share in the "ongoing flux" (Schutz 1964: 170) of the musical process.

Although everyone in the temple is supposed to contribute to the music, this ideal is never achieved. On the periphery of the gathering are people who are not directly involved with the proceedings. This group, made up mostly of young men and women but also including some older people and children as well, constitutes the closest thing to what we would call an audience, although there is no performance specifically directed at it. These people are not patients but have come to the temple to socialize or to escape the sometimes mundane existence they experience at home. Life can get boring in villages, many young men told me, and the goings-on in an *nchimi*'s temple offered, if not entertainment, then at least a welcomed break in the daily routine. These people are minimally involved in music making, at most adding handclaps and occasionally contributing to the singing. Often, though, they merely watch what is going on, or mingle together outside.

Everyone, however, is expected to sing, and because every night in the temple brings new patients and their relatives, there is, in a sense, a new performance group each night. People come from all over the Northern Region, and although some songs have a common currency over wide areas of Tumbuka-speaking country and thus are known to most people, many are local to a particular healer or small group of healers who live in the immediate vicinity of one another.

In order to accommodate this constant flux of new performers, the choral responses of songs are structured for easy access. They are, for the most part, simple diatonic melodies that are easily assimilated and mastered so that participants can join fully into the group's music making. Making music together can be a powerful experience, a fact that most ethnographers concerned with healing rituals have overlooked. For the Tumbuka, as we shall see—or perhaps I should say, hear—it is fundamental to the construction of a clinical reality inside the *thempli*.

When Chikanje dances, those who are about to be divined take on the dual role of involved participant (patient, relative, or adept) and performer—they are those whom Rouget calls "musicants."[6] As part of the *kwaya*, patients sing and clap to help heat an *nchimi*'s *vimbuza* so that he may divine the cause of their illness or misfortune—a reciprocity between patient and healer; in the present context, a musical transaction between singer and dancer. Transactions—unlike communications, which may be one-way—are reciprocal arrangements that require something from each side involved. From the very beginning of their entry into the clinical reality of an *nchimi*'s compound, patients are active participants—specifically, in the case of divination, musical participants—in their own healing. This is in sharp contrast to the almost complete passivity of patients who are diagnosed within the Western medical system.

As the singing, drumming, and clapping intensified, Chikanje's *vimbuza* began to heat. Wearing his special lion's mane headdress (symbolic of *nkharamu*), *mboni* beads strung together with pieces of special roots wrapped across his chest bandolier-style, two *mang'wanda* belts of tin around his waist, the *nyisi* iron jingles around his ankles, and

Fig. 10. Nchimi Chikanje
dancing *vimbuza* to heat his
spirits

holding in either hand a fly whisk (*machowa*) made from the tail of a
horse, a symbol of chiefly authority and the power of healers, Chikanje
rose to "dance his disease" (fig. 10).

   Nkharamu has been coming to Chikanje for a long time, and as a
result of his familiarity with the spirit, his dancing is strong and controlled. But it was not always this way. When Chikanje first became
sick with the disease of the prophets, many *vimbuza* would come out
and he "would dance all over the place." Not surprisingly for Chikanje,
a dream played an important part in the development of his dance style.

   It was during the time he was at Nyakavumbe's (the woman *nchimi*
who trained him), when he was just beginning to "see," that Chikanje
received a powerful dream from his *mizimu:*

   My mizimu came to me and spoke of a certain village where
   there was a crazy man. I was told that I should enter this man's
   nyumba [house] with my drums, and face the west and begin
   to dance. When I danced, the mizimu said, it would be in a
   new way.

When I awoke I found this village and asked if there was such a man, and was told that one of the villagers had recently gone crazy [*chifusi*]. They showed me the man's hut, and as my mizimu had instructed, I went inside with my drummers. But the man was in another room and would not see me. I asked the man's wife if I could dance in the hut anyway, and she agreed. I faced the west, the drums played fumu za pasi, and when I danced it was nkharamu who came. This time I did not dance all over the place but stayed in one spot.

People in the village saw that I was dancing, and some of them came inside the hut to be "seen." The first man who stood before me was from Zambia, and I recognized him as someone I had dreamt about years before when I first got sick.[7] I told the man what I had dreamed, and he said it was all true. I saw a few more people and then was through, but before I left I gave the wife of the crazy man some roots to help cure her husband. . . .

It was after this that more and more I danced only fumu za pasi, which is the kind of vimbuza that nkharamu is under. *When I dance now I have a pattern in my head. When you dance without a particular pattern, your head is not settled. The pattern settles the head.*

Over the years, Chikanje's *nthenda* has matured (*kudankha*), and spirits that once afflicted him now release their energy in the *vimbuza* dance so that he may divine the ills and misfortunes of the patients who have come to his *chipatala* seeking help. On the night of my *mboni*, Chikanje danced *nkharamu*, but contrary to his usual practice, he did not dance in one place.

Chikanje always begins his dance in the same way, shaking the *nyisi* jingles attached to his right ankle by moving his heel up and down while the ball of his foot remains in contact with the ground. Each movement of the heel sounds the *nyisi* once over a two-pulse span. The pulse is articulated by the *mphiningu* drum, whose name is an onomatopoeia of the supporting part it plays to the *ng'oma* master drum (see chapter 5, note 10). Drum phrases played by the *ng'oma* almost always cover six pulses; therefore, Chikanje sounds the *nyisi* three times during one six-pulse phrase. The beat composed of two pulses crosses the often implied beat of three pulses sounded on the *ng'oma* in the rhythmic mode of *fumu za pasi*.

After this start, Chikanje changes his leg work, now using both feet so that the *nyisi* of the right ankle sound on pulses 6 and 1 and the *nyisi* of the left ankle sound on pulses 3 and 4, effectively coming into synchrony with the implied two-beat, three-pulse pattern on the *ng'oma*. Simultaneous with this change in the *nyisi*, Chikanje begins to shake his hips, sounding the *mang'wanda* in a six-pulse pattern: "My feet follow the *ng'oma*, my hips the *mphiningu*." Throughout the dance he shifts back and forth between the two kinds of beats, in essence becoming a human hemiola—a complex rhythmic gestalt.[8]

This same kind of shifting between beats can also be heard in the clapping of the *kwaya*. Although everyone does not sing, virtually everyone adds rhythmical clapping to the musical texture. (Sometimes people augment the sound of their clapping by using wooden blocks or other idiophones.) Two-pulse and three-pulse beats are co-present at all times in the rhythmical structure of the music, and people freely articulate both, changing beats not as a group but as individuals. As a result, at any one time in the musical texture there is the possibility that some people will be clapping in "two" while others will be clapping in "three." This free shifting of beats suggests a fluid musical relationship of the *kwaya* to the rhythmic structure of *vimbuza* that has potentially significant ramifications in the creation of a clinical reality with sound and motion as its experiential parameters, something explored in greater detail in the following chapter.

After about ten minutes of dancing, Chikanje stopped and began to sing one of the songs he frequently uses when he is divining:

> *Uyo nimwana wa Nyakavumbe*
> That is the child of Nyakavumbe.
> *ßalikuzgeba Mayiro*
> She disappeared yesterday [died].
> *Ati mwana ßalira ßa nyina*
> They say the child is crying for its mother.
> *Mwana ßakupenja ßa nyina sono*
> The child is looking for his mother now.
> *ßa nyina mba Nyakavumbe mayo*
> The mother is Nyakavumbe, cry for mother.

Nyakavumbe—his mother in the sense that she is the *nchimi* who trained him—had died the year before, and that is when the spirits brought him this song in a dream. The song reminds him of the past and makes him feel sad, for he misses Nyakavumbe. According to Chikanje, sadness (*chitima*) helps to heat his *vimbuza*, and this in turn helps him to "see."

Muhone soon took up the call, and Chikanje once again began to dance. But instead of staying in one place, he started to dance across the room to where I was seated. I had witnessed him do this only once before, the first night I saw him divine in the temple, and it was to happen only once again, the last time I saw him dance before I left the North. All three times I felt as if he was directing the energy of the *vimbuza* from himself into me through his dancing. With his lion's mane headdress and the rest of his *vimbuza* "kit," Chikanje presented a striking and charismatic figure when he danced. As he got closer, the singing, drumming, and clapping intensified, several women added high-pitched ululations (*nthunguru*), and the whole energy level in the temple moved a notch upward. I found my heart beginning to race and my legs feeling light.

Now dancing right in front of me, Chikanje reached down and shook my hand. As he held my hand he continued to dance, his spirits paying respects to mine. I was no longer merely listening to the music and watching Chikanje dance but felt myself being drawn into a commonality of space and time, into a shared reality created in the temple through musical means.

Suddenly Chikanje knelt down in front of me and signaled for the drumming and singing to stop. The senior adepts joined him and they began to clap *nkufi* for my spirits. This *nkufi* was much like the one earlier in the day, but now I had the distinct feeling—and it was a feeling more than a thought—that Chikanje was talking past me to my spirits. As he spoke to them, asking them to accept the *mboni* that was being offered, he wrapped the strand of white beads four times around my wrist and tied it. Always the pragmatist, he told me he was leaving it loosely tied because he had "seen" that I was going to get a lot fatter. After Chikanje was through presenting the *mboni*, he returned to his chair to reheat his *vimbuza*, for he was "seeing" many patients that night. *Mboni* beads are never taken off—after six years I am still wearing mine, though they are starting to get a bit tight.

That night in the *thempli* changed my social status at the compound. I may still have been an Mzungu, a white man who for some reason wanted to watch, record, and film *vimbuza*, but I was now an Mzungu who was also a fellow patient and, in the eyes of some, a fellow adept. If the Tumbuka had any doubts about me before, when they saw me walking around Rumphi wearing *mboni* they were now convinced that, strange as it was, this Mzungu was in fact afflicted with *vimbuza*.

Mr. Hunga the Drummer

In the days after I received *mboni*, my dreams took an interesting turn: I began to dream almost exclusively about people in the compound, but I was no longer a player in any of my own dreams. When I informed Chikanje of this, he didn't seem the least bit surprised, and said it was to be expected now that I wore *mboni*. When I told him my dream about Mr. Hunga, the drummer, he said nothing.

It was a concise dream. It was night, and Mr. Hunga was standing around a fire with many people. He began to dance *vimbuza* and was trying to divine but could not. Because Chikanje offered no interpretation, and nothing seemed particularly special or noteworthy about the dream, I thought no more about it.

Another Saturday night came, and the sequence of events followed pretty much the same general format I have already described, except that instead of receiving *mboni* I was busy tape-recording the proceedings. Shortly after sunset, the divination session began in the temple with a prayer and the singing of hymns, but because there was no special business to take care of, Chikanje immediately began to heat his *vimbuza* in order to divine. Chikanje does not always heat his *vimbuza* by dancing to songs about *nkharamu*, and on this night the *kwaya* raised one of the current *vimbuza* "hits," one of the few songs I heard no matter what *nchimi*'s temple I was in:

> solo   *Kome kome ßana*
> Kill kill children,
> *ßanikomera kamwana kane*
> You have killed my little child,
> *kamwana kane kambura mulandu we dada*
> my little child who is without a kiss
> [i.e., a child who is innocent].
> *Dandaule*
> Complain.

> chorus   *Dandaule dandaule kwakwa Chikanje*
> Complain, complain to Chikanje.
> *Dandaule dandaule kwakwa Chikanje dada*
> Complain, complain to father Chikanje.

> solo   *Male male ßana mwe*
> You [witches] finish children.
> *ßalipapano pano dada*

> They are right here father.
> *Dandaule*
> Complain.

> chorus　*Dandaule dandaule kwakwa Chikanje*
> 　　　　Complain, complain to Chikanje.
> 　　　　*Dandaule dandaule kwakwa Chikanje dada*
> 　　　　Complain, complain to father Chikanje.

> 　solo　*Ati lowe lowe ßana mwe*
> 　　　　They say you bewitch children.
> 　　　　*ßalipapano pano dada*
> 　　　　They are right here father.
> 　　　　*Dandaule*
> 　　　　Complain.

> chorus　*Dandaule dandaule kwakwa Chikanje*
> 　　　　Complain, complain to Chikanje.
> 　　　　*Dandaule dandaule kwakwa Chikanje dada*
> 　　　　Complain, complain to father Chikanje.

The verses of songs are loosely structured. Other verses may be added, the order of verses changed, or the name of the *nchimi* switched, but the relationship between the call and the response is inviolate.

This song is typical of more recent *vimbuza* songs, the overwhelming majority of which deal with issues of witches and the *nchimi*'s fight to stop their evil deeds. Interestingly, the older *vimbuza* songs rarely speak of witches, probably because *vimbuza* possession was not originally tied so closely to battling witchcraft. The Tumbuka, like many peoples in this part of Africa, used the *mwabvi* (*Erythrophleum suaveolens*, Williamson 1974: 108–110) poison ordeal to catch witches (see Elmslie 1899; Fraser 1914; Marwick 1965), and it seems that only after the British outlawed this practice did *vimbuza* and the "seeing" of *nchimi* become so involved with ferreting out witches and witchcraft. So far as the Tumbuka were concerned, something still had to be done about witches, for they were not eliminated just because the British banned them. The Tumbuka probably turned more to *vimbuza* and its music when the *mwabvi* poison ordeal was made illegal, for *vimbuza* music gave *nchimi* the gift of divinatory sight.

When the *vimbuza* and *mizimu* spirits come together through the transformative properties of the *vimbuza* dance, according to Chikanje, he can see the heart of a patient and can tell from the way it beats what is troubling that person. "When I dance I feel sad and then I can see the person's heart." Chikanje speaks of this "seeing of hearts" as an empathy with the patient's suffering and an identification with a kind of existential sadness of being in the world.[9]

Patients and their relatives—illness is never a solitary affair in Tumbuka society—sit on the floor of the temple in a loosely defined semicircle as they wait to be divined. Chikanje dances in the space circumscribed by this group, and while he dances he points to the next person to be divined, who then stands before him. He continues to dance until he is ready to speak of what he has seen. Although he stops dancing during the actual divination, generally the music continues while he is divining. After a patient is "seen," Chikanje starts dancing again, and the whole process is repeated. Throughout the night, Chikanje dances and divines in this way.

This night Mr. Mkandawire, another drummer whom Chikanje often used, was playing *ng'oma* instead of Mr. Hunga, who, for the past week, had been sick with a "bad stomach." Mr. Hunga was, in fact, one of the patients waiting to be "seen" by Chikanje. When it was finally his turn, he stood before Chikanje, who placed his hands on Hunga's shoulders and began to dance. Suddenly, he stopped dancing and signaled for the music to cease. I was sitting on the other side of the temple adjusting recording levels, and at that moment wasn't paying much attention to the divination, when I heard Chikanje call out my name. At first I didn't understand what he was saying—this had never happened before and I was a little confused—but I soon realized that he was asking me to repeat to those assembled my dream about Hunga.

Unsure what was happening, nonetheless I complied and told of Hunga dancing in front of the fire but unable to "see." As soon as I finished, Chikanje turned to Hunga and told him that my dream was a warning that one of his relatives was trying to "witch" him and that was why he was sick. I had unwittingly just made my first public witchcraft accusation.

Chikanje did not specifically name the witch—although *nchimi* often do—for "that would cause confusion" among Hunga's family. He merely let it be known through my dream that what had been a hidden agenda carried out against Mr. Hunga by one of his relatives was now brought out into the open, and if whoever was responsible did not stop the witchcraft, he or she would suffer dire consequences.

Chikanje informed Hunga that the next day he would give him *mankwhala* (medicine) to counteract the witchcraft and then would

cut him with protection medicine. This medicine, which is rubbed i
small incisions made on the forehead, hands, and feet with a razor
blade, is believed to send the witchcraft back onto the sender. Now
that Hunga had been bewitched, however, his *vimbuza*, which had lain
dormant for many years—the *nthenda* (disease) usually weakens as
people enter old age—had become active, and in the coming weeks he
would need to dance *vimbuza* in order to cool the spirits.

Phineas the Patient

Of the patients who stand before Chikanje, many are bewitched and as
a result are afflicted by the *vimbuza* spirits who have come to help
fight the witchcraft (see chapter 2). Once the witchcraft has been neutralized, then the *vimbuza* must be cooled through dance. *Vimbuza*
dance has the dual purpose of being part of a diagnostic technology for
nchimi and a medical therapy for those afflicted by the spirits.

At Chikanje's, Sundays are usually reserved for these patients to
dance. Although the *thempli* isn't nearly so crowded for such occasions
as it is on divination nights, the atmosphere is still intense and emotionally charged. The following is an account of how one young man
came to dance for the first time at Chikanje's. I cite it for its typicality
in the experiential contours it foregrounds for a majority of *vimbuza*
patients. When I met him, Phineas was twenty years old and had been
at Chikanje's for three months:

"On a Saturday night I was brought in front of Chikanje, who divined that I had been bewitched, and that the only thing protecting me
from dying was the vimbuza and mizimu spirits. I was told that I
needed to come live at the compound and that after the witchcraft had
been cooled down they would try me dancing.

"The following day I was given mankwhala to sniff. I sniffed this
medicine every day for two weeks and was feeling better when Chikanje gave me another medicine to take that was milklike. He said
that this medicine was to remove all the ufwiti [witchcraft] that had
accumulated in my body because someone had put nyanga in my food.
I took that medicine for a month, but Chikanje saw that I was still
weak so he gave me another medicine. This medicine was made from
greenish leaves and made me vomit. I only took it for one day.

"Chikanje decided that I had lost some blood and sent me to the
government hospital in Rumphi. Before I went to the hospital I stopped
at the mission-run dispensary in Bwengu, and they gave me vitamins

and told me to go on to Rumphi. At the hospital they tested me by taking samples from my spinal cord and stool. The doctors found that I wasn't lacking blood, so they gave me tablets for headaches. I stayed at the hospital for one month to treat the headaches and then came back to Chikanje's. When I got back he suggested that they try me to dance.

"The first night that I danced they sat me down in the middle of the temple next to the drums and covered me with a cloth. The singing and drumming began and they tried several different vimbuza, but it took some time before I could be aroused. It started to feel like the drums were beating inside of my head. My heart began to speed up and I started shaking. When the people saw that I was shaking, they took off the cloth and put the mang'wanda [belt with dangling tin] and mazamba [animal skin or cloth skirt] around my waist, and tied nyisi [iron jingles] around my ankles. They picked me up and started moving me in a dancelike motion. After that I danced to a few songs: 'Muharure,' 'Kalulu,' and 'Nowa' [see appendix C]. I remember the songs because the vimbuza hadn't heated up fully yet. But after these songs, I don't remember dancing at all.

"I was told by other people that I danced for a while longer and was presented with mboni plates with a silver coin inside. This was given to my mizimu so that the nthenda would be good. If they don't plead to the spirits with the mboni, the vimbuza might come in a bad way. After this I danced to a few more songs and that was it. The next day I was given msisi [drinking medicine made from roots] to stabilize the vimbuza.

"I still get headaches, and when I do I dance vimbuza, which makes them go away. I'm getting fewer headaches, though, the more I dance and as time goes by. In the near future I will probably do chilopa, and that will be the end of it."

Phineas's story is typical of the stories of many of Chikanje's patients. Like Mr. Hunga, he was bewitched by one of his relatives, the *vimbuza* came to help, and after the witchcraft was dealt with he needed to cool the *vimbuza*. His first time dancing was also typical of many patients' experiences.

Most patients who dance for the first time are covered with a cloth placed over their entire body as they sit in front of the drums (fig. 11). Chikanje explained that this was to help generate more heat, and—again the pragmatic side—to help people who were particularly shy. Although Phineas didn't mention it, *mankwhala* (medicine) to help heat the *vimbuza* is often burned underneath the blanket so that the

Fig. 11. A new patient, covered with a cloth, who is being tried for dancing

patient will breathe in the smoke.[10] There are many different kinds of *vimbuza* medicine, some that help to heat the *nthenda*, others that cool it, and still others that are meant to stabilize the *vimbuza* at a particular energy level—a kind of medicinal governor. Chikanje, for example, when divining would often chew on a particular root during breaks in his dancing precisely for this purpose.

As the patient sits under the blanket, the drummers begin to play in the different rhythmic modes of the *vimbuza* to ascertain which *vimbuza* are afflicting the person. *Nchimi* can divine that a person is afflicted by the *vimbuza* spirits but cannot tell which *vimbuza* are involved. This is something only *vimbuza* drumming can achieve— truly a musical diagnosis. This diagnosis, however, is much more than merely a process of naming and identification. The way the *vimbuza* manifest themselves through dance reveals much about the intensity and nature of the affliction.

A resonance exists between rhythmic mode of drumming and mode of spiritual energy. If the drummers play in a rhythmic mode that does not relate to one of the *vimbuza* spirits afflicting the patient, then nothing happens. Drummers usually play in one mode for at least fifteen minutes, giving the *nthenda* ample opportunity to heat up before they change modes. But if the mode matches the type of one of the afflicting spirits, then the patient will begin to show signs of becoming possessed: arms and legs will begin a fast shaking, the heart will begin to race, and often a distinctive high-pitched cry—"He! He! He!"—is emitted.[11]

People are never afflicted by only one *vimbuza* spirit, so once the patient begins to dance, other rhythmic modes are tried. Again, if the mode matches the spirit, the person will dance. If it does not, the patient usually just stands in front of the drums waiting for a different mode to be played. For a new patient, this process goes on for an hour or so until all the *vimbuza*, or at least most of them, have been given a chance to possess the patient and come out and "play with their children"—that is, dance.

Drummers—musicians who are intimately involved with producing trance states in healers and patients—are rarely afflicted by the *vimbuza*. And if they are, as Hunga was, they virtually never become possessed while drumming.[12] If they do become possessed, something I witnessed only a few times, they are immediately relieved of their duties as drummers and someone else takes over. It is a simple dictum in Tumbuka culture: those who are possessed cannot drum.

Trance in Africa, specifically spirit possession, is not a uniform experience throughout the continent but is highly differentiated both between and within respective health care systems. In the temple of a Tumbuka healer, trance dancing happens sequentially; one dancer is "featured" at a time, and all attention is focused on this person. Drummers play and the *kwaya* sings and claps for an audience of one. This is a distinctive feature of *vimbuza* spirit possession that differentiates it from, for example, the divine horsemen complexes of West Africa. When the *orisha* spirits enter the phenomenal world of the living, many people go into trance simultaneously. The social dynamics of group possession are of a different order from those of individual possession, something that needs more comparative research.[13] They both, however, are entranced modes of being-in-the-world.

Occasionally, *vimbuza* spirit possession does occur in more than one person simultaneously. Especially when the moon is in the west, a time when the *vimbuza* spirits are supposed to be particularly active, many people may spontaneously go into trance.[14] Significantly, and in direct contrast to West African–style possession, in these types of spontaneous possessions people are not allowed to dance.

Among Kunde adepts of the Brekete shrine in the Volta Region of Ghana, for example, each person who becomes possessed is taken into the inner chamber of the cult house to transform his or her attire into that of the possessing god.[15] They emerge to dance with the other gods of the Kunde pantheon, enacting an almost dramaturgical scene, complete with dialogue between the different spirits. But when someone at a *vimbuza* dance who is not featured begins to show signs of becoming entranced, others attempt to cool down the spirits either by fanning the person with the *nchimi*'s fly whisk or by pulling the person's hair. If the possession is serious enough, the person may be chosen to dance later that night, but usually there is only one possessed dancer at a time. It seems that the spirits must learn when it is their time to dance—something that is chosen by the Tumbuka, not by the *vimbuza*.

People who are afflicted by the *vimbuza* spirits also display different levels of sensitivity to *vimbuza* music. Chikanje can now pretty much choose when his *vimbuza* will heat to the drums. When he is not divining, he can sit in the temple for hours listening and watching *vimbuza* without his spirits becoming affected in the least. Phineas, the patient just discussed, on the other hand, couldn't even listen to my tape recordings of *vimbuza* music without his spirits starting to heat. For most people, there are also times when they are more sensitive to the music than they are at others.

Generally, though, the longer someone has had *vimbuza* and has been dancing as part of a therapy, the more control he or she gains over the onset of possession trance when *vimbuza* music is present. This seems to have a resonance with Rouget's (1985: 323) basic point that music socializes trance states, bringing them under cultural control. Perceiving musical experience as a socialization process, however, enables us to understand only a small part of the phenomenal reality of the *vimbuza* musical experience.

Patients dance not to become possessed but because they are possessed. *Nchimi*, however, who regularly dance two or three times a week, control not only the onset of their own trance but also the nature of that trance. Healers are lucid trancers, consciousness-doublers, who dance not because they are possessed but to become *nchimi*—prophet healers who are manifestations of the *vimbuza*, the ancestors, *and themselves*.

Through music, dancer becomes spirit and spirit becomes dancer. Edward Bruner's (1986: 6) categorical separation of "life as lived (reality), life as experienced (experience), and life as told (expression)" collapses in the world of *vimbuza*. The lived experience and expression of music and spirit are one inseparable reality. Spirit possession is not expressed through a retelling or a reliving but is externalized, revealed simultaneously through the music and dance of *vimbuza*. This kind of telling is not symbolic but existentially real. To paraphrase John Blacking (1973: 28), trance is not a flight from reality but a journey into it. For the Tumbuka—as for virtually all peoples who undergo *ng'oma*-type spirit afflictions—the journey is a musical experience.

The musical experience of trance is a complex affair of overlapping meanings and tendencies that are built up through repeated lived experiences. This is not a passive process on the part of patients and healers, something that happens to them as if a tradition were over against them—something to be encountered—but it emerges through an active music making informed through sedimentations that include, but are not limited to, such things as performance practices, musical structures, and rhythmic modes. Repeated experiences with this kind of music making do not result in a fixed practice but rather in a horizon of possibilities.

"Growing Older Together"

When the Tumbuka make music together inside the *thempli*, they construct a reality that is deeply felt. Chernoff (1979) calls it a sensibility, Feld (1982) a sentiment, but I believe Schutz (1964: 175) captures the essence of the phenomenon when he states that making music with one or more persons is "growing older together." It is a unique experience in which "performer and listener are 'tuned-in' to one another, are living together through the same flux, are growing older together while the musical process lasts" (ibid.: 174–75). Within this *performed* auditory field, an intersubjective objectivity becomes possible that binds people together in a commonality of experiential space and time.

In Schutz's (1973) phenomenology of the *Lebenswelt*, making music together is a particularly powerful example of pre-reflective social intercourse, involving a relationship that "originates in the possibility of living together simultaneously in specific dimensions of time" (1964: 162). Following Bergson's concept of *durée*—which for Schutz is "the very form of existence of music" (ibid.: 170)—he conceives of musical experience as a pluridimensionality of inner time. This kind of musical passage cannot be quantified in clock time, nor is it merely the succession of abstract musical beats. It is a thick time that allows consociates to share more than "the inner durée in which the content of the music played actualizes itself; each, simultaneously, shares in vivid present the Other's stream of consciousness in immediacy" (ibid.: 176). It both structures inner time and is a "gearing into the outer world," which

creates the possibility of an objective intersubjectivity between in
viduals.

Kapferer (1983: 181) speaks directly to this point in relation to the
music and dance of Sinhalese exorcisms: "An essential property of the
time-structure of music and dance is that it constitutes a continuous
present. Musical time is movement and passage filled out in its existential immediacy. Because of these aspects, members of the ritual gathering who are engaged within the musical context of the patient can
share the same vivid and continuous present, which is an experiential
possibility of music." Music becomes a shared time for those involved
in one way or another with its processes. In this way, *vimbuza* and
the music of Sinhalese exorcisms are phenomena that transcend the
individual experience of them. For *vimbuza*, it is precisely this sharing
of sacred time that is objectively presented as a clinical reality during
the enactment of trance dance.

A major difference, however, between the Sinhalese sharing of a
vivid and continuous present at an exorcism and the Tumbuka experience of a musically constructed clinical reality is that in Sinhalese
exorcism only the priests and drummers are active musical participants
(see Kapferer 1983: 149–55). In *vimbuza*, everyone is supposed to partake musically. When Kapferer speaks of the sharing of a vivid present
by those who attend a Sinhalese exorcism, he is basically referring to
the passive experience of listening to music together. For the Tumbuka
in an *nchimi's thempli*, growing older together is *making* music together.

People who gather in the temple on divination nights are not passive spectators but are expected to be musically active. Everyone should
participate in the music making, and although this ideal is never
reached, it doesn't alter the underlying premise, which is one of universal participation.[16] Through making music together, a condition of communitas—"a relational quality of full unmediated communication,
even communion, between definite and determinate identities" (Turner
and Turner 1978: 250)—is possible, and this is precisely what *nchimi*
strive for. Coming together in the musical experience creates a powerful
source of cultural energy. When it is directed at a patient who is dancing, this form of musical communitas may have important healing
properties. When it is directed at an *nchimi*, it becomes the "battery"
for "seeing." For the people gathered in the temple, music becomes the
process that particularizes the universal and universalizes the particular
(Kapferer 1986: 191), making possible a profound intersubjective experience.

In the temple, patients, healer, and, from a Tumbuka perspective, spirits as well become part of a focused gathering, "a set of persons engrossed in a common flow of activity and relating to one another in terms of that flow" (Geertz's [1973: 424] reading of Goffman). That common flow of activity in a healer's temple is the musically mediated series of transactions—in Goffman's terms (1961: 7–8), the "focused interactions"—that occur between patient, healer, spirits, and, sometimes, Mzungu researcher. The music and dance of *vimbuza* are, to follow Goffman (1974: 57) one step further, "the engrossables . . . which generate a realm of being." Within the confines of the mud walls and thatched roof of the *thempli,* this realm of being is a sacred clinical reality constructed through musical means.

Musical experience in *vimbuza* spirit possession—as well as in Sinhalese exorcism, Kaluli weeping (Feld 1982), and the ethical sensibilities of Dagomba drumming (Chernoff 1979)—is the objective anchor of an intense intersubjective experience. By saying this, I do not mean to imply that all musical events are musical experiences that manifest these intersubjective potentialities. Listening to a young student struggle through a piano recital is, after all, a completely different experience from that of drumming for the spirits. The intersubjective nature of the former is extremely limited, whereas the latter tends toward a kind of communitas. This kind of musical experience can annihilate interpersonal distance—the distance between "I" and "thou," creating a concrete "we-relation" (Schutz 1973: 63). It is this concrete relation, the intensity of making music together inside the temple of a Tumbuka healer, that is the center of a sacred clinical reality.

Musical experience such as this, to cite Blacking, artfully enhances human consciousness. As he reminds us: "There is a difference between music that is occasional and music that enhances human consciousness, music that is simply for having and music that is for being. I submit that the former may be good craftsmanship, but that the latter is art, no matter how simple or complex it sounds, and no matter under what circumstances it is produced" (Blacking 1973: 50). For Tumbuka healers and their patients, the art of music making inside the *thempli* has the possibility of creating a direct and powerful effect on the processual nature of lived experience. Its immediate presence can shape the very fabric of the ongoing experience of the lifeworld. In this way music becomes an authentic mode of being-in-the-world. Instead of falling into the world away from the existential reality of existence, music making projects a clearing, a place in which people can encounter the world and each other in all their reflexive immediacy.

Musical experience imparts a timbre—to use an aural metaphor—to the proceedings inside the temple. Dancer and spirit, drummer and singer are first and foremost music makers. And in their music making, spirit and Tumbuka meet, and both are transformed. As the *vimbuza* modes call out to the numinous, they simultaneously invite people in to give up one socially defined self for another, perhaps deeper, persona

five

In the *Vimbuza* Mode

sound systems "all up in you"

Many, if not all, of music's essential processes may be found in the constitution of the human body.

—JOHN BLACKING,
HOW MUSICAL IS MAN?

Mulaula says that when the drums sound, he feels their wind enter through his legs, rise up into his chest, and heat the *vimbuza*. Drums are powerful in that way, and one must be careful to protect this power. That is why he puts a special *mankwhala* (medicine) in the fire used to heat the drumheads (fig. 12). Sometimes witches try to bewitch the drums so that an *nchimi*'s "seeing" becomes "clouded." The *mankwhala* counteracts the witches' *nyanga* (potions) so that the drumming will be strong. When the drumming is strong, the *vimbuza* are strong, and as Mulaula puts it, when the *vimbuza* are strong, "the *mizimu* come too much." Musical experience for Mulaula is first and foremost a bodily experience.

The visceral sensations of drumming felt in the chest, the sheer intensity of good singing, the motional power of trance dancing all contribute to a physical encounter with the aural reality of *vimbuza*. This is not subsidiary material, interesting only to musical specialists, but is the very form of existence of a Tumbuka clinical reality. How can we achieve a phenomenology of *vimbuza* if we cannot gain access to this very fabric of its lived experience?

In chiTumbuka, to "hear," *kupulika*, is to "understand," *kupulika*. Only when we begin actually to "hear" the music of *vimbuza* instead of just listening to it will we begin to understand the *vimbuza* experience. In order to begin to hear, we must enter into the existential structure of the music itself, where dancing prophets and drummed spirits are brought forth into an embodied phenomenological presence.

Fig. 12. Saza heating the drumheads for tuning

The Dance of Drumming

Of all the musical phenomena present during *vimbuza,* it is the sound
of drums that is most closely associated with the spirits. A theory of
correspondence relates spiritual energy to rhythmic mode. Only the
rhythmic mode of *vyanusi* will heat the spirits of the Ngoni and transform ordinarily shy young women into spear-wielding Ngoni warriors.
Similarly, only the rhythms of *fumu za pasi,* with its distinctive combination of open and stopped strokes, will call forth the *mphepo* (spirit-
wind) of the lion, which brings the threat of violence but also the prom-
ise of great divinatory power.

Without drumming there would be no dancing, and without dancing, the *vimbuza* would be unable to "play with their children." The
drum modes are the core of *vimbuza* music; they stand out, in a phenomenological sense, from the acoustical field as the noematic corre-
late—that to which intentionality is directed—for both patient *and*
spirit.

When a person is first afflicted by the *vimbuza,* it is the drumming
that initially calls forth the spirits (patients usually sit with their head
almost touching the *ng'oma* drum when they first begin to heat the
vimbuza), and thus it is through drumming that a diagnosis of spirit

affliction is made. When *nchimi* are dancing and want to intensify the heat of their *vimbuza,* they often signal for the singing to stop, and dance only to the drums. It is the drumming that both fuels the trance state and helps to stabilize it.

An equivalent system of melodic specificity—like that, for example, found in *zar* cults (Boddy 1989: 155), where spirits have particular "threads" that are sung—is not operative in *vimbuza.* This is not to say that singing is not of utmost importance, for it is in singing that the maximum level of group participation occurs inside the *thempli.* The sound of song, the direct result of singing—"growing older together"—is a primary part of the *vimbuza* experience. What people are singing about, however, is decidedly epiphenomenal.

Contrary to the emphasis and importance that folklorists, anthropologists, historians, and other researchers, including ethnomusicologists, place on song texts when dealing with musical phenomena in ritual settings—perhaps in part due to the problematics of constructing meaningful musical analyses—the Tumbuka do not seem particularly concerned with or interested in the meaning of songs. This is not to imply that there is little information contained in song lyrics or that they are not worth analyzing (see Vail and White's [1991] recent work), but rather that they often have been overemphasized in the literature at the expense of more important musical issues. Regardless of the sophistication of textual analysis, the words of songs are not, in themselves, musical phenomena. As Alan Merriam (1964: 237) reminds us, "Texts are not music sound and, though shaped and modified by music, they are inevitably linguistic rather than music behavior as such." Analyses that restrict themselves entirely to explication of textual content in songs cannot, therefore, offer us access in any meaningful way to the lived reality of musical experience.[1]

That words of songs are secondary in the experience of a musically constructed clinical reality is evident not only in what the Tumbuka have to say about the matter—which was abundantly clear in my many discussions with people while I was translating these texts—but also in what they do. People sing in languages they do not understand, many songs are made up almost entirely of vocables (syllables without referents), and for the most part, the meanings of song texts have little to do with the action taking place. I have heard songs about the latest soap, Vinoria, sung during *chilopa* blood sacrifices (and they were not about cleansing in any metaphorical sense). Although certain songs are associated with certain spirits—for example, "Mugwede" is always a *vyanusi* song, and the song about the *msoro* tree reproduced in chapter

4 is always related to *nkharamu*—usually there is no strong identification between spirit and song. It is not that lyrical content has no social or cultural function, for there are songs of censure, morals, promotion, witchcraft, politics, and so forth, but rather that this content is most often secondary to the lived experience of music making inside an *nchimi*'s temple. It is the drumming that defines the systematic relationship between dancer and *vimbuza* spirit.

Drumming has a primacy in *vimbuza* that provides a natural focal point from which to begin a phenomenological inquiry. It is something that the Tumbuka themselves acknowledge as being foregrounded in their experience of clinical reality. To describe *vimbuza* drumming phenomenologically, however, requires attention not only—to use Kubik's (1962: 39) terms—to the acoustic image but also to the motor image, or the motional aspects of performance. Attention to motional aspects necessitates a focus on the music-making potential of the human body. This is a matter not of investigating the techniques of playing a musical instrument but of understanding the possibility of the body itself existing in a musical mode.

The importance of the body is nothing new in the ethnomusicology of African musics. In 1928, Erich von Hornbostel (1928: 52–53) wrote that "African rhythm is ultimately founded on drumming. Drumming can be replaced by hand-clapping or by the xylophone; what really matters is the act of beating; and only from this point can African rhythms be understood. . . . We proceed from hearing, they from motion." The "act of beating," of course, involves movement of the human body, but Hornbostel is suggesting that this motion has structural implications in the understanding of musical phenomena. Gerhard Kubik (1962: 33), in his formulation of inherent rhythms, follows a similar theme when he stresses the sometimes dissonant relationship between musical sound and performance: "*The image as it is heard and the image as it is played are often different from each other in African instrumental music*" (italics in the original). "Heard image" and "played image" are both acoustic terms, while the "motor image" may or may not produce an acoustic image (Kubik 1962: 39–40). These theories suggest a realization that an adequate description of much African music must go beyond acoustical phenomena into the realm of bodily action.[2]

Sound and motion are not independent phenomenal streams in *vimbuza* but are multilayered and complexly interrelated. This interaction between sound and motion extends from the obvious—that the motion of dance produces a sound that is an important part of the musical texture—to the not-so-obvious—that drumming is a dance

Fig. 13. Saza
drumming in the
temple

unto itself. The more I learned about drumming, the more I began to
realize how dancelike it is in its motional configuration. In *vimbuza*
drumming there is a dialectic between what is heard and how it is
played. My experience of drumming involved both, for not only did I
listen, but I also drummed.

Saza

Although I learned from many different drummers, it was Saza (fig. 13),
Mulaula's younger brother, who taught me the essentials of *vimbuza*
drumming. He was his brother's main divination drummer and was
well known for his strong style of playing. When I met him, he was
living with his two wives and four children at his brother's compound

and had just signed a waiting list to go work in the mines of South Africa. Saza was still young, only twenty-five, and wanted to make more money than he could in Malawi. Mulaula was not happy about the prospect of losing him, and neither was I. But fortunately for both of us, Saza was not called up right away, and after a while he seemed to lose interest in leaving for what was, to say the least, a dangerous way to make a living (many who went to the South African mines never returned). Part of his decision to stay may have had to do with a rumored increase in "gifts" from his brother—drummers are not formally paid as professionals—and perhaps another part had to do with this white man who, of all things, wanted to learn how to drum, and who was also willing to reciprocate with "gifts."

Most days during my stay at Mulaula's compound, Saza and I would sit by the side of my hut in the afternoons and drum. Patients who had come to Mulaula's *chipatala* to be divined would usually stop and stare. An Mzungu trying to learn to drum *vimbuza* was an unusual sight, but perhaps even stranger was the sight of Saza, one of the finest drummers in northern Malawi, playing the drums in slow motion.

Saza was rare among *vimbuza* drummers in that he was able to break down drumming patterns into their constituent parts and play them, as it were, in slow motion, something extremely helpful to me in my learning process. After working together for a week or so, we had developed a fairly effective procedure in which Saza would start playing and I would hear an interesting rhythmic pattern and ask him to show me the stroke configuration. He would then demonstrate the particular pattern on the *ng'oma*, the master drum, slowly, stroke by stroke, and I would try to reproduce it. This was, needless to say, also beneficial in producing rather precise transcriptions.

Although this was not a traditional way to learn drumming—there is no formalized student-teacher musical relationship in Tumbuka society—it was traditional in at least one respect: I learned by imitating what I saw. Young boys who want to drum do not go to a teacher but learn mainly by watching other drummers play. They try to imitate the motional configurations of drum patterns—a mimetic process—initially paying more attention to what the hands do than to what the acoustic image is.[3] The acoustic image is not ignored, but rather takes a back seat to the physicality of drumming in the initial stages of learning. From this perspective, drumming is as much a dance as it is music making.

As I learned this "dance" of drumming, I began to realize that there was an interactive tension between the acoustic and motor images that produced a rhythmic depth in *vimbuza* drumming not entirely discernible from audition alone. Once I began to experience this depth, the music became multidimensional—in certain ways analogous, in the visual realm, to the new computer-generated, three-dimensional, random dot stereograms popularly called "magic eyes." Anyone who has experienced this illusion will recognize the almost magical quality of seeing a two-dimensional pattern blossom into a three-dimensional form that pops out from the page. Such is the case with *vimbuza* music, for once you can *hear* the rhythmic depth in the drumming, musical experience is transformed into a kind of multidimensional hearing that transcends acoustical phenomena, reaching out and into the world of bodily motion.

The Motional Structure of Sound

The art of *vimbuza* drumming—and again I use "art" in Blacking's (1973: 50) sense of "music that is for being," as opposed to "music that is simply for having"—is capable of producing in the listener attuned to its rhythmic complexities a mode of being-in-the-world. Being-in-the-world musically, in its ontological sense, does not mean that there is a world and that musical experience somehow happens within its confines, as if the world were a container filled with a substance called music. It means, instead, that music and world are given together. There is no distance between the two; they are equiprimordial. The clearing that musical experience projects is both the world and the being-in-it. For *vimbuza*, being-in-the-world is not a diffuse experience but has specific existential features that are particularly amenable to ethnomusicological analysis.

Inside the temple of a Tumbuka healer, a world of shifting rhythmic perspectives is constructed out of polymetrical structures of both sound *and motion* (motion can be polymetrical; take, for example, Chikanje's dancing as described in chapter 4). The following description of this musically phenomenal surface, while interesting in itself as a musical analysis, is given here for the purpose of revealing the tissue of musical reality constructed inside an *nchimi*'s temple. To describe this reality and, in describing it, to move "nearer" to this world of sound and motion requires a radical narrowing of focus, a turn to that which is given first inside the *thempli* during those moments when the drums are sounded to call forth the *vimbuza*. This kind of description necessitates, at the outset, a move not to musical sound but to the physicality of drumming.

The Drummer's Hand

Drummers use two basic playing techniques when they drum *vimbuza:* a palm stroke played in the center of the drumhead with the full hand, which is slightly cupped from the base of the palm to the tips of the fingers, and a hand stroke played mostly with the fingers, the heel of the palm aligned with the edge of the drum. Either of these strokes may be open—in other words, letting the drumhead vibrate freely after a stroke—or stopped, damping the drumhead immediately after the stroke by pressing down on the head. *Vimbuza* drumming is, to a large degree, a matter of being able to control the timbral differences produced by these playing techniques. Timbre—and I include dynamic accents under this term because dynamic levels have timbral ramifications—articulates variation and mode in *vimbuza* rhythmic praxis.

When Saza drums for his brother inside the *thempli,* you can physically feel the sound in your chest. This sensation is not just a result of decibels—although when Saza drums he does push a lot of air—but it also has to do with a technique of focusing the sound. Saza refers to this as "making the *phula* sound." The *phula* is a doughnut-shaped lump of propolis (a resinous substance used by bees in constructing their hives) that is affixed concentrically to the *ng'oma* drumhead (fig. 14). It seems to facilitate the control of timbral nuances, which are essential to *vimbuza* drumming. When palm strokes are played, the *phula* helps to bring out the low fundamental of the drum.[4] When open hand strokes are played, optimally with the first three fingers hitting the side of the *phula,* it gives them a clear, ringing sound. Saza would tell me to try to focus my sound by making the air of the drum come out the small hole of the *phula.*[5] "If you cover the *phula,* you can't sing on the drums." It took me a while to master this technique, but once I did, it was as if I could feel the vibrations of the drum coming out the center of the *phula* on my fingertips.

Once I had these basic techniques literally in hand, Saza began my drumming apprenticeship by showing me the core *vimbuza* pattern. I call it the core pattern because its motional and timbral configuration expresses the essentials of *vimbuza* rhythmic praxis. This motto—I use Rouget's term here to designate the basic rhythmic figure of a mode—generates the rhythmic mode that calls forth a kind of generic

Fig. 14. The *phula* of an *ng'oma* drum

vimbuza referred to as *vimbuza waka* (lit. "just *vimbuza*"), which, most likely, are the spirits of the autochthonous people the Tumbuka encountered when they first came to northern Malawi. Significantly, this rhythmic motto, related to what are possibly the original *vimbuza* spirits, is the core pattern from which virtually all other *vimbuza* rhythmic mottos are derived.

The figure consists of a palm stroke played in the center of the drum followed by two open hand strokes played on the edge of the *phula*. The whole figure is then repeated, creating a core pattern covering six pulses (fig. 15). When this figure is played, as is the case in virtually all *vimbuza* drumming—and in contrast to many other drumming traditions—a strict alternation of hands is maintained.[6] Even if a pulse is not articulated—that is, the pulse is silent, which is characteristic of many of the modes—the alternation of hands is still maintained as if the silent pulse were a sounded stroke. This is an important structural feature of *vimbuza* drumming to which I will return.

A Western-trained musician, upon hearing this core *vimbuza* pattern, would, I think, immediately assume that the figure was constructed around a straightforward duple compound meter of 6/8. In other words, the alternating palm strokes naturally produce an implied two-beat, three-pulse metrical structure, 1 2 3 4 5 6 = 1 2 3 / 1 2 3

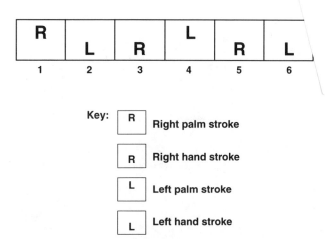

Fig. 15. The core *vimbuza* drumming pattern

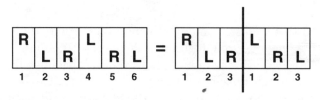

Fig. 16. Implied meter of the core pattern

(fig. 16), but without the pattern of stressed beats associated with Western meter.[7] If the core pattern was heard in the context of a full performance, this perception would be reinforced by the handclaps of the *kwaya*, the *mphiningu* supporting drum pattern, and the beats articulated on the *mboza drum*, when it is used.[8]

When I first encountered *vimbuza* drumming in actual performance, however, I found it somewhat puzzling that when playing the core *vimbuza* pattern, drummers would find their initial rhythmic orientation in the musical texture by sounding the pattern shown in figure 17. This three-stroke figure, 1 2 3 4 5 6 = 1 2 / 1 2 / 1 2 (palm, hand, hand), which may be repeated several times, is played with only one hand and clearly delineates a *three-beat*, two-pulse meter rather than two beats of three pulses each. Notice again that a strict alternation of hands is maintained, for each nonarticulated pulse would be a left-hand stroke, which is why this pattern is played entirely with the right hand. This "threeness" is also reinforced during performance by some members of the *kwaya* who alternately clap in three, and I have already

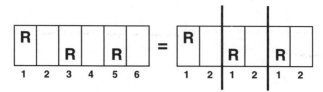

Fig. 17. The *vimbuza* orienting pattern

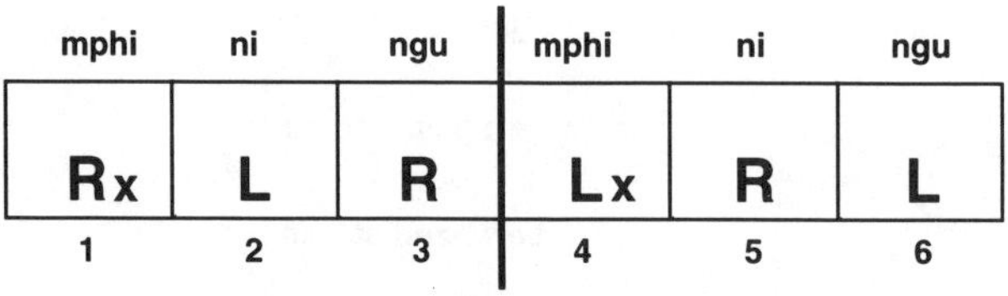

mphi	ni	ngu	mphi	ni	ngu
Rx	**L**	**R**	**L**x	**R**	**L**
1	2	3	4	5	6

Fig. 18. The *mphiningu* supporting drum pattern. Rx indicates a right-hand stopped stroke, Lx a left-hand stopped stroke

mentioned that Chikanje and other dancers often start their dancing by sounding the *nyisi* iron jingles to a three-beat structure.

What really caught my interest, however, was that not only *ng'oma* drummers used this three-beat pattern to find their place in the musical texture, but so did the drummers for the *mphiningu* supporting part.[9] These drummers play an unchanging rhythmic figure on the *mphiningu* that is virtually the same as the core pattern and thus carries a strong implication of a duple meter, 6/8 (fig. 18).[10] Aligning this pattern to that of the *ng'oma* lead and to the call and response of the choir is crucial to correct drumming. If the *mphiningu* pattern is not in the correct relationship to the other parts, the *vimbuza* spirits will not come and no one will dance. I have seen more than one *nchimi* and patient stand with their hands on their hips, refusing to dance because the *mphiningu* was off.

What puzzled me was why both *ng'oma* and *mphiningu* drummers oriented themselves to the core pattern, which obviously was in "two," using a three-beat structure. Was there something inherent in the core pattern that produced this "threeness," or was it just a strange quirk of *vimbuza* drumming?

When I questioned Saza and other drummers about this three-beat pattern, they responded with that familiar phrase most field researchers have encountered: "That's just the way we do it." The Tumbuka do not verbalize a rhythmic theory; they play it every time they drum. It is a bodily praxis.

What I am suggesting is that in the very motions of *vimbuza* drumming is revealed a way of being-in-the-world that itself is a kind of
musical understanding. This kind of understanding is most clearly laid
open in the core pattern itself. In what follows, I seek not a musical
analysis of a *vimbuza* drum pattern but a phenomenological description
of *vimbuza* drumming. To get at this kind of description, I follow Don
Ihde's (1977, 1983) use of Husserl's technique of "imaginative variations," a process that will give us an initial opening to the essential
presence of the *vimbuza* modes.

Vimbuza *Variations*

According to Ihde (1983: 82), the phenomenological technique of imaginative variations constitutes a kind of systematic "logic of discovery"
that opens up experience to a full range of descriptive possibilities. The
variational method, however, is not entirely a free play of imagination
but is circumscribed by the caveat that all variations "*must be fulfilled
or fulfillable in actual experience*" (ibid.: 83, italics in the original).
The criterion for empirical evidence is this fulfillability.

Not only is the variational method a means to get at the "essence"
of a phenomenon, but it also, according to Ihde (ibid.: 82), approximates
what takes place in certain kinds of artistic activity:

> It may also be noted from a philosophical point of view that
> the arts actually exercise the practice of variational discovery.
> Through the possible the actual is revealed.
>
> In the arts the characters in a novel are "possible" people;
> the steps of a dance are, at least in relation and in contrast to
> more mundane movements of our bodies, "possible" move-
> ments; and the plays of form, figure, light and color are varia-
> tions of the possible in visual art. Thus one might say in this
> respect that the arts are latently "phenomenological" in their
> primary use of variations.

In the art of *vimbuza* drumming, phenomenological possibility is not
a latent characteristic but is overtly manifest, for drummers use a variational method of discovery to construct the rhythmic modes of the
different *vimbuza* spirits.

Ihde believes in "doing phenomenology" (1977: 13–27), and I take
the same approach here. One way to an understanding of the *vimbuza*

Fig. 19. Face/goblet illusion

rhythmic modes is to enter into the phenomenological possibilities of *vimbuza* drumming through a kind of "doing," which includes experiencing its motional aspects. But before entering this world of sounded motion, I want to take, as a parallel example, a digression into Ihde's examination of visual illusions. To demonstrate phenomenological "doing," he focuses on a series of line drawings that have the unique properties of the kind of visual illusion that Gestalt psychologists call multistable.

In these types of illusions, figure and ground spontaneously reverse themselves, creating perceptual shifts. The familiar face-goblet illusion (fig. 19) is one example. In this line drawing, it is possible to see either two faces in profile as figure with the middle space between them as ground, or the middle space as a goblet that is foregrounded. Although one can shift between the two perspectives, according to Gestalt psychologists only one configuration can be seen at a time; hence the term multistable.

Ihde's choice of multistable illusions as an example of how the variational method operates serves well our purposes here, for it parallels in visual terms the creative (read artistic) activity taking place in *vimbuza* drumming. Metrical shifting, which is characteristic of all the *vimbuza* modes and which in essence binds them together into a coherent system, is the acoustical *and motional* equivalent of multistable visual illusions.

Faces and goblets, however, are not Ihde's concern, but rather two-dimensional line drawings depicting three-dimensional cubes, something widely known in the field of psychology as Necker cubes (fig. 20). Psychologically, the interesting thing about these cubes is that they may spontaneously reverse themselves. That is, each cube may be seen from at least two perspectives. For example, the cube in figure 20 may be viewed as either a cube tilted downward (facing forward, in Ihde's terms) or a cube tilted upward (rearward). If we stop our description of the cube at these two perspectives, according to Ihde (1983: 86–87), we have remained in the realm of the ordinary, or what Husserl would call the "natural attitude."

To expand into other possibilities, again with the caveat that they have the potential to be fulfilled in actual experience, brings us into the realm of the "phenomenological attitude," an attitude that is a "seeking [of] all possible variations on the figure" (ibid.: 87). To demonstrate this variation technique, Ihde (pp. 87–89) points out two additional perspectives, each elucidated by a story: one is about a peculiarly shaped insect inside a hexagonally shaped hole (the middle section is the body, with six legs [the lines] protruding from it), which gives a two-dimensional view of the cube; the second takes us back to a three-dimensional perspective, this time of an oddly cut gem, with the central configuration being a facet of the gem and the other facets sloping downward away from the viewer. Like the other three-dimensional configurations, this one can also be reversed, giving us another variation.

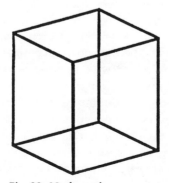

Fig. 20. Necker cube

In this reversal, the central facet of the gem is facing away from the viewer and the other facets slope toward the viewer, as if one were looking up at a ceiling.

Although this process of variation raises questions—Is the series "finite, indefinite, infinite"? Do the "ordinary variations," the ones perceived from the "natural attitude," have a privileged position in a topography of possibilities (Ihde 1983: 89)?—for the moment I want to focus on certain conditional features that are inherent in the process. In a sense, all the aforementioned possibilities are present at one time within the figure. Only one perspective, however, can be perceived by one person at any one instant. It is possible to shift rapidly back and forth between an upward-tilting and a downward-tilting cube, but it is impossible, at least according to Gestalt theory, to see both perspectives at once—they are mutually exclusive, and hence multistable.

Yet the shifting process can involve a certain intentionality on the part of the observer. Whereas upon first glance at a Necker cube, the shifting occurs more or less spontaneously, it is possible, with practice, for the viewer to gain a certain amount of control over this shifting process. (Try it: focus first on the upper left corner, then on the lower right corner). By concentrating, one can *make* the cube shift back and forth, not only from front to back but also from insect to gem.[11] This is an important point which Ihde overlooks and which, we will see, has much to do with the performance of *vimbuza* drumming.

What happens when we take this same "phenomenological attitude" and apply it to the rhythmic praxis of *vimbuza* drumming? In this case we are dealing with a phenomenon that, unlike the visual Necker cube, is perceived temporally through an intersense modality— that is, it is performed. We hear *vimbuza* drumming, but we may also *see* it. Ihde's description of the Necker cube, by contrast, does not include who drew it or how it was drawn, although perhaps it should. This consideration leads us to yet another element absent in the description of the cube: not only may I watch someone play *vimbuza* drums, but I may, in fact, be the person playing—which adds another dimension, that of my intent with respect to both the physical and acoustic properties of my drumming.

Something that *vimbuza* drumming and Necker cubes do share is that they are both multistable phenomena. Multistable illusions have been explored almost exclusively in relation to the visual.[12] This is not surprising, given the overall bias in Western culture for visual modes of representation.[13] I believe, however, that an analogous structure, one that is presented through the acoustical channel, is operative in *vim-*

buza drumming and is utilized by Tumbuka healers to create realities conducive to transformations of consciousness. The essence of *shifting* is still there, but it is experienced through sound.

Although the Tumbuka do not talk about drumming in terms of acoustical illusions, they do refer to multiple layers of beat, which are the basis for this phenomenon. When I asked women about the differences between their clapping in "two" and clapping in "three," they would often reply that the "two" beat followed the *mphiningu* drum and the "three" beat followed the *ng'oma.* And when I inquired whether there was a set procedure or pattern for doing these two kinds of clapping, they commented that it was up to each individual to decide how to clap and when to change. This response implies that both rates of motion (i.e., beat) are available at all times. In the same vein, as already mentioned, Chikanje once told me that his feet followed the *ng'oma* drum and his hips the *mphiningu.* These statements, which clearly indicate that two rates of beat occur simultaneously, when combined with my own observations, particularly regarding the orienting three-beat pattern drummers use, opened the way to this analysis of multistable acoustical phenomena.

For auditors who are perceptually aware of acoustical illusions—it is possible to hear *vimbuza* drumming and miss this phenomenon altogether—*vimbuza* drumming presents a fluid polymorphous structure that is perhaps conducive to loosening up perceptual boundaries between object and subject.[14] This loosening up of perceptual boundaries seems to be a significant factor in the promotion of trance states and thus in the construction of a sacred clinical reality inside the *thempli.* This observation raises issues essential to a phenomenological description of *vimbuza,* something I will return to later. For now, I want to turn to one of the fundamental motional realities of drumming, something so basic it has been overlooked by most researchers.

Part of the physiological makeup of humans is two-handedness. For *vimbuza* drumming, it is the hand as a unit that makes contact with the playing surface of the drum. In other words, the hands are not differentiated into more playing parts through the articulation of individual fingers, as happens, for example, in playing the tabla. The hand itself may change shape—it can be made flat, can be cupped, and so forth—but it still plays as a single unit. And since there are two hands, there is a certain "dupleness" inherent in the playing mechanism.

While two-handedness may seem so obvious that one might wonder why it needs stating, I believe that its very obviousness has, in fact, obscured an important generating feature of much African percussion music. In *vimbuza* drumming it is one of the keys to understanding how the motional and timbral configuration of the core pattern generates multistable acoustical illusions. To illustrate my point, I will tell a brief story, like Ihde's story of strangely shaped insects and oddly cut gems—a myth about the first *vimbuza* drummer.

Mupa's Knee

Sitting under a baobab tree long long ago, in the distant past, a time the Tumbuka call "backtime," Mupa was absentmindedly passing the day. Letting his imagination run freely, he started to experiment with playing rhythms, his hands hitting his thighs (this was long before the first drum was invented). Using just one hand to hit his thigh was not very interesting; it made a grouping of only one. And not much better was the grouping of two he made when he added the other hand and alternated hits. There was little inherent interest in a pattern that repeated right, left, right, left, ad infinitum. But then Mupa had (with my apologies to Robert Farris Thompson [1983]) a flash of the spirit. What if he applied a mental pattern or grouping of three, but played it with his two hands in strict alternation (right left right / left right left)? The result was not merely the addition of one more stroke but the opening up of a whole new world of rhythm. (For a clearer understanding of this process, I invite the reader to follow along with Mupa's discovery and try these procedures.)

Mupa's first realization was that it took six strokes to complete one cycle of the pattern and return to the starting position. The six strokes naturally divided themselves into two halves, each half a mirror of the other. This in turn created a rhythm that, in a sense, shifted across the hands (RLR/LRL). The first pattern started with the right hand, and the mirrored repeat began with the left. In order physically and acoustically to accentuate this pattern, Mupa began to play the first and fourth strokes with greater force on his knees, still playing the other strokes on his thighs. Transfer this pattern from hitting one's legs to playing the *ng'oma*, the master *vimbuza* drum, and you have the core *vimbuza* rhythmic figure. Mupa's knee hits are equivalent to the palm stroke, and his thigh hits are equal to the two open-hand strokes.

As a result of this shift in playing, Mupa realized he was now, through dynamic accent and the physical change in which he hit his

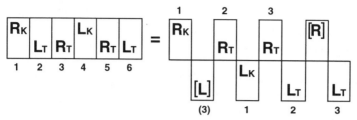

Fig. 21. Mupa's staggered rhythmic pattern. Rk indicates right knee;
Lk, left knee; Rt, right thigh; Lt, left thigh.

leg, playing a duple pattern generated by applying a triple grouping to
the strict duple alternation of right-left hand hits. He played this pattern for a long time, finding the alternation of hands, played against
the crossing generated by a triple grouping, inherently interesting and
aesthetically satisfying.

But as Mupa watched his hands, now almost as a disinterested
observer, he came to another realization, one that moved him farther
from a "natural" attitude and toward a "phenomenological" attitude,
for now his perceptions were becoming a matter of a play of potential
variations. Like the Necker cube, where the configuration of lines suggests a polymorphous structure, the acoustical and motional patterns
Mupa was generating had an inherent possibility of multiple interpretations.

If he kept the pattern going but concentrated on only one hand at
a time, he realized that each hand was separately outlining a motional
pattern of three. The right hand started with an accented stroke on the
knee and then, disregarding the left-hand strokes, played two unac-
cented strokes on the thigh before the pattern was repeated.

The left hand articulated the same motional configuration, starting
with the accented left-knee hit, which came two pulses after the right-
knee hit. Therefore, over six pulses, the right and left hands each separately outlined a motional pattern that divided the time span into three
equal parts (1 2 / 1 2 / 1 2).[15] The more Mupa concentrated on this
aspect of the pattern, the more his hands began to take on the motional
qualities of two distinct entities playing the same figure, with one part
staggered so that it fit into the spaces of the other part, like cogs in a
gear (fig. 21).

With the addition of this motional perception, Mupa could shift
his perspective in a manner similar to that which happens when someone looks at a Necker cube. He could see *and hear* the six strokes of
his hands either as a duple three-pulse configuration outlined by the

hits on his knees or as a triple two-pulse grouping with each hand
playing this figure (knee, thigh, thigh) in a staggered time relationship.
This by no means exhausted the possibilities, but it was enough for
one day. Mupa had discovered a generating rhythmic principle that
could serve as the basis for an entire rhythmic praxis.

The first operation that Mupa performed with his two-handedness,
applying a conceptual grouping of three, produced a dissonance between
the motional image and the intentional image, but in a sense it left the
acoustic image neutral—that is, the alternation of hands, sans accents,
produced a stream of neutral pulses.[16] In other words, an auditor would
have no clue to Mupa's intention and could group the pulses any way
he or she chose—in twos, threes, fives (2 + 3), and so forth—or could
not group them at all (although some psychologists say the brain is
"hardwired" to group undifferentiated pulses, hence the ticktock of a
clock).

When Mupa applied the second operation, however, playing the
first pulse of each grouping of three on his knee, it realigned, as it were,
the three levels, bringing into synchroneity Mupa's concept of three,
his motional pattern, which now articulated a triple configuration (this
is also visible to an auditor), and the acoustic image, which, however
slight—there is not much difference between thigh hits and knee hits—
nonetheless produced enough timbral and accentual change to produce
an audible grouping of three.[17]

Vimbuza drummers do not, of course, just play the core pattern,
which is equivalent to what Mupa played on his thighs and knees.
But this core pattern does generate most of the modal variations that
constitute *vimbuza* rhythmic praxis. Through various transformations
of the core pattern—which include the application of strong acoustic
accents, a filling-in process that I will talk about shortly, and timbral
manipulation—rhythmic configurations are foregrounded against a
shifting metrical base. The way these variations are generated concep-
tually, however, has much to do with Mupa's final perception, which
involved a shift to the phenomenological attitude.

This shift was a free play with potential variations that were inherent in the pattern. When Mupa concentrated on one hand at a time, an
interlocking motional pattern of three emerged that tended to separate
the hands, creating a polyrhythmic and, for lack of a better term, polykinetic structure. Therefore, over the six-pulse time span, his hands were
outlining both a motional pattern that divided the time span into two
equal parts (1 2 3 / 1 2 3)—the core pattern—and a motional pattern
that divided this same time span into three equal parts (1 2 / 1 2 / 1 2)

—which *is the three-beat pattern used by ng'oma and mphiningu drummers to coordinate their parts.*[18] As in the Necker cube, both patterns are present simultaneously, and like the viewer of the cube, Mupa could choose which pattern to focus on, or he could shift back and forth between the two, including the perspective of the other hand that is outlining a separate but interlocking motional pattern of three (fig. 21).

What Mupa discovered in fiction, Saza performs every time he drums. An expert drummer like Saza seems to employ all of these perspectives when he plays, which in itself is the empirical evidence that these variations are indeed fulfillable in the actual experience of *vimbuza*. Saza, however, doesn't sit under a baobab tree or hit his knees when he plays—he sounds the *ng'oma* in the *thempli* for his brother, Mulaula, so that the *vimbuza* spirits will heat.

In the Zambian Mode

When Saza drums for Mulaula, it is mainly spirits from Zambia such as the *vimbuza ßaßiza* and *ßaßemba* who heat up and provide the energy for Mulaula's divinatory trance. It is not surprising that these spirits are important to Mulaula, for he has a long personal history with this country. Although he was raised in Malawi and is a Tumbuka, he was born in Zambia, and when he became sick with the disease of the prophets, after trying many different *nchimi* in Malawi he finally went to apprentice under a well-known healer in Zambia. Filled with the energy of these spirits when he dances, Mulaula often speaks in chiBemba, a Zambian language, and many of the *vimbuza* songs that have come to him in dreams contain phrases in that language.

The rhythmic modes of these Zambian spirits are dominant when Saza drums for his brother. He constructs the Zambian modes, as virtually all *vimbuza* modes are constructed, through a four-dimensional motional axis. The motional elements—two-handedness, the inherent threeness of the core rhythmic pattern, the back-and-forth motion of the palm and hand strokes, and the open and stopped variants of these strokes—intersect in various combinations and recombinations, creating complex patterns of motion and sound that produce multistable structures. When one adds dynamic accenting to this process, a fifth dimension is opened up that is not merely one more element but part of a series that offers a geometrical progression of possible realizations.

The *vimbuza* mode *ßaßiza* is a paradigm of how these multistable

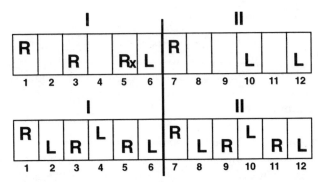

Fig. 22. The *ßaßiza* motto (top) in relation to the core *vimbuza* pattern

forms—that is, acoustical illusions—are drummed. Sounded for the spirits of the Biza ethnic group of Zambia, this motto covers the time span of two core patterns (fig. 22). This doubling of the pattern forms a gestalt which is separable for purposes of variation but which good drummers are sensitive to as a whole. Each half of the *ßaßiza* figure is a slightly different transformation of the core pattern: there are now gaps where there were strokes, and strokes that have been altered, producing timbral changes.[19]

This transformation from core pattern to *ßaßiza* motto seems to confirm Mupa's variational discovery of interlocking motional patterns of three (fig. 21). In order to foreground the fulfillability of this variation in actual practice, it will be necessary to delve into musical particulars. I learned these musical particulars from Saza during those afternoons in front of my hut, and from watching and listening to him drum inside the *thempli*. He didn't use words to explain these rhythms but articulated their structure through his drumming.

The first half of the *ßaßiza* figure is based on a motional pattern of three that is outlined by the right hand. It is basically the same configuration as Mupa's knee-thigh-thigh pattern, except that in the third beat the pulses are articulated—a stopped-hand stroke followed by an open-hand stroke. Stopped strokes can be played very quietly, serving more as a timekeeper than as an acoustical phenomenon, but in this case they are played with a good deal of force. The resulting timbre is a higher-pitched, almost slapped, kind of sound. The second half of the pattern suggests Mupa's staggered three-beat motion, although only two of these beats are actually played—significantly, both with the left hand. This sets up a kind of internal call and response between the two parts, one being a motional mirrored version of the other—that is, the right-hand strokes in the first half of the motto are answered by the left-hand strokes in the second half, both of which are part of the interlocking pattern of three that in our story moved Mupa to a phenomenological perspective. This figure, taken as a gestalt, is a prime example of a multistable structure that internally shifts rhythmic perspectives—it is an acoustical illusion.

Developing these metrical shifts and their accompanying acoustical illusions is basic to the art of *vimbuza* drumming. After I could play a rhythmic motto such as *βaβiza over an* extended period, Saza would then begin to show me how to vary the pattern. And after I could handle several variations, putting them in different combinations, he would usually invite people who were passing by to stop and listen to this Mzungu play the drums. They would offer their opinions on what was working and, more often, on what was not, but I did begin to gain some credibility as an Mzungu who at least knew what a *vimbuza* rhythm was and could play the mode in a limited way.

One of the basic ways Saza showed me to vary the rhythmic motto of a *vimbuza* mode was through a process of filling-in "empty" pulses. This technique, which has much to do with constructing acoustical illusions, involves a musical sensitivity to gaps or empty spaces in the musical texture. From this perspective, it is not so much the resultant pattern that is important for the construction of a mode but the spaces created by the rhythmic motto of a mode and how those spaces get filled in.

Although he is speaking of a different musical praxis, John Chernoff's (1979: 114) comment on West African drumming seems applicable here: "The music is perhaps best considered as an arrangement of gaps where one may add a rhythm, rather than as a dense pattern of sound." *Vimbuza* modal variations, with their characteristic arrangements of gaps, can be understood only within the context of the musical environment in which they are being produced. In its unfolding, music is hearkening both backward (its quality of "having been") and forward (its setting up of anticipations) at the moment of its presence. Schutz (1964: 170) makes a similar point in regard to the compositional process of Western art music:

> The composer, by the specific means of his art, has arranged it in such a way that the consciousness of the beholder is led to refer what he actually hears to what he anticipates will follow and also to what he has just been hearing and what he has heard ever since the music began. The hearer, therefore, listens to the ongoing flux of music, so to speak, not only in the direc-

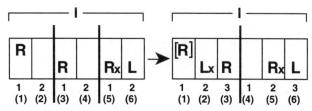

Fig. 23. *ßaßiza* variation 1

tion from the first to the last bar but simultaneously in a reverse direction back to the first one.

This point is particularly important for the identity of modal patterns in *vimbuza* precisely because of the filling-in process, for what
has come before and what will come after a particular pattern affect
how that pattern is perceived. This process does not follow a prescribed
order but rather constructs a variational set—a rhythmic mode—that
is open to a wide range of interpretation by individual drummers. Each
variation is based on a kind of modular cell that can be combined and
repeated in numerous different configurations, creating a highly stable
yet extremely fluid rhythmic form.[20]

In the *ßaßiza* mode, gaps occur on pulses 2, 4, 8, 9, and 11, and
these spaces may be filled in a number of different ways in order to
generate shifting acoustical illusions. For example, an accented
stopped-hand stroke may be added to fill in the second pulse. This
addition of just one stroke produces in the first half of the *ßaßiza* figure
a more motional feeling of "twoness" (fig. 23). It involves a shift in
metrical perspective from the implied configuration of three played in
the original motto. Indeed, Saza sometimes leaves out the first palm
stroke, further enhancing this metrical change. Pulses 2 and 3 are now
articulated in the same way as pulses 5 and 6, which produces, in Western musical terms, an off-beat eighth-note triplet figure. Although it is
doubtful that Saza thinks or feels rhythmic patterns in terms of "on"
or "off" beats, this does not mean that he doesn't construct patterns
metrically. With the filling in of this one stroke, the initial call and
response shifts from a mirrored type of structure to more of a call and
response between a metrical two and a metrical three (see the set of
numbers in fig. 23). And with this metrical shifting, the motto is transformed into a complex gestalt that is not only multifaceted but also
multistable, with its possibilities for figure-ground metrical reversals—
the acoustical equivalent of changing cubes and gems.

If a drummer wants to bring out the "three" side of the equation (i.e., the response), he might, as Saza often did, merely fill in an open-hand stroke on pulse 8, thus articulating the basic strokes of Mupa's staggered motional pattern of three (fig. 24).[21] These procedures are ingeniously elegant in that simple means—for example, the addition of one stroke—produce complex results.

The overwhelming majority of *vimbuza* modes are constructed in the same way as *ßaßiza:* their rhythmic mottos are transformations of the core pattern, cover the span of twelve pulses or two core patterns, and, through gaps and timbral nuances, construct multistable structures (see appendix B). The *vimbuza* mode of *ßaßemba,* spirits of the Bemba ethnic group of Zambia, who are a particularly important category of *vimbuza* spirits for Mulaula, illustrates this congruity of structure between the different modes.

The motto for *ßaßemba* displays more differences with the core pattern than does the *ßaßiza* motto, but it is nevertheless identifiable as being generated from this pattern (fig. 25; especially notice the congruence of palm strokes between the two patterns on pulse 7, which divides the figure into two equal parts). The same strict alternation of hands and the filling-in variational process is used in *ßaßemba,* but this time empty pulses occur on 3, 8, 11, and 12, which gives the mode its characteristic sound.

Sometimes, however, the exact identity of a mode can be confusing. For example, *ßaßemba,* as I was to learn from Saza, often has the same rhythmic motto as *fumu za pasi* (see Appendix B for an alternate version). This is not a musical coincidence but entails a historical connection that is also expressed musically. Under the category of *fumu za pasi,* "chiefs of the ground," comes the *vimbuza nkharamu,* the lion, which has the same modal signature as *ßaßemba.* In one of its manifes-

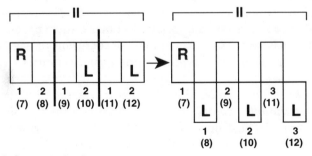

Fig. 24. *ßaßiza* variation 2

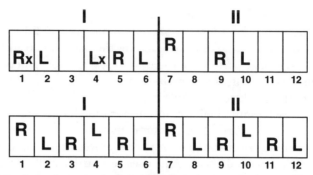

Fig. 25. The *ßaßemba* motto (top) in relation to the core *vimbuza* pattern

tations, the lion, as chief of the animals, is related by the Tumbuka to the spirit of the historical hereditary chief of the Bemba, Chitimukuru, who is said to have had the spirit of the lion inside of him, which made him a great chief (see chapter 2).[22] It is through this connection with Chitimukuru that *fumu za pasi* is related to the Bemba people of Zambia and thus to the *vimbuza ßaßemba*—a relationship the Tumbuka express musically by giving both kinds of spirits the same rhythmic motto.[23]

Not only do some *vimbuza* spirits use the same motto and essentially the same mode, but because of the filling-in and cellular nature of the variational process, modes that start out as distinct and different often end up with many of the same variations. In other words, various filled-in versions of *ßaßiza* can also be heard as variant patterns in *ßaßemba, fumu za pasi,* and, for that matter, *vimbuza waka.* This is why what comes before and after a particular variation is so important. This kind of congruity between modal variations is further enhanced by certain stock rhythmic gestures that can be inserted into virtually any mode. For example, playing open-hand or open-palm strokes with one hand in a simple reiteration of a two-pulse–based beat is not spirit-specific but can be heard as a variation in many different modes.

All this has resulted in a fair amount of confusion among Tumbuka about which mode belongs to which spirit. I have had various Tumbuka tell me that what I am calling *fumu za pasi/ßaßemba* was really the *vimbuza kachekuru,* and still others that it was *virombo,* the general category of *vimbuza* spirits of wild animals (perhaps this also relates to *nkharamu*).[24] The dance is usually no help in identifying the mode, for people dance to most of the different modes in exactly the same way, using the core dancing movement, the shaking of the hips described in chapter 1. I might add that I was the only one concerned about these discrepancies. Tumbuka, for the most part, do not seem to be particularly interested in identifying which *vimbuza* spirit is present during the dance. Usually, no special ritual actions are taken inside the *thempli* if one *vimbuza* spirit is possessing a patient instead of another. The important thing is that whichever *vimbuza* spirit is possessing the patient "comes out" and dances in order to dissipate spiritual heat.

I believe this indifference speaks to a general lack of specificity in the system, which is important because it allows for quite a bit of individual elaboration. The *vimbuza* are not, for the most part, gods with specific traits, as are the *orisha* Shango or Ogun, who, when riding their mounts, induce spirit-specific behavior complete with costuming and accoutrements. Rather, the *vimbuza* are more loosely defined configurations of spiritual energy that can be shaped according to particular circumstances. There are *vimbuza* who do have special characteristics, such as *nkharamu* and *vyanusi*, but they are more the exception than the rule. In keeping with the overall ethos of *vimbuza*, there seems to be a structural ambiguity in the musical and behavioral identification of specific spirits. This may be an important factor that delimits a southeastern Bantu spirit-possession complex distinct from the better-researched possession cults of West Africa and African-based cults in Latin America and the Caribbean.

In the Vyanusi Mode

As I have mentioned before, not all of the drumming modes are derived from the core pattern, and in these cases there is rarely any confusion over which spirit is being invoked. Not only is the drumming distinct, but so is the dance. These counterexamples are instructive in their differences from the core pattern and the modes derived from it.

Among the most distinctive *vimbuza* drumming patterns and dances is that of *vyanusi*. Not surprisingly, *vyanusi* is unlike any other *vimbuza* mode or dance, for it is derived from Ngoni musical practices based on an Nguni musical style (see Merriam 1982: 139), a style significantly different from those of the Tumbuka and other neighboring peoples in southeastern Africa. With enough research in this part of Africa, perhaps a type of musical archaeology of *vimbuza* would be possible, in which certain musical elements of the different modes could be traced to the music cultures of the ethnic groups to which the *vimbuza* spirits are related. At the time of my writing, such research

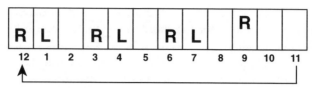

Fig. 26. The *vyanusi* motto

is lacking for most of the modes, but for *vyanusi*, many relationships are obvious.

Many *vyanusi* songs are still sung in chiNgoni, even though no one knows what they mean. And Tumbuka generally agree that the drumming of *vyanusi* and its dance are transformations of the *ingoma* dances performed traditionally by returning Ngoni warriors in the royal cattle kräal (see chapter 1). I was told by one of the advisors to the Mbelwa, the paramount chief of the Ngoni, however, that the rhythm of *vyanusi* is in fact not derived from the *ingoma* but rather is based on the beating of the cowhide shields with spears that *izanusi* did when they went into trance.

Not only is this *vimbuza* mode not based on the core figure, but it is also the only rhythmic figure that is an exception to the motional rule of strict alternation of hands (fig. 26). If strict alternation were followed, the stroke on pulse 3 would be played with the left hand. Moreover, the twelve-pulse pattern does not naturally divide itself into two equal halves, as most of the other modes do. Therefore, variations, if they are played at all—this figure is usually played in its pure form without variation—are based on the full twelve pulses.[25]

The dance figure to *vyanusi* is also very different from the core dance movement, for there is no shaking of the hips. In *vyanusi*, the dance follows almost exactly the basic motion of the drumming, so that the movement of the drumming hands closely mirrors the motion of the dance steps (or, vice versa, the motion of the dance closely follows that of the hands).[26] Perhaps this is one reason why the strict alternation of hands is not followed in drumming the *vyanusi* motto.

Although *vyanusi* is an important dance for adepts and new healers, which is not surprising given the whole connection it has with the Ngoni witchsmellers and diviners called *izanusi*, it is rarely danced by established healers such as Mulaula or Chikanje. I never saw either one of them dance this *vimbuza*, although both said that when they were *mutwasa* (new healers) they danced *vyanusi* often. In addition, patients rarely dance *vyanusi* when they first begin to heat their *vimbuza*. They usually wait until the initial stages of heating are concluded before the *vyanusi* mode is invoked. Significantly, part of this delay may have to do with the fact that in the *vyanusi* mode there is not the same level of figure-ground shifting that occurs in most other *vimbuza* modes, and therefore it is not as conducive to one's initially entering into a possession state—an issue I will return to shortly.

Musical Motion

For all practical purposes, it is impossible to separate *vimbuza* music from *vimbuza* dance, because in a very real way they are music/dance. We do not have a gloss in English that adequately captures the essence of this phenomenon. It is particularly evident in *vyanusi*, where drumming motion and dance motion are so closely linked. But it is also true for the core *vimbuza* dance movement, even though there is not always a precise fit between drumming motion and dance motion as there is in *vyanusi*. Both the drumming and the dancing of the core pattern, however, are based on a polykinetic structure that emanates from a rhythmic structure based on a ratio of 3 to 2. Dancers play it with their bodies, and drummers (and singers, through their clapping) dance it with their hands.

The *vimbuza* modes are neither music accompanying dance nor dance accompanying music, but rather, to borrow a phrase from Kubik (1979: 227), "a system of movement patterns" that transcends distinctions between dance and music. Perhaps this is one reason why I was able to dance *vyanusi* and *vimbuza* without ever having tried them before (see chapter 1). By the time I danced at Lußemba's compound, I had been drumming for some time, and my body, through my hands, already knew the motion of the dance.

The layers of complexity in the *vimbuza* modes are many, and the foregoing examples give only a glimpse of their depth. Nevertheless, these examples, I believe, express the essence of the phenomenon. A mode such as *vyanusi* is unique but has been adopted within the overall scheme of *vimbuza* drumming. Modes such as *ßaßiza* and *ßaßemba* are musically and motionally paradigmatic in that they are derived from the core motional figure and have an inherent capacity to generate multistable forms. A description of these acoustical illusions must be an essential part of a phenomenology that attempts to describe the musical experience of a Tumbuka clinical reality.

It is possible, however, to listen to *vimbuza* drumming and be completely unaware of this aspect of the phenomenon, which is one very important reason for paying explicit attention to such musical detail. Shifting metrical patterns of "twos" and "threes" are cultural constructs, and therefore the perception of them must, in a sense, be learned. Being unaware of acoustical illusions may have to do, in part, with cross-cultural differences. Unfortunately, we have no data on this subject. In regard to visual illusions, however, "evidence seems to point to cross-cultural differences in visual inference systems learned in response to different ecological and cultural factors in the visual environment. . . . The cross-cultural differences in susceptibility to geometrical illusions seems best understood as symptomatic of functional differences in learned visual inference habits" (Segall, Campbell, and Herskovits 1970: 682). The same thing may occur in the perception of acoustical illusions. Once these acoustical illusions have been experienced, however, it is impossible to return to a naive perspective.

This statement is equally true of visual illusions. Some people will see only one figure in an ambiguous, multistable visual form and will be completely blind to the other possibilities—that is, until they are pointed out to them. For example, one person might initially have trouble seeing that figure 27 is not only a picture of an old woman but also,

Fig. 27. Old woman/young woman illusion

simultaneously, the profile of a stylish young woman (the old woman's nose is the young woman's chin, the nostril her jaw line, and the line representing her mouth becomes a choker around the young woman's neck; the young woman is facing away from the viewer). Other people, of course, might see the young woman first. Either way, once the reversal is experienced, it is impossible to return to the naive position of being aware of only one figure.[27] This loss of naiveté is nothing less than the move from the natural attitude to a phenomenological one. This same process, I believe, holds true for *vimbuza* drumming. It is possible to hear all the variations in a 6/8 compound meter, even with an occasional hemiola thrown in for good measure, but one will be hearing only the equivalent of an old woman, and thus the depth that is inherent in *vimbuza* rhythmic praxis will be lost.

The analogy also holds true, but perhaps even more vividly, for the "magic eye" three-dimensional illusions mentioned earlier (fig. 28). The stereogram pictured in figure 28 is called "raindrop" and depicts a

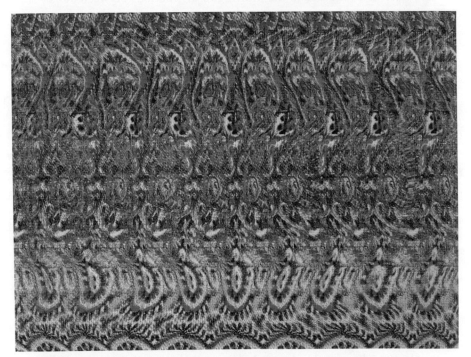

Fig. 28. Three-dimensional stereogram ("Raindrop"). From *Magic Eye* © by N. E. Thing Enterprises, Inc. Reprinted with permission of Andrews & McMeel. All rights reserved.

ɔunded shape projecting from a circular trough, as if a raindrop had rebounded off a hard surface. The original illustration is in color, but the three-dimensional effect is still discernible in black and white, and, indeed, for some people this makes it easier to see the intended picture. Many, however, find it difficult to see the illusion whether in black and white or color. Those who cannot make the two-dimensional pattern transform into its three-dimensional configuration—it has been reported that adult males have the hardest time—will experience only a flat perspective and in fact may refuse to accept that there is another possibility at all. It often takes some time, effort, and especially patience, but if you can see the "raindrop," the transformation is truly striking.[28] I take this visual transformation as a direct parallel to the experience of *hearing* the "three-dimensionality" in vimbuza drumming.

In *vimbuza*, dancer and spirit, drummer and singer encounter each other within a field of shifting rhythmic figures. Here, musical structure itself is conducive to the blurring of distinctions between subject and object—and between inner and outer time. *Vimbuza* drumming is seductive in this way, and it is structured to be so through its shifting rhythmic perspectives. Spirit and Tumbuka meet in the music of *vimbuza*, and both are transformed as a result.

Drum Time

> **When I listen to the vimbuza *drums I begin to lose track of whether they are outside or inside my head.***
> —*VIMBUZA* PATIENT AT MULAULA'S COMPOUND

When Saza drums for his brother inside the *thempli* (fig. 29), the music is both heard and physically felt. The sound of the drums has a "surroundability" to it that is penetrating, and thus one can feel pervaded by the sound on both the outside and the inside.[29] To try moving "nearer" to this experience of *vimbuza*, I asked Mulaula if I could try some of the *mankwhala* he gave his adepts to smoke when they danced. On nights when Mulaula divined, typically one or two of his assistants would be "featured" before the official proceedings got under way. And on these nights, as the drums began to invoke the *vimbuza* spirits, the adepts would be given a special medicine to smoke (fig. 30). I was interested in experiencing its effects, for according to Mulaula, it helped

Fig. 29. Saza drumming for Nchimi Mulaula inside the temple

to heat the *vimbuza*. He said he could see no harm in letting me try this *mankwhala* and would make the necessary arrangements.

On the next divination night, as always, before Mulaula entered the temple several hymns were sung, a prayer was said, and one of the women sprinkled *ufu*, white maize flour, on the floor in the shape of a square. Inside the square she drew a cross with the *ufu*, and on this cross sat the adept, a young man in his twenties, who was to dance. He was handed a medicinal cigarette, and on this night, so was I. As Saza began to drum, we both smoked.

By the time the adept finished his cigarette he was possessed by the *vimbuza* spirits and up and dancing. I was still sitting in my chair

Fig. 30. An adept
smoking medicine to
help heat her spirits

searching for the effect. Whatever this medicine was made of, it was
not a potent psychoactive substance, and if its effects were of a more
subtle nature, they were totally lost on me.[30] Although this first time
was disappointing, I decided to continue trying the *mankwhala* on subsequent divination nights on the chance that if there were subtle effects, they would become more apparent.

The second time I tried this medicine, hymns were again sung,
prayers said, and an adept—this time a woman in her late twenties
who had been living at Mulaula's compound for the past two years—sat
on the white *ufu* cross inside the square, and again nothing seemed to
happen when I smoked. After a while, however, I began to notice that
there were moments when I was getting lost in the shifting patterns of
the drumming. "Threes" were becoming "twos" and vice versa, and I
found myself becoming fascinated by this shifting phenomenon. I was

already aware of metrical shifting, for I would often focus on Saza's playing, following the way he constructed the modes and trying to pick out what I had learned that day, but this "fascination" with the process was something different.

The drums on this night seemed to have a special presence to them, as if the sound was very close to my ears, something I may have experienced before but was not consciously aware of. This sensation of "closeness," in which the physical and psychical distance between myself and the sound of the drums seemed to collapse or be enfolded, became more pronounced. My boundaries between self as subject and drum sound as object were losing their meaning. I began to experience, it seems to me, something similar to what Mulaula's patient had described: I could no longer tell whether the drumming was coming from outside or inside my head. When I smoked, I had been looking for the visual, expecting some kind of hallucinatory phenomenon, but instead I found the acoustical.

I did not become possessed, but I believe I was having a parallel experience, or at least a glimpse of what it is like to hear the drums on the "inside." For the adept who was "featured" that night—as for the young male adept the previous night—this kind of musical experience led to possession by the *vimbuza* spirits. This woman, however, unlike the male adept, had been a *mutwasa* for some time and was already beginning to "see." Her dancing was much more controlled, and when the *vimbuza* heated she did not become completely possessed and amnesic, as is usually the case with adepts who have just started their treatment/training, but was on her way to becoming a trance doubler, a prophet healer.

Mulaula says that he can tell how an adept's *nthenda* (disease) is progressing by watching the person dance. The dance of a novice is usually wild and uncontrolled—"new ones are always falling down"—compared with that of a *mutwasa*. As the *nthenda* matures (*kudankha*), the dance stabilizes, and the energy of the *vimbuza* is channeled into divination. According to Mulaula, *it is the drums that cause the* nthenda *to mature.* "The drums make the disease get matured; before, it is tender." If drumming is crucial to the enabling of the divinatory trance, then multistable acoustical illusions seem to be a prime agent in this transformation.

The metrical doubling inherent in *vimbuza* drumming is mirrored, in a sense, in the consciousness-doubling of the healer's divinatory trance. There the amnesic aspect of spirit possession is transformed into the lucid trance of an *nchimi*. The same shifting rhythmic figures that initially helped to bring on a total spirit possession now act as a kind of anchoring of consciousness, a focusing device that helps to stabilize the trance state and thus produce the doubling phenomenon. There seems to be an inherent aesthetic interest in this shifting that, for those who are aware of it, captivates consciousness, inviting it to radically narrow its focus.[31]

This is precisely what Chikanje is referring to when he says that you need to "dance with a pattern in your head." Music shapes both spiritual and human energy into the same modal pattern. Drumming in the *vimbuza* mode constructs a time so deeply felt that its flow can become the flow of inner time—that which Bergson calls *durée*. Musical experience becomes both noema and noesis—phenomenal focus and the mode of focusing. In the *thempli* that night, drum time was becoming my time.

CONCLUSION

An Ontology of Energy

. . . the experience of art is the most insistent admonition to scientific consciousness to acknowledge its own limits.
—HANS-GEORG GADAMER,
TRUTH AND METHOD

Charles Keil offers, I believe, some good advice. He suggests that we shift our analytical focus from "emotion" to "motion," from "beauty" to "energy," from "esthetics" to "ontology," and in the process perhaps we will begin to shed some of our "basic ethnocentric cataracts and ear plugs" (Keil 1979: 199). This is what I have tried to accomplish in this book. I have written, for the most part, not of emotion but of the transcendent motional patterns of music and dance. I have written not of beauty—though these motional patterns are indeed beautiful—but of sources of numinous energy, and not of an aesthetics but of a clinical reality that by its very nature is part of an *nchimi's* healing art. This musically constituted clinical reality, part of the Tumbuka health care system, is not an abstract construction but a living process, and as such it has more to do with an ontology of energy than with an aesthetics of music.

I am not implying that the concepts motion, energy, and ontology are somehow less cultural in their construction than are emotion, beauty, and aesthetics. I am saying, however, that perhaps the former concepts are more universally applicable than the latter. It matters not if they turn out to be more local, for the Tumbuka tell of their experience of spirits, music, witchcraft, disease, and illness within these conceptual frames. It is this "telling," expressed by the Tumbuka in both word and action, that I have attempted to describe in the preceding pages.

Spirits, Wind, and Music

The Tumbuka say that spirits are like the wind, *mphepo:* both can be discerned only through the effects they create. The invisible wind may be felt on the face or seen in the rustling of leaves on a tree, just as the invisible spirits may be felt as an illness in the body or seen through the possession dance of *vimbuza.* For the Tumbuka, the existence of both wind and spirits is part of the background understanding that constitutes the everyday world.

We don't *believe* in wind, we take it for granted as part of our natural environment. In the same sense, the Tumbuka don't *believe* in spirits; they don't have to, for spirits are part of their natural environment and so play an important role in everyday life. They can experience the *vimbuza* in an illness or hear them in a dance. The sacred as part of the everyday has an existential reality for the Tumbuka. Spirits are not "otherworldly" but "this worldly."[1]

This "everydayness" of *vimbuza,* however, does not reduce the spiritual to the mundane. Rather, it elevates the quotidian world to a more intense level of reality, one that involves a compelling engagement with the spirits. Phenomenologically, the *vimbuza* are *the things themselves.* This liminal world, betwixt and between the numinous and the mundane, is precisely where *nchimi* and their followers enact a clinical reality. Into this musically created liminality comes the possibility of a communitas that has the potential to release cultural forces of healing—the *meta*-power Turner (1986: 43) speaks of as resulting from "social arousal, however produced."

The enactment of *vimbuza* is a special case of social interaction in Tumbuka culture—one that is transitory, repeatable, and deep in its affect. In the community of Tumbuka healers, people regularly transform their consciousness, by their own account, through musical means. Within the acoustical *and motional* properties of singing, clapping, drumming, and dancing, people experience profound modes of being-in-the-world. This is not the sharing of an interior state of consciousness but a gathering together of intersubjective experience through the objective process of making music together.

I use the term "intersubjective" here and elsewhere in this book, not in the Husserlian context of a derived sharing of individual intentional states—our belief "that others have beliefs about our beliefs about their beliefs" (Dreyfus 1991: 148)—but in Heidegger's (1962a: 155) sense of *Mitsein,* Being-with: "The world is always the one that I share with Others. . . . Being-in is *Being-with Others.*" If making music together is truly intersubjective, then it is a transcendent process, and in this sense its presence is objective. The invisible spirits are refracted through the bodily music of the trance dancer, and *vimbuza* and Tumbuka, as equally viable presences, partake of the same experiential realm of sound and motion.

In the constitution of the invisible made present through music, the Tumbuka approach seems very close to other phenomenological approaches. The Tumbuka are not the only ones who meditate on the invisibility of such things as wind and sound. In Don Ihde's (1976: 51) phenomenology of sound, we find a striking parallel:

> I stand alone on a hilltop in the light of day, surveying the landscape below in a windstorm. I hear its howling and feel its chill, but I cannot see its contorted writhing though it surrounds me with its invisible presence. No matter how hard I look, I cannot see the wind, *the invisible is the horizon of sight.* An inquiry into the auditory is also an inquiry into the invisible. Listening makes the invisible *present* in a way similar to the presence of the mute in vision. . . . What is the wind? It belongs, with motion, to the realm of verb. The wind is "seen" in its *effects,* less than a verb, its visible being is what it has done in passing by. (Italics in the original)

"Mute" objects are objects at rest, and in this sense Ihde claims they make silence *present.* I look at a piece of rectangular wood on my desk, and as it sits there it is silent. If I tie a string to it, however, and whirl it around my head like a bullroarer, it "sounds," but only through motion is this "sounding" accomplished. " 'Visualistically' sound 'overlaps' with moving beings" (ibid.: 50). Without movement of some sort, objects are indeed mute. Paralleling this formation, the invisible, which is the horizon of the visual, is made *present* in sound. In this way we can see silence and hear the invisible, a phenomenological fact not lost on the Tumbuka.

Musical Technology

Spirits are essentially part of a Tumbuka ontology of energy that also encompasses the music of *vimbuza.* Music, however, unlike the foreign *vimbuza* spirits, is a source of energy that is under the cultural and social control of the Tumbuka—in other words, it is a technology.

When Tumbuka compare this music to batteries and trance dancing to X rays, they are making explicit their technological concerns. The music of *vimbuza* is an energy source that is harnessed for specific ends, namely, the heating of the *vimbuza* spirits. This kind of musical technology seems, in fact, to be a widespread and perhaps delimiting feature of indigenous health care systems in southeastern and southern Africa. One need look only to the boiling energy of the !Kung bushmen (Katz 1982) for a prototype (and perhaps historical grounding) of this conception of the technology of musical heat.

Understood as technology, music both reveals and creates a clinical world for the Tumbuka. Dancing prophets, singing patients, and drummed spirits populate its environs, navigate its ways. In this clinical world there is more than just a connection between a healing art and technology. What have become two totally separate phenomena for Western medicine—the aesthetic and the technological—have become for the Tumbuka a singular mode of existence.

What could be farther from the aesthetic realm of art, where, in traditional Western philosophical thought, function is not in play, than the world of technology, where everything is predicated on an instrumentality of means and ends? Yet according to Heidegger (1977: 3–35) there is a fundamental connection between the two, for both are a mode of revealing. By conceiving of technology in its most obvious manifestation as a means to an end (instrumentality) and as a human activity (the anthropological definition) ruled by the fourfold nature of causality revealed in Cartesian duality, we are not looking at the essence of technology but viewing its concealment. This technological "enframing" is not only true for modern machine technology and science but also holds sway for every other aspect of contemporary life, wherever human beings, as the self-conscious, representing subject, rule.

The essence of technology, for Heidegger, paradoxically, has nothing to do with the technological. Essence to him is neither a Platonic ideal nor a Husserlian transcendental *edios;* it is a "bringing-forth" that in its most authentic presence is an art. True, Heidegger plays the differences between art and technology off one another to mark the ontological structure of Western technology. But Heidegger ultimately seeks a phenomenological basis for their mutual inclusion. He finds his answer in the early Greeks, for whom technology was an art that brought forth the radiance of the gods. I find mine in a world of dancing prophets, where the *vimbuza* spirits are made present in sound.

The music of *vimbuza* is part of a medical technology, and thus musical experience becomes a particular mode of being-in-the-world. Music may in fact be a privileged mode of being, a way of being-in-the-world that is beyond or before linguistic phenomena and therefore is especially worthy of serious ontological investigation. Language, despite Heidegger's claim, may not be the only house for Being. To reverse the analytic direction, an analysis of musical experience, the temporal art par excellence, may indeed make an important contribution to a fundamental ontology whose very essence is temporality.

Musical Possibilities

In this account of spirit and human, trance and music, I have, of necessity, adopted a kind of radical empiricism. The anthropologist and novelist Michael Jackson (1989: 3) has extended William James's notion into the world of ethnography:

> The importance of this view for anthropology is that it stresses the ethnographer's *interactions* with those he or she lives with and studies, while urging us to clarify the ways in which our knowledge is grounded in our practical, personal, and participatory experience in the field as much as our detached observations. Unlike traditional empiricism, which draws a definite boundary between observer and observed, between method and object, radical empiricism denies the validity of such cuts and makes the interplay between these domains the focus of its interest. This is the same focus as in quantum mechanics. It is the *interaction* of observer and observed which is crucial. (Italics in the original)

To assume less—or, for that matter, more—in the ethnographic situation is a distortion, especially concealing in a musical world. For music is not an object to be encountered but is itself an *interaction*, a fusion of horizons that dwells in the possibilities of *having been.*

What I have sought to uncover in this book is an ethnomusicology of a clinical reality. Musical experience for Tumbuka healer and patient, for ethnographer as participant and observer, both occurs within a lifeworld and *is* that world. Making music together projects a clearing, and the world *is* that clearing. This reality is circumscribed through sedimentations of previous musical experiences that, taken together, form the recurrent lived experience of trance dancing. For *nchimi* healers and their patients, not only are the sick made well, but a world is won in the process.

What ethnographers have overlooked time and again in their investigations into the world of African healing is this musical dimension of experience. It has been my focus not so much because I am an ethnomusicologist and therefore have simply found what I was looking for. Rather, it is a result of *doing* phenomenology. Tumbuka clinical reality is saturated with the musical; it is unavoidable. Therefore, not surprisingly, this reality was for me, at its "nearest," a musical experience. The same would hold true, I believe, for any researcher who spent time in an *nchimi*'s temple and did not have in place a set of "ethnocentric cataracts and ear plugs." To ignore musical phenomena in Tumbuka healing is to flatten this world into a mere semblance of itself.

Musical experience for the Tumbuka is more than just an acoustical phenomenon; it penetrates directly into the realm of bodily existence. The categorical separation of music and dance becomes meaningless in a world of possessing spirits, spirits moved by music. When the spirits are made present in the temple of a Tumbuka diviner-healer, their existential reality is always an embodied, sounded presence. The immediate understanding that arises from this musical corporeality is a meaning wholly submerged in action, what Merleau-Ponty terms a "practognosis" (cited in Kwant 1963: 28). This is not an awareness produced through some kind of mystical union of different modes of being—a melding of mind and body—but rather a single reality that resides in the "chiaroscuro" of the "body-subject" itself (ibid.: 62). When Tumbuka healers divine, their dance is more than an actuality; it is a self-transcending movement in the density of Being. Trance dancing becomes the locus of projected possibility—a futural clearing that is simultaneously the gathering-together of tradition.

Musical experience in a healer's temple is *there* as a possibility of "living in the tonal sphere as though this sphere alone existed" (Dilthey 1985: 17). If this is indeed a possibility of existence for trance dancers, then musical structure reveals itself as a mode of being-in-the-world that can be understood in formal terms, an important onto-phenomenological opening not available to all modes of being. This is precisely what makes a phenomenology of musical experience of the kind found in indigenous healing systems a particularly powerful form of ontological description.

In *vimbuza*, multistable acoustical illusions constructed out of a polymetrical framework may be heard as an overt expression of what amounts to a basic binary opposition, namely, that of even and odd. To paraphrase Lévi-Strauss, it is something good to musicate with. "Twos" and "threes," even and odd meters, are co-present in the rhythmic structure of *vimbuza* drumming at all times—sometimes overtly, sometimes implicitly, but always available to musicians to create shifting rhythmical forms. Music mediates this rhythmic binary opposition, and in doing so its very structure becomes a paradigm of doubling: the rhythmic doubling of acoustical illusions is reflexive with the doubling of spirit type, which itself is the prerequisite for a doubling of consciousness. In all of these, doubling is both a splitting apart and a bringing together.

The *vimbuza* rhythmic modes bring together the "two" in the "three" and the "three" in the "two"; they mediate between the "I" and the "thou." And through the *chilopa* sacrifice, these modes bring into the correct relationship the energy of the foreign *vimbuza* and the power of the ancestral *mizimu*. Music is the transformer of spiritual heat, turning affliction by the spirits into the disease of the prophets. It is the means by which worlds are mediated, revealed, *and constituted.*

If mediation is a musical paradigm that resonates throughout the *vimbuza* complex, then we need to address the question, What is the essence of this phenomenon? This is not a question of what something *is*, but a matter of what is brought forth. In mediation, what is brought forth in its initial emerging is the foregrounding of boundaries, the splitting apart. In this sense, what is explored in *vimbuza* drumming is the multistable boundaries between polyphonic and polykinetic configurations; in the trance dance of *vimbuza*, the boundaries between human and spirit; ontologically, that which separates objects from subjects.

Tumbuka musical experience tells us that boundaries are the locus of phenomenological possibilities: they are stable but fluid, multifaceted, and shifting. But most importantly for the Tumbuka, musical boundaries bring forth the invisible spirits. Without music, Tumbuka healing would be fundamentally a different art.

EPILOGUE

On my last day in the field, I awoke at three in the morning in order to drive to Chikanga's compound. It was located in the Mpompha Hills, and from where I was staying it was a good forty-five-minute drive— dirt roads pretty much all the way. I wanted to arrive at the compound early, for at sunrise, Edita, Chikanga's third wife and herself an *nchimi*, was going to sacrifice a cow as a *chilopa* for her *vimbuza* spirits.

A messenger from Chikanga had arrived the day before to inform me that the *chilopa* was finally going to take place. It had originally been scheduled for two weeks earlier but had been canceled because Edita had started her period, and a woman cannot do a *chilopa* while in menses. I was disappointed at the time because it seemed as though my last chance to witness this rarest of *vilopa*—only healers with the most powerful *nthenda* do the *chilopa* of a cow—and to capture it on videotape—something I had wanted to do for the past year—was lost. When I received word that everything for the *chilopa* was now in place and that the sacrifice would indeed be performed the next morning— the very morning I was planning on leaving—I had the distinct feeling that Edita's *chilopa* would somehow be a fitting end to my stay in northern Malawi.

For the past few months, Edita, a woman in her early fifties, had been very ill, so ill that she had gone to the mission hospital in Mzuzu to see if the doctors there could help her. The traditional treatments that she had tried had not worked, and her condition was deteriorating rapidly. The doctors at the mission hospital told her that she was suffering from high blood pressure and an irregular heartbeat. They gave her medicine, but it seemed to help only a little. It was finally decided by both Chikanga and Edita that perhaps her *vimbuza* were unexpectedly heating up, something unusual for an established healer like Edita, who danced regularly. The two agreed that a particularly powerful *chilopa* needed to be performed in order to cool her spirits.

Not every *nchimi* can afford the *chilopa* of a cow, but Chikanga was not just any *nchimi*. He was, after all, *nchimi ya uchimi*, prophet of prophets, considered by all to be in a league of his own. No one could match his powers of witchfinding, and at the height of his fame thousands would visit his compound each week. Even though he had only recently returned from internal exile, he was already beginning to reestablish his dominance, and with that dominance came a thriving business in witchcraft protection medicine. Many who visited Chikanga were comparatively well-off and paid generously for this kind of *mankwhala*. Therefore, money was no object when it came to Edita's *chilopa*.

When I finally arrived at Chikanga's compound, Edita was still in her *nyumba* (house). She had not yet entered the *thempli* to begin to heat her *vimbuza* so that the spirits would be prepared to receive the blood from the *bongwani* (young bull) that had been chosen to be the sacrificial animal. While I waited for Edita to come out, I inquired about where the sacrifice would actually take place and what the general progression of events would be. My bags were packed and in the car, and because I knew that this was going to be my only chance to videotape such an infrequent event—most Tumbuka have never seen the *chilopa* of a cow—I wanted to find a good spot to film it. I was shown the place where the bull would be killed and was told that Edita would stab the animal with a spear and drink the blood from the wound. This explained one question I had, for I couldn't figure out how she was going to suffocate the bull (the usual method of sacrifice) that was tied to the tree next to the temple.

About an hour after I arrived, Edita finally emerged from her *nyumba* dressed in her red *nchimi* outfit and carrying her special witch stick, which she called *chatonda* (lit. "conqueror"). She had dreamt about this stick when she was a *mutwasa*, and Chikanje, the *nchimi* who trained her, had commissioned a local carver to make the stick according to Edita's dream. Not only does Chikanje interpret dreams, but he also takes action as a result of them (as he did, for example, after my dream about *mboni* beads).

At the top of the stick is carved a lion, symbolic of the *vimbuza nkharamu*, an important spirit for divination. In the middle there is a carved rooster (*tambala*) representing the light of dawn, and toward the end of the stick is depicted an Ngoni warrior, which is for the *vyanusi* spirits. In the bottom of the stick there is special *mankwhala* that contains *mwabvi*, the traditional poison used in the poison ordeal to discover witches. This medicine helps to fight witches but, according to Edita, is mainly there to stabilize the *vimbuza*.

Because Chikanje had been the *nchimi* under whom Edita apprenticed, he was invited by Chikanga to be master of the *chilopa*, even though there was some friction between the two. Chikanje had originally planned to marry Edita, and the fact that she had left him to seek Chikanga's help and eventually married him was still a source of tension. But for a *chilopa* of this magnitude it is customary for the person who is doing the sacrificing to have his or her "father" (the trainer *nchimi*) be "master of the chilopa." Edita was truly sick, and neither Chikanga nor Chikanje was willing to jeopardize her health by failing to help.

With Chikanje officiating, Edita entered the *thempli*, which was packed with people. It wasn't every day that the *chilopa* of a cow took place, and the fact that it was to be carried out by Chikanga's wife drew even more people. She sat down in one of the chairs positioned in the front and began to raise that favorite of Tumbuka hymns, "Charo Nchinonono." The people joined in the singing, which seemed that morning to be particularly strong. After a few more hymns were sung and a prayer offered by Chikanga, the *vimbuza* drums began to call forth the spirits. At Chikanga's compound, Edita is pretty much responsible for treating *vimbuza* patients, and usually when she dances he leaves the temple. But Chikanga cared for Edita deeply and wanted to see her get well, so he was willing to take part actively in the proceedings.

Chikanga is an anomaly among *nchimi*, for he does not dance *vimbuza*. When he divines he uses only *kwaya*. Part of his claim to being *nchimi ya uchimi* is that his spirits are so powerful that he does not need to dance in order to "see." It is not unusual for the holders of top positions in such systems to differentiate themselves from other practitioners, and this was one way Chikanga separated himself from other *nchimi*.

According to some healers, however, Chikanga used to dance when he was first sick with *nthenda ya uchimi*. It was rumored that he had done the *chilopa* of a duiker, a small deer, which, if true, is very unusual because *chilopa* are invariably domesticated animals. In many ways other than his not dancing, Chikanga was outside the mainstream of *nchimi* healers. He was famous in Tanzania (see Redmayne 1965), Zambia, Zimbabwe, and South Africa as a witchfinder, and he took on more the persona of a one-man quasi-religious witch eradication movement than that of merely a healer of illness. This was precisely why the government feared him and exiled him to the city of Blantyre in the south. On this morning, Chikanga did not leave the temple when the *vimbuza* drums were sounded, but stayed close by Edita's side because he wanted to make sure everything went smoothly.

After listening to the drums for a few minutes, Edita stood up to dance her disease. Several of her women assistants gathered around her, forming a circle as they sang and clapped. When Edita danced there was no mistaking whom she had trained under, for her dance style was almost exactly like Chikanje's.

About thirty minutes into Edita's dancing, I decided to go outside in order to be able to film as she came out of the *thempli*. I didn't want to miss anything that was going on inside, but I also wanted to capture the entire *chilopa* on videotape, and I had to conserve my battery power. Shortly after I got myself situated at the place where I was told the sacrifice would take place, Edita's senior woman assistant came out of the temple with a few of the men to discuss how the sacrifice should proceed. The sacrifice of an *ng'ombe* (cow) was so uncommon that it seemed no one was entirely sure how to go about it. After a few minor disagreements, it was decided that the bull would be brought over to Edita, and following a formal presentation of the animal to the spirits, it would be laid on its side for the sacrifice.

Some thirty minutes later, as a crowd began to gather immediately outside the temple where the *chilopa* would be performed, the drumming stopped and Edita walked out into what by now was becoming a bright sunny morning. She sat down on a straw mat that had been laid on the ground, and *nkufi* clapping was performed for the spirits inside of her. The *vimbuza* were officially informed of the sacrifice and were asked to accept in a good way what was being offered to them.

After the *nkufi*, the rhythmic mode of *vyanusi* was played and Edita danced. She did not hold the short spear customary for dancing this *vimbuza*, but instead held a long, slender one with a fairly large iron spearhead. Protecting the point was a corklike cap. She danced over to the bull and put her head to the bull's forehead. Looking through the camera, I was at first confused, for I thought she had put her mouth over the bull's nose, reminiscent of what happens when a goat is sacrificed for a *chilopa*. But I soon realized she was only touching forehead to forehead.

Following this presentation of the sacrificial animal to Edita, she was led by her senior assistant back to the straw mat, where Chikanga and Chikanje joined her. More hymns were sung, and once again Chikanga offered a prayer. This was the only time I had heard Christian prayers and hymns introduced into the ritual this close to the actual sacrifice. Then something even more unusual happened: an *nkufi* was done over the bull. I had neither seen an *nkufi* performed for an animal nor heard of its being done. At the conclusion of this paying of respects, the drums were sounded and Edita rose to resume her dancing.

When she stood up to dance, the drumming and singing intensified, and there was much ululation from the other women. There was an almost chaotic atmosphere in the crowd as people pushed and shoved to get closer to the center. I fought to maintain my space in the front row of the circle of people that now surrounded Edita and the bull.

As Edita continued to dance, several of the men turned the bull on its side and held it down as it struggled to get back on its feet. The cork was removed from the point of the spear. Edita danced closer to the animal and then stood over it with the spear poised in midair, ready to strike. All the energy and attention of those gathered for the sacrifice seemed to be focused on the raised spear. It was a moment of intense power, for in her hand Edita held life and death.

I always realized, when I filmed a *chilopa*, that I was, in a sense, once removed from the action. I would see the sacrifice through the camera's viewfinder—blood wasn't red, it was in black and white. But when Edita stabbed that bull, the power of the moment overcame the camera's distancing effect. The spear went into the animal's heart, and Edita immediately knelt down to drink the blood that flowed from the wound. Like the moment of sacrifice in the first *chilopa* I had seen at Mzimu's compound, this moment seemed to me, amid all the blood, to have a certain tranquillity to it, perhaps because there was a kind of equanimity to the events.

After a minute or so, the woman assistant pulled Edita away from the bull and collected some of the flowing blood into a bowl. This was mixed with special *mankwhala* and stirred into a froth. It was then given to Edita to drink and was poured over her body. Unlike in other *vilopa* I had seen, where the blood was immediately cleaned up, this time blood seemed to be everywhere. As Edita danced, the bull finally died, and the men quickly pulled the body away. They returned shortly with a small piece of the heart, which was given to Edita to eat.

After this final act of the blood stage of the sacrifice, Edita went back inside the temple to let all of her *vimbuza* come out and dance.

But for some reason, I didn't follow her inside; instead, I said my good-byes, got in my car, and left the North.

For several days after I left the Henga Valley, the feeling of intensity that I had experienced at Edita's *chilopa* stayed with me. No other *chilopa* I had witnessed had affected me in quite this way, so I decided to take a look at the videotape of the sacrifice. This was something I rarely did because I didn't have many C-cell batteries to run my small portable television. I had watched many of the other videos I had shot, but that was in a research context, when I showed them to people at the compound in order to discuss what was on the tape. But now my field research was pretty much finished, and I didn't need to worry about saving my batteries. This time I could watch the video for myself.

I turned on the television and watched as Edita walked out of the temple accompanied by Chikanga and Chikanje. The events that followed were still vivid in my mind. But as she lifted the spear and prepared to kill the young bull, suddenly the sound on the video began to cut out and the picture started to break up—long streaks of white horizontal drop-out lines appeared. I could barely make out Edita stabbing the bull and drinking the blood, and by now the sound was completely gone.

My first reaction was one of disbelief and anger—this had never happened before. Out of some sixty hours of videotape that I had shot, all were fine. Would this, perhaps my best piece of video, turn out to be the only defective tape? I immediately stopped the video, rewound the tape, checked my equipment, and played it again, but the same thing happened. I even tried a different tape to make sure the interference wasn't in the playback system but was actually on the videotape itself. Unfortunately, the other tape played just fine. This meant that either my camera had malfunctioned while I was shooting or the tape itself was flawed. I put the video of Edita's *chilopa* back on, and as I watched I became more and more upset as the picture got progressively worse.

As the video continued, I still could barely make out Edita standing up and beginning to dance after drinking the blood. Then, just as suddenly, the picture started to clear up and the sound returned. It was as if nothing had ever been wrong with the video. How could this be the only part of the tape that was damaged? At the time I was amazed at the coincidence that out of an entire year's worth of filming, not only was this the only defective tape, but it was only these five minutes of the most intense and dramatic part of the *chilopa* that were ruined.

Yet in a way, I wasn't surprised. Coincidences like this had followed me throughout my stay in northern Malawi. I remember once sitting with Chikanje in the afternoon. It was early in my research, and I was telling him that I had heard about goat sacrifices and I hoped to be able to see one of these *vilopa*. A few moments later, two men walked by with a goat. As we soon found out, the goat was for a *chilopa* that was to take place the next day. I didn't think much about it other than being pleased that I would get my chance sooner than I had expected. But Chikanje casually mentioned that I must have strong ancestors because I asked for a *chilopa* and my *mizimu* provided one. Coincidences like this always seemed to keep my experiences one step ahead of my research. This writing has been one way of catching up.

APPENDIX A
Glossary of *Vimbuza* Spirits

ßaßemba	Bemba ethnic group (Zambia).
ßaßiza	Biza ethnic group (Zambia).
ßachota	Spirits who like to eat fire or raw eggs.
ßamunkwele	Monkey; a *virombo* spirit.
ßaMwera	(lit. "wind from the lake") Spirits of people from across the lake; sometimes related to spirits of the lakeshore Tonga.
ßaSenga	Senga ethnic group (Zambia).
Chitimukuru	Hereditary chief of the Bemba.
Fumu za Pasi	(lit. "chiefs of the ground") Spirits of chiefs. Sometimes the spirit of the lion, *nkharamu*, is included in this category of spirits.
Geremani	Germans who were in Tanzania in World War I. (Lußemba was the only person I saw possessed by these spirits.)
Kachekuru	Spirits of old people who have stiff joints.
Kalulu	Hare; a *virombo* spirit.
Magambura	A spirit related to *ßaßiza*.
Makahwango	A *virombo* (wild animal) spirit?
Mangwera	Swahili spirits possibly from Tanzania.
Muharure	Spirits who like to eat beef. There is some indication that these spirits are related to the Ngoni.
Mukarachitutu	This *vimbuza* is silent. "When it is 'on top,' nothing comes out."
Mulaula	(lit. "speaker of hidden or forbidden things") Tumbuka were not clear who these spirits were; however, most agreed that they came from the east and were associated with Lake Malawi.
Munjiri	Wart hog; a *virombo* spirit.
Muryavivisi	Spirits who like to eat things raw.
MuSwahili	Swahili ethnic group.
Mzungu	Europeans or white people.
Ngoma	Similar to the *vyanusi* spirits of the Ngoni.
Nkharamu	Lion; sometimes associated with chiefs.
Singo	(lit. "the neck") It is not clear what this spirit is related to. When it comes, people dance on their hands and knees, swaying their necks back and forth.
Umphanda	Spirits from Zambia. It is not clear which peoples this type of *vimbuza* refers to.
Vimbuza waka	(lit. "just *vimbuza*") Most likely the spirits of the autochthonous

people the Tumbuka encountered when they first came to Malawi.

Virombo Spirits of wild animals. It seems likely that these spirits are related to the *malombo* (wild animal) spirits that possess members of the Nyau secret society found among the Chewa people of central Malawi. More than one Tumbuka, however, denied this association.

Vyanusi The Ngoni ethnic group originally from South Africa. The name is derived from *izanusi*, who were Ngoni witchsmellers.

APPENDIX   B
Vimbuza Rhythmic Mottos

A Note on Transcription

What follows is a representative sample of *vimbuza* rhythmic mottos. The mottos
are not static constructs meant to be repeated without change, but definitions of
musical motion, hence their modal character. Rather than dictate a structure, the
mottos suggest a "feel" for musical space, one defined by gaps as much as by sound.
To bring out this element in the transcriptions, I used a modified form of the TUBS
(Koetting 1970) notation system.

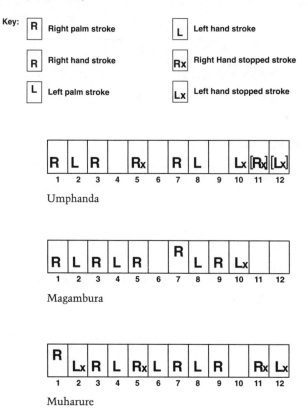

Key:

R Right palm stroke   L Left hand stroke

R Right hand stroke   Rx Right Hand stopped stroke

L Left palm stroke   Lx Left hand stopped stroke

R	L	R		Rx		R	L			Lx	Rx	Lx
1	2	3	4	5	6	7	8	9	10	11	12

Umphanda

R	L	R	L	R		R	L	R	Lx		
1	2	3	4	5	6	7	8	9	10	11	12

Magambura

R	Lx	R	L	Rx	L	R	L	R		Rx	Lx
1	2	3	4	5	6	7	8	9	10	11	12

Muharure

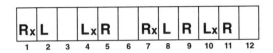

Fumu za pasi
(Fuma za pasi can be played the same way as the *ßaßemba* motto. This is an alternate version used by some *nchimi*.)

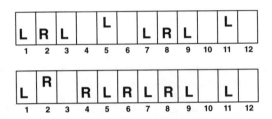

Kalulu
(*Kalulu* is one of the few mottos that cover two twelve-pulse phrases.)

ßaßiza

ßaßemba

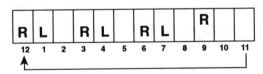

Vyanusi

APPENDIX C
Vimbuza Song Texts

ßaßiza

Mwana wambelele walira kombwe.
The child of a sheep cries for the cock.
Sekalera kußaßiza.
Get happy for the Biza.
Note: The *vimbuza ßaßiza* wants a *chilopa*. This does not mean, however, that this song is sung only during one of these sacrifices.

ßaßemba

Kuli ßemba; nkhutali we lero.
There are ßemba; it is far today.
Ho Lußemba,
Ho Lußemba!
Ho Lußemba,
Ho Lußemba!
Ati mwanijabira kuwalo lero.
They say you have shut me outside today.
Palußemba mphatali lero.
At Lußemba it is far today.

ßaSenga

Ati ßaSenga nawo.
They say *ßaSenga* too.
Ati ßavwara madumbo.
They say put on madumbo.
ßakana kuwonjera ßaSenga nawo.
They refuse to copy *ßaSenga.*
ßavwara Mazamba nawo!
Put on *mazamba!*
Note: *Madumbo* is the chiSenga word for *mazamba*, the skirt made of animal or cloth strips worn by *vimbuza* dancers.

ßaMwera

He kavunza mwera he
Cover the wind from the lake,
Mwera he
Wind from the lake.
He nkhagwade ine
I go kneel,
Namuniyino nkhagwade kuvißwanda
I my friend, I go kneel to ghosts.
Amama nthenda nikavuluvulu
The disease is a whirlwind.
Note: *Vißwanda* literally translates as "ghosts," but here refers to *vimbuza* spirits.

ßaMwera

Ja Muzungu kuMwera
Of Europeans from Mwera
Muzungu wapamaji wanimulozi
Europeans from the water come like witches
Tangali nayo (chiBiza)
to play with them.

Kachekuru

Kaponda ponda, Kaponda kayikama.
He stamps stamps, Stamps he is kneeling.
Note: An old person dances using his knees. If this spirit comes in a young person, he or she should dance in that way.

ßachota

Chota lero
Fire today,

181

Chota muliro wavißanda
Fire of ghosts.
Note: *Nchimi* Lußemba explained that
Chota was an Ngoni *isanusi* (witchsmeller) who was asked to find the
cause of rampant bush fires around a
village. He divined that it was due to *vißanda,* not witchcraft. The *vimbuza*
spirit *ßachota* is generally considered
to be a *vimbuza* who likes to eat fire.
"Muliro" is a chiNgoni word.

Fumu za Pasi

Ati nipani kang'oma
They say give me the good sounding
drum.
Nichinkikulire mwezi wathwa
I dance, the new moon has come out.
Waßala
It has shone.
Mwezi wathwa
The new moon has shown.
Note: The "ka" of "kang'oma" refers to
beautiful or good sound. When the new
moon is in the west, the *vimbuza* are
particularly active.

Fumu za Pasi

*Ati mwayiwona mwayiwona mwe ku-
dambo*
They say you have seen it in the river,
Yawa kumitambo
In the clouds.
Ati mwayiwona ndege
They say you have seen an airplane.
Yikulira kumitambo
It is roaring in the clouds.
Para yalira yalira mwe
When it roars
Ati yikulira kumitambo kwale
It is roaring in the clouds.
Para mukuti nkuteta he
If you say I am lying
mukafumbe a Chißeza
go ask Chißeza,
munyane Chitimukuru

my friend Chitimukuru,
munyane fumu za pasi
my friend *fumu za pasi.*

Fumu za Pasi

ßahaßi
Witches.
Ahe sendelela uko sendelela
Let's go that way.
He ßakwenda munthowa
They are walking on the path.
He ßakupenja banyawo
They are looking for their friends.
He ßamara banmyawo
They have finished their friends.

Fumu za Pasi

Iyaya lero, mujima ngolo
Iyaya lero, a digger of holes
Heleliya heleliya we
Heleliya heleliya we [vocables]
Ine, amama, bayankhu mujima ngolo?
Me, mother, where have they gone, the
hole diggers?
Note: No one knew what this song
meant. *Ngolo* is a Phoka word. The
Phoka are related to the Tumbuka and
have a reputation for witchcraft.

Fumu za Pasi

Wayi kata muchira.
You have cut its tail.
Nkharye mwana.
I eat the child.
Note: This is a very old song and no
one was sure of its meaning. Some peo-
ple suggested it might have to do with
chilopa.

Nkharamu

Iyaya nkharamu zauluma ku Mombwa
The lion roars at Mombwa [a hill near
Njakwa]
Nipani mwana. Ndirye!
Give me a child. I eat!
Note: The lion spirit is said to want to
eat young children. When this spirit

comes in a fierce way, people will often run out of the temple, especially mothers with babies.

Nkharamu

A Zamangwe mwarya mwana
Zamangwe, you have eaten the child.
Mwarya mwana mwtenge ning'ombe
You have eaten the child; you thought it was a cow.
Note: This song is about a woman named Zamangwe who thought she was doing a *chilopa* sacrifice but actually killed a child.

Munjiri/Virombo

Ati ßamunjiri Jimanga, ßamunjiri ji-manga.
They say wart hog Dig, wart hog, dig.
Ho ßana ßane!
Ho my children!
Jimanga, tiwerenge!
Dig, let's go!
Note: When people have this *nthenda* (disease) they imitate the digging of a wart hog.

Virombo

Ho Kayipale!
Ho Scratch!
Wiza kayipale pale wiza.
Scratching [disease] has come.
Note: This is a kind of *vimbuza* that causes people to scratch when they dance.

Virombo

Mwalembera
Floating in the air
ßachipungu
Eagle
Note: In this *vimbuza*, people dance like eagles. The song refers to an eagle floating in the air looking for food. When this was sung at Nchimi Mseka's, everyone ran out of the them-

pli. Mseka explained that the *nthenda* (disease) is looking for food, and that is why everyone was scared.

ßamunkwele/Virombo

ßamunkwele ßamunkwele ßachema.
The monkeys, the monkeys are calling.
Amunkwele ßakulira kunyanja ako.
The monkeys are crying there at the lake.

Kalulu/Virombo

Kalulu, kalulu, tirye nayo.
Hare, hare, we eat with him.
Kalulu kuchenjera; wazgoßera kurya yekha.
The hare is clever; he is used to eating alone.
Awo useßele nawo.
You play with them.
Kalulu, useßele nayo.
Hare, you play with him.

Geremani

Kuli nkhondo lero chitima nkhondo yama Geremani
There is war today, sorrowful war of the Germans.
Yikaßako iyaya iyaya
It was there, iyaya iyaya [vocables].
Note: During World War I there was combat in northern Malawi between the British King's African Rifles and the German *Schutztruppe,* who were based in German East Africa (Tanzania).

Vyanusi

Wayiwona vula para mukwambuka dambo ilo.
I have seen the rain when crossing that river.
Note: This song refers to the Ngoni's crossing the Zambezi River when they first entered Malawi.

Vyanusi

Kuthwasa ungathwasa we thwasire we
New moon, even if you can be a new
moon,
Mwalowana mwekha
You have bewitched each other.
Wathwasa namaboza we thwasire
He has become a new moon with lies.
Mwathwawsa nautesi we thwasire
You have become a new moon with
lies.
Note: New moons are new *nchimi* heal-
ers, some of whom are bad and de-
ceitful.

Mungoma

Hoya hoya mungoma
Hoya hoya [vocables] mungoma
Sißaßa zamungoma!
Preach [tell] about the [disease]
mungoma!
Note: Mungoma is a form of *vyanusi*.

Vimbuza

Nkhalelenkhu mwana lero hele
Where do I raise my child today?
Mwana ine ßadada mbahaßi we
My child, father is a witch.
Ndiwo ßakumara ßana heliye we
He's the one who finishes children.
Inya ßadada mbahaßi we
Yes, father is a witch.

Vimbuza

A Wyness zaluma njuche.
Wyness, the bees have stung her.
Zaluma njuche zaluma!
Sting, bees, sting!
Note: A witch can send bees to sting
someone.

Vimbuza

Aka mwe kalimuliwunda.
That is around the waist.
Kalimuliwunda dekani ßanjake ßaku-
kalikera.

Around the waist, that is why others
leave it to him/her.
Note: A person has a venereal disease
that causes boils around the waist. He
or she is ashamed to tell, but it is up to
her to not hide the illness and tell the
doctor.

Vimbuza

ANyirongo weramko,
Mr. Nyirongo come back,
ANyirongo lero he.
Mr. Nyirongo today.
Iyaya lero, ANyirongo lero he.
Mr. Nyirongo today come, come today.
ANyirongo wera wera!
Mr. Nyirongo come come!
Lekani k̇unidelera, ANyirongo we!
Stop undermining me, Mr. Nyirongo!
ßali kutola gozole, ANyirongo.
He has caught gonorrhea, Mr. Ny-
irongo.
Gozole wamara mphapo, ANyirongo
we.
Gonorrhea has finished fertility, Mr.
Nyirongo.
ßaNyirongo weraniko, ANyirongo!
Mr. Nyirongo come back, Mr. Ny-
irongo!
Note: Gonorrhea is used here to mean
venereal disease in general.

Vimbuza

Ati yeßo, yeßo, yeßo, mama.
They say thank you, thank you, thank
you, mama.
Pakwiza ßakayowoya ßaMseka kuli
nkhondo; nkawela!
When coming they said at Mseka's
there is war; I am going back!
Ati yeßo, yeßo, yeßo, mama.
They say thank you, thank you, thank
you, mama.
Tikwimba namuzungu, mama.
We are singing with the white man,
mama.

Nkhondo iyo kwaMuseka, kuli doli.
War at Mseka's, there is a "hurrah."
Yeßo, yeßo, yeßo
Thank you, thank you, thank you
Ati AChikanga ßakuchema we.
They say Chikanga is calling.
*Mulaula ßalikuko; nayoso ßakuchema
usiku wose.*
Mulaula is there; he too is calling all
night long.
ßaMuseka chemaninge chomeni!
Mseka keep on calling a lot!
ßaMuseka nikatunda;

Mseka is a lord [expert];
ßakuwona nyamuchisi.
he sees things from the dark.
Mbaya, mwana wane tora we!
Please, my child catch!
Tiyeni tikaßa wone.
Let's go and see them.
Ati, tilute kwaChikanga!
They say, let's go to Chikanga!
Note: *Nchimi* Mseka calls this an
uchimi song. It is for bringing the *miz-
imu* up for purposes of divination. The
song, however, can be sung for anyone.

NOTES

Preface

1. This is Kleinman's term (1980: 38) for the health-related aspects of social reality (see chapter 4). Clinical reality, for Kleinman (ibid.: 42), is mediated through a symbolic reality that connects the social environment with physiological processes.

2. Some Tumbuka also referred to *vimbuza* spirits as *mashave*, although this was not common usage (see Chilivumbo 1972).

3. Katz's (1982) ethnography on !Kung healing is a notable exception, as are Stoller's (1989a) work on the Songhay and Besmer's analysis of *bori* (1983). Outside of Africa, Roseman's (1991) ethnography on Temiar music and medicine and Kapferer's (1983) analysis of Sinhalese exorcisms (although I take issue with it here) are among the few monographs that give musical experience important consideration.

4. This neglect of music is due, in most cases, to anthropologists' lack of training and expertise in dealing with musical material, combined with a theoretical bias that relegates music to the realm of superstructure. This explanation does not, however, negate the significant gap that exists in the literature on medical technology and techniques in indigenous healing systems—a gap found not only in ethnographies of Africa but in those of cultures worldwide.

5. The criticisms I make here regarding Victor Turner's work (and later Bruce Kapferer's) could, of course, be applied to most ethnography. I have chosen these two ethnographers not as particularly glaring examples of deficiency but because their work deals specifically with ritual performance and yet overlooks or ignores significant aspects of the phenomena under investigation.

6. Someone has yet to write, à la Jan Vansina, the etymological and cultural history of this important term. Although Janzen (1992) has dealt with *ng'oma* institutions, the ethnomusicological significance of the term remains an issue for further investigation.

7. See Don Ihde's introduction, "Doing Phenomenology," in his book *Experimental Phenomenology* (1977).

Introduction

1. Everyday life, which for the Tumbuka includes such phenomena as spirit possession, trance dancing, and flying witches, can indeed sometimes be extraordinary.

2. I am appropriating Victor Turner's term "liminal," which he adopted from van Gennep's model of *rites de passage*. "Liminal" is taken from the Latin term

limin, meaning threshold. As Turner (1969: 95) explains of "threshold people": "Liminal entities are neither here nor there; they are betwixt and between the positions assigned and arrayed by law, custom, convention, and ceremonial." I am extending this meaning to include the in-between of ethnographic encounters.

3. Speaking to the issue of the ontological ground of "historicality," Heidegger makes the point that "[*Dasein*'s] own past—and this always means the past of its 'generation'—is not something which *follows along after* Dasein, but something which already goes ahead of it" (1962a: 41; italics in original).

4. I take ontology to be essentially a phenomenological project. As Heidegger states: "*Only as phenomenology is ontology possible*" (1962a: 60, italics in the original).

5. The use of hyphenation here refers to Heidegger's ontological terminology and is meant to distinguish and set off this term from the long history of travelers' accounts (and the more recent tradition of reflexive ethnography) of "being there."

6. By using the term *Erlebnis*, I follow the lineage fathered by Dilthey (1976), extended to the lifeworld by Schutz (1973), and brought into the world of ethnography by such scholars as Turner and Bruner (1986).

7. In *Being and Time*, as Dreyfus (1991: 34–35) points out, "[Heidegger] does not discuss what it means to be a human being in specific cultures or historical periods, but rather attempts by describing everyday life to lay out for us the general, cross-cultural, transhistorical structures of our self-interpreting way of being and how these structures account for all modes of intelligibility." Along with critiquing other sciences such as psychology and biology, Heidegger (1962a: 71–77) critiques anthropology's narrow empirical focus and its neglect of the ontological question. ("Philosophical anthropology" is a different issue for Heidegger [1962b: 215–21]). He questions whether ethnology can supply the phenomenal data required for such an investigation, especially given anthropology's traditional focus on the ontic and its general lack of concern with the ontological. While distancing his analytic of *Dasein* from traditional anthropology—which for Heidegger is a mixture of Christian theology, personalism, and life philosophy—he nevertheless discerns a positive significance for ethnography:

> To orient the analysis of Dasein towards the "life of primitive peoples" can have positive significance as a method because "primitive phenomena" are often less concealed and less complicated by extensive self-interpretation on the part of the Dasein in question. Primitive Dasein often speaks to us more directly in terms of a primordial absorption in "phenomena" (taken in a pre-phenomenological sense). A way of conceiving things which seems, perhaps, rather clumsy and crude from our standpoint, can be positively helpful in bringing out the ontological structures of phenomena in a genuine way. (1962a: 76)

Anthropology and ethnographic inquiry have come a long way since Heidegger wrote these words in the 1920s. If we seek beyond the ethnocentric prejudices embedded in this discourse—primitive equals simple; innocents lost in a kind of Levy-Bruhlian *participation mystique*, their conceptions clumsy and crude, never to attain the analytical power of the Western mind—we can indeed discern a positive significance. The significance, however, is not so much in the "simplicity" of primitive life—itself a construct of nineteenth- and early twentieth-century anthropology driven by concerns with social evolutionary theories—but in an ontological investigation into the lived experience of other ways of being-in-the-world.

Chapter 1

1. Just before I arrived in northern Malawi to conduct my research, a long drought was broken, according to local sources, because of rituals that had recently been carried out at this site.

2. The first Bantu speakers arrived in Malawi probably around A.D. 300 as part of the early Bantu migrations. They were iron-working and pottery-making agriculturalists (Cole-King 1972: 71) who most likely came into Malawi via a natural corridor that exists between Lake Tanganyika and Lake Malawi. The Henga Valley is located at the southernmost extreme of this corridor, and it can be assumed that these early peoples found the valley a suitable place to settle, given its highly fertile soil and favorable climate (Pike and Rimmington 1965: 87). This corridor, which was "an ancient crossroads of Africa, with movement of peoples from west, east, north and south" (Wilson 1972: 136), experienced an almost continual flux of peoples moving through its confines. These were not mass migrations but the wanderings of small groups, some of whom stayed in the North while others moved farther south. In the eighteenth century this movement of peoples into northern Malawi intensified, owing to disturbances in the regions from which these people came. Vail (1972: 153) cites Bemba expansion in the west and northwest and disturbances in the Uhehe-Ubena area of southern Tanzania as likely sources for this increased migration. By the middle of the eighteenth century, there was in place an indigenous Tumbuka-speaking population that was a mixture of many groups and clans from different regions of Africa. Tumbuka country was characterized by a lack of centralized political or religious institutions, with localized clan groups holding autonomy over restricted areas of land.

3. Many of the patients of nchimi are strangers from outside the general vicinity of the *nchimi*'s compound. This may have to do in part with what Shorter (quoted in Ranger and Weller 1975: 9) calls a "mystical geography," a notion "which ascribed special power to areas outside one's own and which often emphasized the mediating or cleansing role of the uncommitted outsider."

4. Chikanje is his *nchimi* name; it is the name of a colony of mushrooms that are bitter and inedible. Its symbolic meaning has to do with being bitter and sour against witches.

5. In 1835, on the auspicious day of a full solar eclipse, the Ngoni crossed the Zambezi River and began their long march north into Tumbuka country.

6. Detailed histories of the Ngoni in Malawi have been published elsewhere (see McCracken 1977; Pachai 1972; Read 1956) and need not be recounted here. For our purposes, it should be pointed out that some of the Tumbuka did resist the Ngoni. In 1875, a short-lived rebellion resulted in the Henga Valley Tumbuka's fleeing to the lakeshore. And in the most famous incident, in 1880 a group of rebellious Tumbuka were massacred by the Ngoni on Mount Hora. After this rebellion,

the Henga Tumbuka fled to Ngonde country farther north, leaving the Henga Valley virtually deserted for perhaps the first time in over sixteen hundred years (Tew 1950: 54).

7. Ngoni culture, however, is still alive and strong in the southern part of the Northern Region in Mzimba District, where the paramount chief resides.

8. Shaka is said to have invented this type of spear, and much of his military success has been attributed to its effectiveness in fighting.

9. Rev. William Turner (1952: 88) translates *nkufi* as the palm of the hand. He combines this with the verb *kukuva* to get the phrase *kukuva nkufi*, meaning to clap hands (1952: 55). He indicates that the word *mapi* may be used instead of *nkufi* in this phrase. From my information, *mapi* is differentiated from *nkufi* and indicates the regular clapping style used when singing.

10. The coin does not actually have to be silver, but it must be white (that is, not copper or gold-colored), the color symbolizing the *mizimu*.

11. Brelsford (1944: 10) lists Mpanda as a Bemba chief's territorial district. The area was named after a river where "the white-cheeked otter (Mumpanda) eats the fish caught in the traps."

12. In reading Maya Deren's account of the *loa* (1953: 321n5), I was struck by the similar description she offers concerning her personal experience of spirit possession: "Possession is accompanied by a sense of an explosion upward and outward."

13. See Fraser (1914: 124) on this point.

14. Deren (1953: 249) comes to a similar conclusion regarding Voudoun spirit possession: "To understand that the self must leave if the loa is to enter, is to understand that one cannot be man and god at once."

15. Turner (1952: 159) translates the word *kuwukwa* as "to divine." I, too, heard this term used in the context of divination, but in day-to-day conversation, when people talked about an nchimi's divination, they most often used the term *kuwona*, which literally means "to see."

16. The mission fathers of the Free Church of Scotland translated the Bible into chiTumbuka. It is not clear from my research whether *nchimi* was a term applied to healers before this use by the missionaries.

17. *Nchimi* emphasize the Old Testament, as do most independent African churches. Especially for the independent churches, the Old Testament was used as a justification for the continuing practice of polygyny, which was banned by the Church of Central Africa Presbyterian (CCAP).

18. Psalms 150 (King James Version):

PRAISE ye the LORD. Praise God in his sanctuary: praise him in the firmament of his power.

2 Praise him for his mighty acts: praise him according to his greatness.

3 Praise him with the sound of the trumpet: praise him with the psaltery and harp.

4 Praise him with the timbrel and dance: praise him with stringed instruments and organs.

5 Praise him upon the loud cymbals: praise him upon the high sounding cymbals.

6 Let everything that hath breath praise the Lord. Praise ye the LORD.

19. This scenario of a supreme God who is removed from the everyday concerns of the world, a *deus otiosus*, is not only typical of many cultures in this part of Bantu-speaking Africa and virtually a pan-African religious trait but is, in fact, a worldwide religious phenomenon (see Eliade 1963: 46–50, 1964: 9n3).

20. See Lex (1979: 117–51) for a different physiological theory of trance not mentioned by Rouget. Rouget's (1985) position here is really little more than a re-statement of Rousseau's contention two centuries earlier concerning the airs of the tarantella:

> The healing of tarantula bites is cited in proof of the physical power of sounds. But in fact this evidence proves quite the opposite. What is needed for curing those bitten by this insect are neither isolated sounds, nor even simply tunes. Rather, each needs tunes with familiar melodies and under-standable lyrics. Italian tunes are needed for Italians; for Turks, Turkish tunes. Each is affected only by accents familiar to him. His nerves yield only to what his spirit predisposes them. One must speak to him in a language he understands, if he is to be moved by what he is told. The cantatas of Bernier are said to have cured the fever of a French musician. They would have given one to a musician of any other nation. (Rousseau 1966: 60)

In this nature-nurture debate, Rousseau comes down on the side of culture, as does Rouget (who in fact cites this passage from Rousseau [1985: 167–68]).

21. There was a divergence of opinion, among both laymen and *nchimi*, on whether *vimbuza* dancing during divination was still under the control of the spirits, whether it was under partial control of the spirits, or whether there was a transfer-ence of this control to the *nchimi*. But all agreed on the importance of remembering during trance, for when one begins to remember the dance experience, one begins to "see" (*kuwona*).

22. I first encountered the notion of music as a technology in the lectures of Ter Ellingson at the University of Washington in 1983 (see also Ellingson 1987: 164).

23. One other thing that batteries do in Tumbuka culture, besides powering radios, is to light "torches" (flashlights). Flashlights, however, did not seem as com-mon to me as radios. Most people used paraffin lamps if they needed light. While the metaphoric associations may seem self-evident, I never heard a Tumbuka men-tion them. In other words, it is logical that the Tumbuka could make an analogy between batteries' powering torches, allowing one to see in the dark, and music's providing energy for an *nchimi* to "see." The Tumbuka, however, seem to be a more sound-oriented than a visually oriented people. For example, in chiTumbuka, as in many Bantu languages, to understand (*kupulika*) is to hear (*kupulika*). For a discus-sion of the nonvisual orientation of some African cultures, see Stoller (1989b: ch. 6).

24. The *vimbuza* music was recorded by the brother of Nchimi Chikanje who works for MBC. *Vimbuza* music is played on the radio as part of a government policy to promote traditional African culture.

Chapter 2

1. Because music is an important part of *vimbuza* affliction, "resonance" here is not only metaphorical but ontological.

2. The Tumbuka make a clear distinction between mental illness (*chifusi*) and affliction by the spirits. Both are *nthenda* (disease), but they are different categories of illness: the former is not caused by the spirits but is a naturally occurring illness, that is, caused by God.

3. I use the term "disease" here because this is how the Tumbuka themselves translated their word *nthenda* into English. It is not meant to imply the dichotomous structure many medical anthropologists make between disease—dysfunctional physiological states—and the social construction of illness (see Eisenberg 1977).

4. See Horton's (1967: 56–57) discussion of natural immunity and stress-producing disturbances in traditional African societies.

5. See Yoder (1982), *African Health and Healing Systems.*

6. Music and healing have a long tradition throughout this part of Africa. We have written accounts from as early as the seventeenth century in southern Africa of the use of music and trance in traditional healing (see Oesterreich 1930: 263–64). There seems to be little doubt that these practices have a considerable historical depth.

7. Assimilating a new and foreign type of healer within Tumbuka culture was not without precedent. When the Ngoni invaded northern Malawi in the 1850s, they brought with them not only their own traditional healers but also healers from people they had conquered along the way. These were all eventually incorporated, to varying degrees, into the traditional health care system of the Tumbuka. There is a widespread belief among Bantu-speaking peoples of southern and southeastern Africa that healers from outside the community or localized group can be more powerful than local healers. This is why so many people from outside travel to the Henga Valley seeking the help of a healer.

8. See Vail and White (1989: 164–66) for an excellent discussion of the reasons for the government's restrictive language policy and the effects it has had on the Tumbuka.

9. Specialization of healers in non-Western medical systems generally revolves around the diviner-herbalist distinction (see Foster and Anderson 1978: 101–22).

10. *Sing'anga* who do use divination usually rely on some type of external apparatus (see Wendroff 1985: 125–26n6), while *nchimi* use only divinatory trance and dreams to diagnose the ills and misfortunes of their patients.

11. There are also witchkillers called *seketera*. They are said to have the ability, through the use of special medicines, to trap witches at gravesites. Witches come to graves at night either to eat human flesh or to raise victims from the dead to act as slaves (zombies). Once the witch is caught, the *seketera* is claimed to insert a sharp stick up the witch's anus, which will eventually kill the witch. There are very few

seketera, and they are not considered to be active players in the day-to-day battle against witchcraft and witches.

12. I am retaining the use of the term "clan" here in conformity with standard usage in writings about the Tumbuka. As Vail (1972: 164n17) remarks, however, "the original 'clan' as described in tradition usually includes one leader, the eponymous founder, and a few relatives, usually male only. Thus the term clan is perhaps an overly ambitious description."

13. The following is the witchcraft ordinance introduced by the British in 1912, which is still part of the legal code: "The profession or calling of witchfinder or witchdoctor or a professional maker or mixer of poison is hereby declared to be an illegal calling and every person exercising or pretending to exercise such calling or profession shall be guilty of felony and shall be liable to imprisonment for life" (Section 8, Witchcraft Ordinance, 1912).

14. I am not following the distinction some anthropologists make between sorcerers and witches, which is based on physiology (witches are born that way) and conscious intent (sorcerers know what they do, but witches do not). I have chosen to use the term "witch," even though in Tumbuka ideology it fits the foregoing definition of sorcerer, because that is the terminology the Tumbuka use when speaking English. Douglas (1967: 72) employs the same usage, "for it has always been customary to translate *Nfiti* as 'witch' even though the *Nfiti* behaves in many ways like a Zande 'sorcerer.' " Although witches ordinarily exercise conscious intent, several *nchimi* told me about a special form of witchcraft "stuff" called *mbunguru,* made with parts of hyenas, bats, vultures, owls, and various other ingredients, which is fed to small children and creates a witchcraft substance inside them that makes them become witches without knowing it. This scenario, however, is considered very rare and is not part of everyday explanations about how witchcraft operates.

15. Contrary to the Western conception that all medicines are potentially beneficial, the Tumbuka, when speaking in English, use the term "medicine" to designate any compound that is efficacious, regardless of whether it is intended for good or for evil purposes.

16. The *mizimu* are divided into two subcategories: named ancestors, those blood relatives who have died in the preceding few generations—usually grandparents and great-grandparents—and unnamed ancestors, who function as a kind of combined ancestral group. These are not rigidly defined categories but groups that gradually and logically blend into each other as time elapses and named ancestors are forgotten.

17. An entire dissertation by Arnold Wendroff (1985) focuses on letters *nchimi* receive and send concerning witchcraft. These letters are often addressed to or come from village headmen (traditional authorities) and are seen as one way *nchimi* legitimize and legalize their witchcraft accusations—that is, try to protect themselves from legal recourse by those whom they accuse.

18. All kinds of medicine are administered to patients through small cuts made in the body. This seems to be a widespread practice in southeastern and southern Africa. Schapera (1982: 113), for example, mentions people's using this practice in Botswana when applying strengthening medicine: "The doctoring consists in making

small cuts on every joint of the person's body, and into each cut is smeared a little of the magical ointment."

19. Although it is usually translated as wind, when *mphepo* is used in the context of spiritual energy, we do not have an adequate English gloss. For this usage, with its connotations of wind, air, life force, and spirit, I have coined the compound word "spiritwind" to impart the multivocal nature of the Tumbuka concept.

20. As is typical in spirit-possession complexes populated by foreign spirits in this part of Africa, these spirits are usually identified by ethnic group instead of by individual names (see Colson 1969; Gelfand 1956, 1964b; Junod [1927] 1962). This practice is further evidence of a delimited healing complex in southeastern Africa, distinct from, for example, the West African divine horsemen complexes (see Barber 1981; Bascom 1944; Besmer 1983; Herskovits 1938), in which spirits are individually named.

21. Pike and Rimmington (1965: 211n2) cite *Mwera* as a "South East Trade wind" on Lake Malawi, which dhows traveling from the eastern shores use to head north. In the late eighteenth century, the Balowoka (lit. "those who crossed over") arrived in northern Malawi, probably using these trade winds. They were a small group of Arabized traders who crossed Lake Malawi, looking for ivory. When they reached the Nkhamanga Plains in Rumphi District, they must have felt that they had found "a perfect El-Dorado" (Young 1933: 9), for this region was rich in elephants and the Tumbuka did not know the value of ivory. To the Tumbuka, ivory was merely elephant bones to be used as doors to huts and "to keep away from mud" (Nyirenda 1931: 10), meaning they used ivory instead of logs to raise their sleeping mats off the mud floors. By trading cloth and beads for these worthless "bones," the Balowoka easily established an economic hegemony in the North that made the name Nkhamanga famous throughout eastern Africa—a fame, however, that would eventually undermine the Balowoka's control of the ivory trade as new traders entered the area to exploit this newfound wealth.

As the Balowoka moved into the interior looking for new sources of ivory, they installed a series of subchiefs along the trade route to the lakeshore. This was the beginning of a loose political confederation centered in Nkhamanga that was ruled by a paramount chief called the Chikulamayembe. The reign of the Chikulamayembe was for the most part a peaceful one, and the Balowoka adopted the language and customs of the local Tumbuka (Tew 1950: 52). Contrary to the official Tumbuka dynastic interpretation of history, however, the Chikulamayembe never did exert an effective political dominance over the region. There was no military force to back up the regime, which was based on the economics of trade (Vail 1972: 158). It was much more a mercantile enterprise than a chiefly kingdom.

By the turn of the century, the Chikulamayembe began to lose the monopoly of the ivory trade to Swahili slave traders who dealt directly with the local subchiefs. If the Tumbuka were brought under some measure of centralized political control during the first years of Chikulamayembe rule, by the middle of the nineteenth century a decentralized society based on the autonomy of local clan groups had reasserted itself. When the Ngoni arrived in the 1850s, they "found a land that was politically and socially fissiparous, militarily weak, and an economy in an advanced state of decay because of exploitation by outside traders" (Vail 1972: 161). It was not until some fifty years later, under the auspices of the British colonial administration, that the Chikulamayembe was reinstated as a paramount chief.

22. This theory bears a striking resemblance to that of the boiling energy of the !Kung bushmen of the Kalahari (Katz 1982). According to the !Kung, humans have a substance in their bellies called *num*, which can be heated through music and dance. Once it reaches a boiling point, it can be used to heal. The relationship between music and heat seems to be widespread—think about the metaphorical usage of terms such as "hot" in the musical vernacular of the African diaspora—and it raises interesting questions for further ethnomusicological investigations.

23. *Vimbuza* affliction writ large takes on the classic proportions of a Turnerian social drama (Turner 1974: 38–42, 1982: 215–21). As an episode of illness, it has a definite beginning, which stands out from quotidian life: the onset of socially defined and recognized symptoms ascertained and validated through divination—in Turner's scheme, the breach leading to the crisis. This initiates redressive action involving therapeutic intervention, which includes musical activity in the form of trance dancing. And finally, spirit affliction culminates in one of three possible outcomes: (1) reintegration, a cessation of dysfunctional symptoms; (2) irremediable schism, a failure of therapy that may result in death; or (3) transformation, which, for those who are afflicted by the special form of *vimbuza* known as *nthenda ya uchimi*, disease of the prophets, changes ordinary Tumbuka, both men and women, into diviner-healers.

By using Turner's model, I am not subscribing to its professed universality but rather to its particular fit with rituals of affliction in this part of Africa. I agree with Margaret Drewal's (1992: xiv) basic point that it is not the tripartite structure of the social drama that imparts agency, but rather human beings who, through performance, transform ritual itself. I would not throw out the proverbial baby with the bathwater, however, as Drewal does in dismissing Turner's dramaturgical theory. Spirit affliction among the Ndembu whom Turner studied, as well as among the Tumbuka, is articulated in dramatic modes of experience and therefore seems inherently to follow a dramaturgical scheme. This does not mean that all actions are circumscribed and dictated by some kind of inflexible plot. Rather, the progression of events surrounding spirit affliction seems to coalesce naturally into dramatic structures. These structures take their shape from the possibilities inherent in a theory of illness that is realized in a medical praxis.

24. Meras's case fits a typical accusation pattern in Tumbuka culture. Her affinal relatives were responsible for the witchcraft, and although I am not pursuing a functional analysis of witchcraft accusations here, in the patrilineal society of the Tumbuka, a woman's relations with her affines are a point of stress. Once again there is a kind of cognitive dissonance going on in this pattern, because affines by definition are not blood relatives, yet Tumbuka consistently state that only blood relations can bewitch each other.

Chapter 3

1. The word *chilopa* is a transformation of the class 9 noun *ndopa*, which in chiTumbuka means "blood." This transformation of noun classes is a significant one in that it adds a kind of concretization to the term "blood" by placing it into

noun class 7 with the prefix *chi* (this noun class is often called the "Things Class" [Brain 1977: 18]). Instead of meaning "blood," the red stuff that flows in veins, it has much more the meaning of "The Blood," a self-contained process.

2. Sometimes after an all-night session of *vimbuza*, the next day healers will hold what they call "Kwaya," which does not involve drumming but uses only singing and clapping, often enhanced with concussion sticks and rattles, to "see" remaining patients. *Nchimi* explained that the *vimbuza* were already heated from the night before, and therefore they needed only the *kwaya* (choir) for divination.

3. I have played the *kagan* part many times in Ewe percussion ensembles and was immediately struck by this similarity. In Western musical terminology, the *kagan* plays an off-beat eighth-note triplet figure (see chapter 5, note 6).

4. I use the term "purification" here because the Tumbuka consider menstruation "unclean."

5. *Chilopa* refers only to the actual sacrifice of the animal; *kuskaßiska* (from the chiNgoni word *kuskaba*, "to stab") is the verb used to designate the entire ritual process. By using the term *chilopa* in a general sense for the whole ritual, I am following standard usage by the Tumbuka, who rarely use *kuskaßiska* when referring to the events I am describing. A Tumbuka usually wouldn't say, "So and so is going to (ku)skaßiska," but rather, "He or she is doing a *chilopa*." The Zezuru people of southern Zimbabwe use roughly the same term to refer to a similar blood sacrifice. The final ritual for a new "spirit medium" is called *kudya muropa* (lit. "to drink blood"). See Fry (1976: 32) for a description of the ritual.

6. This is, of course, if the *chilopa* was handled correctly. The *vimbuza* may remain heated or even get hotter as a result of a bad *chilopa*. Determining which scenario applies to which situation is usually left up to the healer, although, as always, a patient who is unhappy with the *nchimi*'s diagnosis of the situation may choose to sever relations with that healer and interpret the outcome in his or her own way. Moreover, both patient and healer may reinterpret events as situations change.

7. To preserve anonymity, I use only this man's surname. Tembo is a typical Ngoni name. His father was Ngoni and his mother, Tumbuka. The Ngoni incorporated many of the peoples they conquered, including the Tumbuka (see Read 1956); there was a lot of interethnic marriage in the North, which still goes on today.

8. This dispute resolution has striking similarities to family-type therapies used in Western psychotherapies such as psychodrama (see Moreno 1946).

9. Chikanje said, "If a person has *vimbuza* mixed with *mizimu*, I get medicine from the Chikopawoli Bridge at Njakwa." This bridge crosses the Njakwa Gorge, which is considered a sacred place often frequented by the spirits. When people cross this bridge, they often throw a coin into the water as a kind of offering to the spirits.

10. Chikanje is probably referring to First Corinthians, chapter 9; in particular, the part which deals with recompense for ministry. See verse 11, which speaks directly to the issue of compensation:

> If we have sown unto you
> spiritual things, *is it* a great thing if
> we shall reap your carnal things?

Chikanje is an nchimi, a prophet healer who sows spiritual things but is also someone who makes his profit as a healer.

11. Before I saw the *chilopa* of a goat, many Tumbuka explained to me that the goat is given a medicine that makes it hemorrhage from the nose. The person doing the *chilopa* was said to suck out all of the goat's blood, so that when they cut the goat open it was completely dry. I saw many *vilopa* of goats and talked with many *nchimi*, but I never saw or heard anything about sucking blood from the nose of a goat. The popular explanation is reminiscent of what in the industrialized world is referred to as an urban myth.

12. *Nyongo* (gallbladder) is a word borrowed from chiNgoni.

13. In northern Malawi, the use of cattle as a means of paying bride price is beginning to be supplanted, at least in part, by the use of cash.

14. In keeping with this kind of grammar of animals, rumor had it that I had done the *chilopa* of a duck because I had come from across a large body of water.

15. See de Heusch (1985) on sacrifice in Africa.

16. Although theoretically it is possible to be possessed by only one spirit, of the more than one hundred people I talked to who were afflicted by *vimbuza*, all were troubled by more than one *vimbuza* spirit.

17. Proverbs 2:1: My son, if thou wilt receive my words, and hide my commandments with thee . . .

18. For example, *sangoma* healers of the Nguni-speaking peoples of southern Africa use the gallbladder in a way similar to that of the Tumbuka for the initiation of healers: "The goat was cut up and . . . the gallbladder was attached to a small square of hide and fastened to the head as a distinctive insignia of a novice [healer]" (Hammond-Tooke 1955: 18). For the ritual use of the gallbladder in Ngoni funerals, see Read (1956: 177). Junod ([1927] 1962: 489–93) also describes the ritual use of a goat's gallbladder in the blood sacrifice performed by the Thonga of Mozambique for patients possessed by a Zulu or Ngoni spirit.

Sibisi (1975) reports a similar custom among Zulus who are possessed by foreign spirits called *indiki*. Speaking of a woman who is possessed, she states: "She withdraws from society, observes various forms of abstinence, wears white strips of goat's skin across her chest, wears skin wristlets, and inflated goat bladders from sacrificed goats, slaughtered to induce possession by her male ancestor. In addition she sings, dances and works herself into ecstasy" (1975: 50–51). The *indiki* spirits are also associated with the color red, and ancestral spirits with the color white, which parallels the color symbolism of the *vimbuza* and *mizimu* spirits. Interestingly, Sibisi states that this was a new kind of possession that came to Natal and "Zululand" at the turn of the twentieth century, a period when many Malawians, particularly Tumbuka, were coming to South Africa as migrant laborers. Not only were Malawians coming to South Africa during this period, but, according to Read (1942: 606), "male labour [from Nyasaland] began to emigrate to the port of Beira, to the Rhodesian Railway, to the Belgian copper mines and the Rand Gold Mines." In all of these places can be found possession cults similar in style to *vimbuza*.

Sibisi interprets the therapeutic process as an exorcism of the foreign *indiki* spirit in order that it be replaced by a male ancestor. This sounds very much like the process used in *vimbuza*, where foreign *vimbuza* and ancestral *mizimu* are brought into a beneficial arrangement, but without the exorcism aspect that Sibisi speaks of. I believe, however, that one may question her interpretation of the process as "exorcism." For example, she states that "even when the alien spirit—the *in-diki*—is thrown out and replaced by an ancestral spirit, the patient is still referred to as *indiki*," and as with an *nchimi*, "such an *indiki* may promote powers of prophecy and healing" (Sibisi 1975: 51).

Chapter 4

1. Beads are not the only kind of *mboni*. The tin plates with *ufu* and the silver coin put in the plates are also called *mboni*. As I have already mentioned, these plates were put under my pillow the first night I danced. They all have in common the aspect of offering and paying respects to the ancestors and the *vimbuza*. When I received my *mboni* beads, all three manifestations of *mboni* were present.

2. Timbre in African musics—and, for that matter, in most musics—is an ill-defined area of scholarship at best and needs much more attention. In general, we use a dyadic metaphorical terminology—warm/cool, bright/dark, liquid/dry—to attempt to describe this important element of musical phenomena. Perhaps this lack of attention to timbre is due, in part, to the tendency in Western music scholarship to treat tone color—itself a visual metaphor—as something that is added on, something not essential to the rarefied musical object that musicologists and theorists so often posit. Of course, this dimension of music is often precisely what many twentieth-century composers focus on (especially given the explosion of synthetic means of tone production), although our analytical musings have not necessarily kept pace with this development.

3. Overlying the indigenous core style is the four-part harmonic style introduced by the Christian missionaries of the Free Church of Scotland. In *vimbuza* singing, the way the parts move—sometimes with simple chorale-type voice leadings—definitely shows traits of Protestant hymnody as taught by the missionaries. This is not to say, however, that the Tumbuka did not have an indigenous harmonic vocal practice. Jones (1959: 226) lists the Tumbuka as using octaves, fifths, and fourths as part of their harmonic style. My research indicates that thirds are also a prevalent harmony, but this may be a result of Bemba and Biza influence. The Tumbuka have had extensive contact with both ethnic groups, and Jones (ibid.) cites both groups as using only thirds in their harmonic practice.

4. See the film *Prophet Healers of Northern Malawi* (Friedson 1989)—the last scene with Nchimi Mseka—for an example of *nkharamu*'s possessing in this way.

5. This is more myth than fact, for lions don't hide their kills in trees or bury them.

6. Rouget (1985: 103–107) distinguishes between "musicians," professionals whose sole purpose at ritual events is to make music, and "musicants," usually adepts and spectators, whose "activity is to make music only episodically, or accessorily, or secondarily." Although making music in the temple is much more than a secondary phenomenon, if we apply Rouget's terminology to the performance of *vimbuza*, then drummers are musicians, and members of the *kwaya* are musicants. The difference is in the multiplicity of roles assumed by patients, their relatives, and adepts, and in the singularity of the role of drummers, *not* in the episodic, accessory, or secondary role of music making, which for *vimbuza* does not hold true.

7. *Nkharamu*, through its relationship to the Bemba hereditary paramount chief Chitumukuru (see chapter 2), is often connected to Zambia.

8. "Hemiola" is derived from the Greek *hemiolios*, meaning "the whole and a half." The ancient Greeks used this term to denote a poetic meter of five units. In early Western musical theory, "hemiola" had two different meanings: one involving the tuning of two strings to the ratio of 3:2, which produces the interval of a P5, and the other, more familiar grouping of time values into a 3:2 relationship. I am using the term in this latter sense. In other words, the two levels of beats that Chikanje articulates with his body are in such a ratio. Simply put, six pulses can be grouped either into two groups of three or into three groups of two, creating the hemiola ratio. This procedure has been exploited and developed by African musicians and is considered by many ethnomusicologists (see Brandel 1959; Jones 1959; Kauffman 1980; Nketia 1974) a pan-African musical feature. By using this term I am not implying the structure of Western metrical practice, complete with bar lines delineating upbeats and downbeats, nor am I embracing the typical terminology in which hemiola is a three *against* two or a two *against* three. In African musical practice, these beats, made up of differing numbers of pulses, are not *against* each other but occur simultaneously.

9. Not all *nchimi* "see" in the same way. Within the general confines of the discipline, there is much individual elaboration in the techniques of divination. Mulaula, for example, does not see the patient's heart but rather feels the wind of the music and spirits of *vimbuza* come into his body simultaneously and "push up" the *mizimu*. When this happens, his soul often travels to the patient's village, where he can talk to the patient's ancestors to "see" the cause of what is troubling the person. Many *nchimi* told me that when they divined it was like seeing a movie before them, sometimes played out on the patient's face. Chikanga, the *nchimi ya uchimi* (the *nchimi* of *nchimi*), claims that when he catches a witch he can see the faces of his or her victims on the witch's forehead.

10. Junod ([1927] 1962: 486) reports a similar practice during possession ceremonies of the Thonga of Mozambique: "The patient was covered with a large piece of calico during the whole drum performance. A first medicinal pellet was burnt under the calico."

11. Rouget (1985: 111) comments that this kind of cry is a typical feature associated with spirit possession throughout the world. This stylized cry, however, is not a universal feature of spirit possession.

12. Rouget (1985: 102–111) has also commented on this phenomenon.

13. By using the expression "group possession," I do not mean to imply that everyone is possessed, but merely that more than one person is.

14. This reference to the west perhaps points to the origin of the *vimbuza* cult. Soko (1987: 2) and Ncozana (1985: 73) believe that *vimbuza* came to Malawi from the Bemba and Biza people of northeastern Zambia in the late nineteenth century. Some, though not all, Tumbuka cite a similar origin for *vimbuza*.

15. This information is taken from my own research in the Volta Region of Ghana in 1993.

16. This concept of universal participation also affects the texts of songs, for, as I mentioned about *vyanusi* songs earlier, the act of singing together is more impor-

tant than what is being sung about. Lyrical content is not important to the creation of this kind of communitas, and in fact may somewhat hinder it if it leads to reflection. Communitas, as Turner explains it, is an immediate experience that is pre-reflective. Perhaps this is why we find songs that consist of a single word, lyrics in languages that no one understands (such as the song about Mugwede in chiNgoni), and extensive use of vocables.

Chapter 5

1. A recent example of this conflation of the musical with textual analysis can be found in chapter 7 of Corinne Kratz's (1994) study of Okiek women's initiation. Despite the chapter's title, "The Musical Molding of Initiation," there is virtually no musical description or analysis. The chapter is entirely focused on the explication of song texts.

2. See Chernoff (1979: 200n16) for a discussion of this issue.

3. Berliner (1978: ch. 6) reports a similar process of concentrating on motional patterns when novices try to learn to play *mbira*.

4. Palm strokes also bring out the sound of the *nembe-nembe*, a spider's nest affixed to a hole cut in the side of the *ng'oma* drum. Not all *ng'oma* have *nembe-nembe*, but when they do, the mirliton gives the sound a buzzing, burred timbre, a widespread African sound aesthetic. This distinctive timbre is especially evident in the low frequency range, characteristic of palm strokes. If the *nembe-nembe* breaks—something that happens frequently owing to its fragile nature—it often will not be replaced. Indeed, the use of the *nembe-nembe* seems to be dying out in *vimbuza*. Drummers often told me that it just wasn't worth the trouble to keep fixing it. The use of spider nest mirlitons is widespread in this part of Africa (see for example Kirby's (1965: 50–51) description of the Venda *mbila* xylophone). A particularly interesting example in northern Malawi, in addition to the *ng'oma* drum, is the *malipenga* gourd trumpets used in *beni*-style kazoo bands (Friedson 1994b; Terence Ranger 1975).

5. The *phula* seems to focus the tone of the drumhead, perhaps operating in a manner similar to that of the black tuning-paste on the drumhead of an Indian tabla.

6. For example, in Ewe drumming from the Volta Region of Ghana, the *kagan* pattern is often, in Western musical terms, an unvarying off-beat eighth-note figure always stroked in the same way—right/left: right/left. This pattern does not follow the strict alternation of hands found in roughly the same pattern that is played in *vimbuza* drumming on the *mphiningu* drum.

```
    Kagan    -  ! !  -  ! !
             R L      R L
Mphiningu    -  ! !  -  ! !
          (L) R L (R) L R
```

In other words, the "rests" in the *mphiningu* part, if sounded, would have been played by alternating hands, thus maintaining the strict alternation.

7. I am using the term "meter" here in Kolinski's (1973: 499) sense as organized pulsation functioning as a framework for rhythmic design.

8. The *kwaya* often articulates this two-beat, three-pulse structure through hand-claps that align with the palm strokes of the *ng'oma* drum. The *mphiningu* supporting drum reinforces this metrical perception because it plays virtually the same core pattern as the *ng'oma*. When a third drum, *mboza,* is used (it is used only occasionally), it also supports a 6/8 metrical interpretation because it plays single open-hand strokes that align with the palm strokes of the *ng'oma* and the "empty" strokes of the *mphiningu* part (see note 10), thus articulating a two-beat structure.

9. In recent research among the Ewe of the southern Volta Region of Ghana, I found the *kagan* drum players using this same technique to orient their part, which is often identical to the *mphiningu* part.

10. The figure consists of three strokes, only two of which are readily audible. *Mphiningu* is an onomatopoeia of the pattern. The first syllable, *mphi,* represents either a rest or a stopped hand stroke that can barely be heard (it is more a timekeeper than an acoustical phenomenon), followed by two open-hand strokes, which relate to the last two syllables of the word, *ni* and *ngu*. If one substitutes a palm stroke on the first syllable, *mphi,* one has, of course, an exact duplication of the core pattern, but with timbral differences because the *mphiningu* drum does not usually have a *phula*.

11. Speaking about another multistable visual structure, a grid of squares, Attneave (1971: 65), too, seems to find that there is a certain ability to control these kinds of illusions consciously: "With voluntary effort one can attain fairly stable perceptions of rather complex figures [multistable illusions]."

12. Since writing this, I have come across Locke's (1987: 7) usage of the term "acoustical illusion" to describe aspects of Ewe drumming.

13. See Stoller (1989b; especially ch. 6), and Ihde (1976) on this point.

14. Being perceptually aware of something does not necessarily mean that one is consciously aware of it or able to verbalize about the perception. I am perceptually aware of three-dimensional perspective rendered in two-dimensional space, for example, something not true of people in all cultures, but I don't have to think about it every time I see a Renaissance painting.

15. Kubik (1962: 38–40), in the only published material on *vimbuza* drumming, ends up with basically the same motional and acoustical pattern (see his fig. 13) of interlocking "threes," though he comes to it in a different way. In his figure 12, the "big tone," which is equal to my "palm stroke," is shown as the second pulse of an eighth-note triplet. Kubik does not offer an explanation for why he places this stroke in that position. He goes on to say, however, that "this inaudible cross rhythm is the clue to the drummer's most subtle joy: with the motor image of his hands he *influences* the metrically different acoustic image at times!" (italics and punctuation as in the original). And when he further states that creating variations is a matter of "applying an inaudible motor image to an acoustic image of different meter or rhythm" (ibid.: 40), I take this as independent confirmation that acoustical-motional illusions are indeed operative in *vimbuza* drumming.

16. This formulation of intentional, motional, and acoustical images has echoes in Merriam's (1964: 32–35) tripartite model of ideation (or concept), behavior, and sound. I am applying it narrowly to the level of musical performance, however, and not in Merriam's broader cultural and social sense.

17. This is where I disagree with Kubik's analysis of the motional image (see Kubik 1962: 39–40). For the *mohambu II* drum—I personally never heard a Tumbuka refer to a *vimbuza* drum using the term *mohambu*—Kubik indicates in his notation a change in playing position on the drum for one stroke of the three-stroke grouping, which is precisely what I am showing in my description of Mupa's pattern. Kubik maintains that the motional image is still duple—he is referring to the right-left alternation of hands—but that the acoustic image is different (creating "two conflicting triple rhythms" [ibid.: 39]). While I agree with Kubik that the acoustic image is different, I maintain that the motional image has also changed. The drummer is no longer playing "strictly in *duplets*," but feels this change physically when he moves his hand to a new position on the drum for this one stroke. An observer would also perceive this motional change.

18. The motional pattern that divides the time span into two is created by the hands articulating each pulse (RLR + LRL). The division of the time span into three for the orienting pattern involves one hand, and therefore each articulation of the hand covers two pulses R (L) + R (L) + R (L).

19. Figure 22 illustrates the relationship between the core *vimbuza* pattern and the *ßaßiza* rhythmic motto. The palm strokes on pulses 1 and 7, which divide the figure into two equal sections, serve as an initial orientation to the core pattern; that is, each core pattern starts with a right-hand palm stroke, and, as in the core pattern, drummers maintain a strict alternation of hands.

20. Good *ng'oma* drummers have an aesthetic of repetition that involves a refined sense of when to change a pattern in order to keep the drumming interesting and intense, but steady. After having worked with Saza for some time, I could play most of the mottos of the *vimbuza* modes, and I knew the basic procedure for constructing variations, but one of the most difficult things for me to learn was this right "feel" for repetitions. Invariably when I listened to Saza drum in the *thempli*, whenever I thought a variation would repeat, he would change it, and whenever a pattern had been repeated numerous times and I "felt" it was ready for a change, the variation would continue until I thought it wouldn't change—and then it would. This kept me off balance and perhaps was part of the aesthetic of repetition, but this sense of repetition also gave the drumming a vitality that transcended the rhythmic energy of the individual variations. Chernoff (1979: 100) seems to have had a similar experience when learning Dagomba drumming:

> A Dagomba drummer has the choice of moving to any stylistic variation he wants and playing it for as long as he wishes. When I had learned to play many of these variations and could change from one to another, I might have considered myself qualified to play, except that I could not "feel" how to vary the variations. . . . It is the duration of time that a drummer plays a particular rhythm, *the amount of repetition and the way the rhythms change*, to which the drummers pay attention, and not so much any particular rhythmic invention. The aesthetic decision which constitutes excellence will be the *timing* of the change and the choice of a new pattern. (Italics in the original)

21. If Mupa's pattern of knee and thigh hits were translated into the core pattern, the only difference would be the open-hand stroke on pulse 10 instead of a palm stroke (see the left-hand strokes on pulses 8, 10, and 12 in figure 24).

22. David Lan (1985: 32–34) reports a similar connection between lions, chiefs, and spirits in his research on the Shona spirit mediums of Zimbabwe who embody the spirits of royal ancestors.

23. Historically, the Biza are also closely related because they were originally a splinter group of the Bemba (see Wills 1985: 56).

24. I am following Saza's classification here.

25. The one common variation that Saza did use involved a transformation of the basic pulse, a procedure unique to *vyanusi*. Saza would change the heavily implied triplet feel of the pulse into an even duple eighth-note articulation, which substitutes two pulses for every three, so that instead of a twelve-pulse pattern, the variation transforms into an eight-pulse pattern. Because they are created by a process of substitution, both versions still cover the same time span. This is the only instance in *vimbuza* drumming in which a 3:2 ratio is articulated at the level of pulse—that is, an exchange of two pulses in the time span it takes to play three pulses. In all the other examples I have been discussing, a ratio of 3:2 is generated from a process of grouping pulses together into gross beats (i.e., of either two or three pulse durations), not one of substituting different rates of pulse. The pulses in variations generated from the core pattern are all equal, whereas in *vyanusi* they are not.

26. The right foot takes a step on pulse 12, followed immediately on pulse 1 by an articulation with the left heel. These two steps are, for all practical purposes, felt as one motion and exactly match the right-left hand motion of the first two strokes of the drum motto. This dance motion is repeated three times, again exactly following the structure of the rhythmic motto. On pulse 7, however, which is a left-heel step, there is an accompanying lifting motion with the right foot, again landing with the right foot on the implied beat on pulse 9. The left foot then starts the entire dance figure over, starting on pulse 12 but now reversed, with the left foot doing the step and the right foot articulating with the heel (the drummer does not reverse hands, however). This alternation continues throughout the dance.

27. When I first looked at this figure, I had a very difficult time seeing the young woman, even after it was described in Attneave's (1971: 66) text. Now, however, I have been surprised that whenever I look at this figure, which has been sitting on my desk for several weeks, I always see the young woman first—a complete reversal of my initial perception.

28. I find the best method for viewing is to hold the picture close to your eyes and allow them to cross, then slowly pull the paper away from your face, while keeping an unfocused perspective.

29. Ihde (1976: 75) comments on the surroundability and the penetrating nature of musical sound: "If I hear Beethoven's Ninth Symphony in an acoustically excellent auditorium, I suddenly find myself *immersed* in sound which *surrounds* me. The music is even so *penetrating* that my whole body reverberates and I may find myself absorbed to such a degree that usual distinction between the senses of inner and outer is virtually obliterated. The auditory field surrounds the listener, and surroundability is an essential feature of the field-shape of sound." (Italics in the original.)

30. Looking back on this experience now, it seems to have been similar to that oft-reported phenomenon in which people smoke marijuana for the first time and "nothing happens," which usually means something did but they didn't recognize the effects (in the vernacular, they got high but didn't know it). This *vimbuza* medicine is made of various plants and roots, but *nchimi* were adamant that there was no *banja* (marijuana) in the preparation, for that causes "confusion and clouds one's ability to 'see.' "

31. This narrowing of focus may have aspects similar to those of the concept of "flow" experience. Discussing Czikszentmihalyi's interpretation of "flow," Peters and Price-Williams (1983: 9–10) state that the flow experience may be operative in "certain forms of play, creativity, meditation states, dance, and religious ecstasy. . . . Flow involves concentration or centering of attention on a single stimulus, a 'narrowing of consciousness.' " In the *thempli* of an *nchimi*, music would seem to be a good candidate as a stimulus capable of producing flow-type experiences.

Chapter 6

1. Horton (1971: 86) characterizes Yoruba religion as essentially "this worldly," in other words, "concerned with the explanation, prediction, and control of space-time events."

BIBLIOGRAPHY

Alderman, Harold. 1978. "Heidegger's Critique of Science and Technology." In *Heidegger and Modern Philosophy: Critical Essays.* Edited by Michael Murray, pp. 35–50. New Haven, Connecticut: Yale University Press.

Armstrong, Robert Plant. 1971. *The Affecting Presence: An Essay in Humanistic Anthropology.* Urbana: University of Illinois Press.

Attneave, Fred. 1971. "Multistability in Perception." *Scientific American,* December, pp. 62–71.

Banda, P. K. 1970. "Some Reflections of the History of the Tumbuka Proper." University of Malawi, Chancellor College, Final Year History Seminar Papers.

Barber, Karin. 1981. "How Man Makes God in West Africa: Attitudes towards the Orisa." *Africa* 51 (3): 724–45.

Bascom, William. 1944. "The Sociological Role of the Yoruba Cult Group." *American Anthropologist* 46 (1): 47–73.

Beattie, John, and John Middleton, eds. 1969. *Spirit Mediumship and Society in Africa.* London: Routledge and Kegan Paul.

Belo, Jane. 1960. *Trance in Bali.* New York: Columbia University Press.

Berger, Peter L., and Thomas Luckmann. 1966. *The Social Construction of Reality: A Treatise in the Sociology of Knowledge.* Garden City, New York: Doubleday.

Berliner, Paul. 1978. *The Soul of Mbira: Music and Traditions of the Shona People of Zimbabwe.* Berkeley: University of California Press.

Besmer, Fremont E. 1983. *Horses, Musicians, and Gods: The Hausa Cult of Possession-Trance.* Boston: Bergin and Garvey.

Blacking, John. 1955. "Some Notes on a Theory of Rhythm Advanced by Erich von Hornbostel." *African Music* 1 (2): 12–20.

———. 1973. *How Musical Is Man?* Seattle: University of Washington Press.

———. 1977. "Towards an Anthropology of the Body." In *The Anthropology of the Body.* Edited by John Blacking, pp. 1–28. London: Academic Press.

Boddy, Janice. 1989. *Wombs and Alien Spirits: Women, Men, and the Zar Cult in Northern Sudan.* Madison: University of Wisconsin Press.

Bourguignon, Erika. 1968. "World Distribution and Patterns of Possession States." In *Trance and Possession States.* Edited by Raymond Prince. Montreal: R. M. Bucke Memorial Society.

———. 1973. "Introduction: A Framework for the Comparative Study of Altered States of Consciousness." In *Religion, Altered States of Consciousness, and Social*

Change. Edited by Erika Bourguignon, pp. 3–35. Columbus: Ohio State University Press.

—————. 1976. *Possession.* San Francisco: Chandler and Sharp.

Brain, James L. 1977. *Basic Structure of Swahili.* Syracuse, New York: Maxwell School of Citizenship and Public Affairs, Syracuse University.

Brandel, Rose. 1959. "The African Hemiola Style." *Ethnomusicology* 3 (3): 106–16.

Brelsford, W. V. 1944. *Aspects of Bemba Chieftainship. Communications from the Rhodes-Livingstone Institute no. 2.* Livingstone, [Northern Rhodesia] Zambia: Rhodes-Livingstone Institute.

—————. 1948. *African Dances of Northern Rhodesia. Occasional Papers of the Rhodes-Livingstone Museum no. 2.* Livingstone, [Northern Rhodesia] Zambia: Rhodes-Livingstone Museum.

Bruner, Edward M. 1986. "Experience and Its Expressions." In *The Anthropology of Experience.* Edited by Victor W. Turner and Edward M. Bruner, pp. 3–30. Urbana: University of Illinois Press.

—————. 1993. "Introduction: The Ethnographic Self and the Personal Self." In *Anthropology and Literature.* Edited by Paul Benson, pp. 1–26. Urbana: University of Illinois Press.

Chernoff, John M. 1979. *African Rhythm and African Sensibility: Aesthetics and Social Action in African Musical Idioms.* Chicago: University of Chicago Press.

Chilivumbo, A. B. 1972. "Vimbuza or Mashawe: A Mystic Therapy." *African Music* 5 (2): 6–9.

—————. 1976. "Social Basis of Illness: A Search for Therapeutic Meaning." In *Medical Anthropology.* Edited by Francis X. Grollig and Harold B. Haley, pp. 67–79. The Hague: Mouton.

Clifford, James. 1988. *The Predicament of Culture: Twentieth-Century Ethnography, Literature, and Art.* Cambridge, Massachusetts: Harvard University Press.

Clifford, James, and George E. Marcus, eds. 1986. *Writing Culture: The Poetics and Politics of Ethnography.* Berkeley: University of California Press.

Cole-King, P. B. 1972. "Transport and Communication in Malawi to 1891, with a Summary to 1918." In *The Early History of Malawi.* Edited by Bridglal Pachai, pp. 70–90. London: Longman Group.

Colson, Elizabeth. 1969. "Spirit Possession among the Tonga of Zambia." In *Spirit Mediumship and Society in Africa.* Edited by John Beattie and John Middleton, pp. 69–103. London: Routledge and Kegan Paul.

Colson, Elizabeth, and Max Gluckman, eds. 1951. *Seven Tribes of Central Africa.* Oxford: Oxford University Press.

Cory, Hans. 1936. "Ngoma ya Sheitani." *Journal of the Royal Anthropological Society* 66: 209–17.

Crapanzano, Vincent. 1973. *The Hamadsha: A Study in Moroccan Ethnopsychiatry.* Berkeley: University of California Press.

Crapanzano, V., and V. Garrison, eds. 1977. *Case Studies in Spirit Possession.* New York: Wiley.

De George, Richard T., and Fernande M. De George. 1972. Introduction to *The Structuralists: From Marx to Lévi-Strauss.* Edited by Richard T. De George and Fernande M. De George, pp. xi–xxix. Garden City, New York: Anchor Books.

Deren, Maya. 1953. *Divine Horsemen: Voodoo Gods of Haiti.* New York: Chelsea House Publishers.

Dilthey, Wilhelm. 1976. *Selected Writings.* Edited by H. P. Rickman. Cambridge: Cambridge University Press.

———. 1985. *Poetry and Experience.* Edited by Rudolf A. Makkreel and Frithjof Rodi. *Selected Works,* vol. 5. Princeton, New Jersey: Princeton University Press.

———. 1989. *Introduction to the Human Sciences.* Edited by Rudolf A. Makkreel and Frithjof Rodi. *Selected Works,* vol. 1. Princeton, New Jersey: Princeton University Press.

Douglas, Mary. 1967. "Witch Beliefs in Central Africa." *Africa* 37: 72–80.

Drewal, Margaret. 1992. *Yoruba Ritual: Performers, Play, Agency.* Bloomington: Indiana University Press.

Dreyfus, Hubert L. 1991. *Being-in-the-World: A Commentary on Heidegger's Being and Time, Division 1.* Cambridge, Massachusetts: MIT Press.

Du Toit, Brian M. 1971. "The Isangoma: An Adaptive Agent among the Urban Zulu." *Anthropological Quarterly* 44 (2): 51–65.

Eisenberg, Leon. 1977. "Disease and Illness." *Culture, Medicine and Psychiatry* 1: 9–23.

Eliade, Mircea. 1963. *Patterns in Comparative Religion.* Translated by Rosemary Sheed. Cleveland: Meridian Books, World Publishing Company.

———. 1964. *Shamanism: Archaic Techniques of Ecstasy.* Translated by Willard R. Trask. Princeton, New Jersey: Princeton University Press.

Ellingson, Ter. 1987. "Music and Religion." In *The Encyclopedia of Religion,* vol. 10. Edited by Mircea Eliade, pp. 163–72. New York: Macmillan.

Elmslie, W. A. 1899. *Among the Wild Ngoni.* New York: Fleming H. Revell Company.

Evans-Pritchard, E. E. 1937. *Witchcraft, Oracles and Magic among the Azande.* Oxford: Clarendon Press.

Fabian, Johannes. 1983. *Time and the Other: How Anthropology Makes Its Object.* New York: Columbia University Press.

Feierman, Steven, and John M. Janzen, eds. 1992. *The Social Basis of Health and Healing in Africa.* Berkeley: University of California Press.

Feld, Steven. 1982. *Sound and Sentiment: Birds, Weeping, Poetics, and Song in Kaluli Expression.* Philadelphia: University of Pennsylvania Press.

Field, M. J. 1937. *Religion and Medicine among the Ga People.* London: Oxford University Press.

Foster, George M., and Barbara G. Anderson. 1978. *Medical Anthropology.* New York: John Wiley and Sons.

Fraser, Donald. 1914. *Winning a Primitive People.* London: Seeley, Service and Co.

———. 1923. *African Idylls: Portraits and Impressions of Life on a Central African Mission.* London: Seeley, Service and Co.

Friedson, Steven M. 1989. *Prophet Healers of Northern Malawi.* Video, 1/2 inch VHS. *African Encounters* series. Seattle: University of Washington, Jackson School of International Studies, Executive Producer.

———. 1994a. "Ingoma Dance of the Ngoni People." Tape 20, 1/2 inch VHS. *The*

New JVC Video Anthology of World Music and Dance. Tokyo: Victor Corporation of Japan, Executive Producer.

————. 1994b. "Malipenga Kazoo Bands." Tape 20, 1/2 inch VHS. *The New JVC Video Anthology of World Music and Dance.* Tokyo: Victor Corporation of Japan, Executive Producer.

Fry, Peter. 1976. *Spirits of Protest: Spirit-Mediums and the Articulation of Consensus among the Zezuru of Southern Rhodesia (Zimbabwe).* Cambridge: Cambridge University Press.

Gadamer, Hans-Georg. 1976. *Philosophical Hermeneutics.* Translated and edited by David E. Linge. Berkeley: University of California Press.

————. 1989. *Truth and Method.* 2d rev. ed. Translation revised by Joel Weinsheimer and Donald G. Marshall. New York: Crossroads.

Garbett, G. Kingsley. 1969. "Spirit Mediums as Mediators in Valley Korekore Society." In *Spirit Mediumship and Society in Africa.* Edited by John Beattie and John Middleton, pp. 104–27. London: Routledge and Kegan Paul.

Geertz, Clifford. 1973. *The Interpretation of Cultures.* New York: Basic Books.

————. 1983. *Local Knowledge: Further Essays in Interpretive Anthropology.* New York: Basic Books.

————. 1986. "Making Experiences, Authoring Selves." In *The Anthropology of Experience.* Edited by Victor W. Turner and Edward M. Bruner, pp. 373–80. Urbana: University of Illinois Press.

————. 1988. *Works and Lives: The Anthropologist as Author.* Stanford, California: Stanford University Press.

Gelfand, Michael. 1956. *Medicine and Magic of the Mashona.* Cape Town: Juta and Co.

————. 1964a. *Lakeside Pioneers: Socio-medical Study of Nyasaland (1875–1920).* Oxford: Basil Blackwell, Oxford and Mott.

————. 1964b. *Witchdoctor: Traditional Medicine Man of Rhodesia.* New York: Fredrick A. Praeger.

Gelven, Michael. 1970. *A Commentary on Heidegger's Being and Time: A Section-by-Section Interpretation.* New York: Harper and Row.

Gillies, Eva. 1976. "Causal Criteria in African Classification of Disease." In *Social Anthropology and Medicine.* Edited by J. Loudon, pp. 358–95. London: Academic Press.

Goffman, Erving. 1959. *The Presentation of Self in Everyday Life.* Garden City, New York: Doubleday Anchor.

————. 1961. *Encounters: Two Studies in the Sociology of Interaction.* Indianapolis: Bobbs-Merrill.

————. 1974. *Frame Analysis: An Essay on the Organization of Experience.* Cambridge, Massachusetts: Harvard University Press.

Government of Malawi. 1983. *The National Atlas of Malawi.*

————. 1987. "Malawi." *Africa South of the Sahara.* 16th ed. London: Europa Publications Limited.

Gray, Robert F. 1969. "The Shetani Cult among the Segeju of Tanzania." In *Spirit Mediumship and Society in Africa.* Edited by John Beattie and John Middleton, pp. 171–87. London: Routledge and Kegan Paul.

Hammond-Tooke, W. D. 1955. "The Initiation of a Baca Isangoma Diviner." *African Studies* 14 (1): 16–22.

———, ed. 1974. *The Bantu-speaking Peoples of Southern Africa.* 2d ed. London: Routledge and Kegan Paul.

Heidegger, Martin. 1962a. *Being and Time.* Translated by John Macquarrie and Edward Robinson. New York: Harper and Row.

———. 1962b. *Kant and the Problem of Metaphysics.* Translated by James S. Churchill. Bloomington: Indiana University Press.

———. 1972. *On Time and Being.* Translated by Joan Stambough. New York: Harper and Row.

———. 1977. *The Question Concerning Technology and Other Essays.* Translated by William Lovitt. New York: Harper Colophon Books.

Heisenberg, Werner. 1958. *Physics and Philosophy: The Revolution in Modern Science.* New York: Harper and Row.

Herskovits, Melville J. 1937. *Life in a Haitian Valley.* New York: Alfred A. Knopf.

———. 1938. *Dahomey: An Ancient West African Kingdom.* 2 vols. New York: J. J. Augustin.

Heusch, Luc de. 1985. *Sacrifice in Africa.* Bloomington: Indiana University Press.

Hornbostel, Erich M. von. 1928. "African Negro Music." *Africa* 1: 30–62.

Horton, Robin. 1967. "African Traditional Thought and Western Science." *Africa* 37: 50–71, 155–87.

———. 1971. "African Conversion." *Africa* 41 (2): 85–108.

Husserl, Edmund. 1931. *Ideas: General Introduction to Pure Phenomenology.* Translated by W. R. Boyce Gibson. New York: Humanities Press.

———. 1960. *Cartesian Meditations: An Introduction to Phenomenology.* Translated by Dorion Cairns. The Hague: Nijhoff.

Ihde, Don. 1976. *Listening and Voice: A Phenomenology of Sound.* Athens: Ohio University Press.

———. 1977. *Experimental Phenomenology: An Introduction.* New York: Capricorn Books, G. P. Putnam's Sons.

———. 1983. *Existential Technics.* Albany: State University of New York Press.

International African Institute. 1930. *Practical Orthography of African Languages.* Oxford: Oxford University Press.

International Phonetic Association. 1949. *The Principles of the International Phonetic Association.* London: International Phonetic Association.

Jack, James W. [1900] 1969. *Daybreak in Livingstonia.* New York: Young People's Missionary Movement. Reprint, New York: Negro Universities Press.

Jackson, Michael. 1989. *Paths toward a Clearing: Radical Empiricism and Ethnographic Inquiry.* Bloomington: Indiana University Press.

James, William. 1977. *The Writings of William James: A Comprehensive Edition.* Edited by John J. McDermott. Chicago: University of Chicago Press.

Janzen, John M. 1978. *The Quest for Therapy in Lower Zaire.* Berkeley: University of California Press.

———. 1992. *Ngoma: Discourses of Healing in Central and Southern Africa.* Berkeley: University of California Press.

Jones, A. M. 1954. "African Rhythm." *Africa* 24 (1): 26–47.

———. 1958. *African Music in Northern Rhodesia and Some Other Places. The Occasional Papers of the Rhodes-Livingstone Museum, no. 4.* Livingstone, [Northern Rhodesia] Zambia: Rhodes-Livingstone Museum.

———. 1959. *Studies in African Music.* 2 vols. London: Oxford University Press.

Junod, Henri. [1927] 1962. *The Life of a South African Tribe.* 2 vols. 2d ed., rev. and enl. London: Macmillan. Reprint, New Hyde Park, New York: University Books.

Kapferer, Bruce. 1983. *A Celebration of Demons: Exorcism and the Aesthetics of Healing in Sri Lanka.* Bloomington: Indiana University Press.

———. 1986. "Performance and the Structuring of Meaning and Experience." In *The Anthropology of Experience.* Edited by Victor W. Turner and Edward M. Bruner, pp. 188–220. Urbana: University of Illinois Press.

Katz, Richard. 1982. *Boiling Energy: Community Healing among the Kalahari Kung.* Cambridge, Massachusetts: Harvard University Press.

Kauffman, Robert. 1980. "African Rhythm: A Reassessment." *Ethnomusicology* 24 (3): 393–415.

Keil, Charles. 1979. *Tiv Song: The Sociology of Art in a Classless Society.* Chicago: University of Chicago Press.

Kirby, Percival R. 1965. *The Musical Instruments of the Native Races of South Africa.* 2d ed. Johannesburg: Witwatersrand University Press.

Kleinman, Arthur. 1980. *Patients and Healers in the Context of Culture: An Exploration of the Borderland between Anthropology, Medicine, and Psychiatry.* Berkeley: University of California Press.

Kockelmans, Joseph J., ed. 1967. *Phenomenology: The Philosophy of Edmund Husserl and Its Interpretation.* Garden City, New York: Anchor Books.

Koetting, James. 1970. "Analysis and Notation of West African Drum Ensemble Music." *UCLA Selected Reports* 1 (3): 115–46.

Kolinski, M. 1973. "A Cross-Cultural Approach to Metro-Rhythmic Patterns." *Ethnomusicology* 17 (3): 494–506.

Kratz, Corinne. 1994. *Affecting Performance: Meaning, Movement, and Experience in Okiek Women's Initiation.* Washington, D.C.: Smithsonian Institution Press.

Kubik, Gerhard. 1962. "The Phenomenon of Inherent Rhythms in East and Central African Instrumental Music." *African Music* 3 (1): 33–42. Corrigenda in *African Music* 4 (4), 1970.

———. 1979. "Pattern Perception and Recognition in African Music." In *The Performing Arts: Music and Dance.* Edited by John Blacking and Joann W. Kealiinohomoku, pp. 221–49. The Hague: Mouton.

———. 1982. *Ostafrika.* Series; *Musikgeschicte in Bildern, Band 1: Musikethnologie, Lieferung 10.* Leipzig: VEB Deutscher Verlag für Musik.

———. 1987. *Malawian Music: A Framework for Analysis.* Zomba, Malawi: Centre for Social Research, Department of Fine and Performing Arts, Chancellor College, University of Malawi.

Kwant, Remy C. 1963. *The Phenomenological Philosophy of Merleau-Ponty.* Pittsburgh, Pennsylvania: Duquesne University Press.

Lakoff, George, and Mark Johnson. 1980. *Metaphors We Live By.* Chicago: University of Chicago Press.

Lan, David. 1985. *Guns and Rain: Guerrillas and Spirit Mediums in Zimbabwe.* Berkeley: University of California Press.

Langan, Thomas. 1959. *The Meaning of Heidegger: A Critical Study of an Existentialist Phenomenology.* New York: Columbia University Press.

Laws, Robert. 1934. *Reminiscences of Livingstonia.* Edinburgh: Oliver and Boyd.

Lee, S. G. 1969. "Spirit Possession among the Zulu." In *Spirit Mediumship and Society in Africa.* Edited by John Beattie and John Middleton, pp. 128–56. London: Routledge and Kegan Paul.

Lévi-Strauss, Claude. 1963. *Structural Anthropology.* New York: Basic Books.

———. 1969. *The Raw and the Cooked: Introduction to a Science of Mythology.* Vol. 1. Translated by John and Doreen Weightman. New York: Harper and Row.

———. 1973. *Tristes Tropiques.* Translated by John and Doreen Weightman. London: Jonathan Cape.

Lévy-Bruhl, Lucien. 1923. *Primitive Mentality.* Translated by Lilian A. Clare. New York: Macmillan.

Lewis, I. M. 1971. *Ecstatic Religion: An Anthropological Study of Spirit Possession and Shamanism.* Baltimore: Penguin Books.

Lex, Barbara W. 1979. "The Neurobiology of Ritual Trance." In *The Spectrum of Ritual: A Biogenetic Structural Analysis.* Edited by E. d'Aquili et al., pp. 117–51. New York: Columbia University Press.

Livingstone, W. P. 1921. *Laws of Livingstonia.* London: Hodder and Stoughton.

Locke, David. 1982. "Principles of Off-Beat Timing and Cross-Rhythm in Southern Eʋe Dance Drumming." *Ethnomusicology* 26 (2): 217–46.

———. 1987. *Drum Gahu: A Systematic Method for an African Percussion Piece.* Crown Point, Indiana: White Cliffs Media Company.

Lovitt, William. 1977. Introduction to *The Question Concerning Technology and Other Essays,* by Martin Heidegger, pp. xiii–xxxix. Translated by William Lovitt. New York: Harper Colophon Books.

Maganga, J. 1983. "Nantongwe: A Spirit Possession Ritual among the Lomwe." In *Papers on Regional Cults (Sources for the Study of Religion in Malawi, no. 7).* Zomba, Malawi: Chancellor College.

Makkreel, Rudolf A., and Frithjof Rodi. 1989. Introduction to *Introduction to the Human Sciences,* vol. 1, *Selected Works,* by Wilhelm Dilthey. Edited by Rudolf A. Makkreel and Frithjof Rodi, pp. 3–43. Princeton, New Jersey: Princeton University Press.

Marcus, George, and Michael Fischer. 1986. *Anthropology as Cultural Critique: An Experimental Moment in the Human Sciences.* Chicago: University of Chicago Press.

Marshall, Lorna. 1969. "The Medicine Dance of the !Kung Bushmen." *Africa* 39: 347–81.

Marwick, M. G. 1965. *Sorcery in Its Social Setting: A Study of the Northern Rhodesian Cewa.* Manchester: Manchester University Press.

———, ed. 1982. *Witchcraft and Sorcery.* 2d. ed. Harmondsworth, England: Penguin Books.

McCracken, John. 1977. *Politics and Christianity in Malawi 1875–1940: The Impact of the Livingstonia Mission in the Northern Province.* Cambridge: Cambridge University Press.

Merleau-Ponty, M. 1962. *Phenomenology of Perception.* Translated by Colin Smith. New York: Humanities Press.

Merriam, Alan P. 1959. "African Music." In *Continuity and Change in African Cultures.* Edited by William R. Bascom and Melville J. Herskovits, pp. 49–86. Chicago: University of Chicago Press.

———. 1964. *The Anthropology of Music.* Evanston, Illinois: Northwestern University Press.

———. 1981. "African Musical Rhythm and Concepts of Time Reckoning." In *Music East and West: Essays in Honor of Walter Kaufmann.* Edited by Thomas Noblitt, pp 123 42. New York: Pendragon Press.

———. 1982. *African Music in Perspective.* New York: Garland Publishing.

Métraux, Alfred. 1972. *Voodoo in Haiti.* New York: Schocken Books.

Middleton, J., and E. Winter, eds. 1963. *Witchcraft and Sorcery in East Africa.* London: Routledge and Kegan Paul.

Moerman, Daniel E. 1979. "Anthropology of Symbolic Healing." *Current Anthropology* 20 (1): 59–77.

Moreno, Jacob P. 1946. *Psychodrama.* New York: Beacon House.

Msonthi, Jerome D. 1982. "Research into Traditional Medicine in Malawi." *Research Digest,* National Research Council of Malawi.

Natanson, Maurice, ed. 1973. *Phenomenology and the Social Sciences.* vol. 1. Evanston: Northwestern University Press.

Nazombe, A. 1981. "Spirit Possession Songs and Social Tension: A Comparative Study of Vimbuza and Nantongwe." Paper presented at the Conference on Literature and Society in Southern Africa, University of York.

Ncozana, S. S. 1985. "Spirit Possession and Tumbuka Christians: 1875–1950." Ph.D. diss., University of Aberdeen.

Needham, Rodney. 1967. "Percussion and Transition." *Man,* n.s., 2: 606–14.

Neher, Andrew. 1961. "Auditory Driving Observed with Scalp Electrodes in Normal Subject." *Electroencephalography and Clinical Neurophysiology* 13: 449–51.

———. 1962. "A Physiological Explanation of Unusual Behavior in Ceremonies Involving Drums." *Human Biology* 4: 151–60.

Ngubane, Harriet. 1976. "Some Aspects of Treatment among the Zulu." In *Social Anthropology and Medicine.* Edited by J. B. Loudon, pp. 318–57. London: Academic Press.

Nketia, J. H. Kwabena. 1957. "Possession Dances in African Societies." *Journal of the International Folk Music Council* 9: 4–9.

———. 1974. *The Music of Africa.* New York: W. W. Norton.

Nyirenda, Saulos. 1931. "History of the Tumbuka-Henga People." Translated and edited by T. Cullen Young. *Bantu Studies* 5 (1): 1–18.

Oesterreich, T. K. 1930. *Possession: Demonical and Other among Primitive Races, in Antiquity, the Middle Ages, and Modern Times.* Authorized Translation by D. Ibberson. New York: R. R. Sinilh.

Oger, Louis. 1972. "Spirit Possession among the Bemba: A Linguistic Approach." Paper presented at the Conference on the History of Central African Religions.

Pachai, Bridglal, ed. 1972. *The Early History of Malawi.* London: Longman Group.

———. 1973. *Malawi: The History of the Nation.* London: Longman Group.

Palmer, Richard E. 1969. *Hermeneutics: Interpretation Theory in Schleiermacher, Dilthey, Heidegger, and Gadamer.* Evanston: Northwestern University Press.

Pantaleoni, Hewitt. 1972. "Three Principles of Timing in Anlo Dance Drumming." *African Music* 5 (2): 50–63.

Peters, Larry G., and Douglass Price-Williams. 1983. "Overview: A Phenomenological Overview of Trance." *Transcultural Psychiatric Research Review* 20: 5–39.

Pike, John G. 1968. *Malawi: A Political and Economic History.* New York: Fredrick A. Praeger.

Pike, John G., and G. T. Rimmington. 1965. *Malawi: A Geographical Study.* London: Oxford University Press.

Prince, Raymond, ed. 1968. *Trance and Possession States.* Montreal: R. M. Bucke Memorial Society.

Ranger, T. O. 1975. *Dance and Society in Eastern Africa, 1890–1970: The Beni Ngoma.* London: William Heinemann.

Ranger, T. O., and I. N. Kimambo. 1972. *The Historical Study of African Religion.* Berkeley: University of California Press.

Ranger, T. O., and John Weller. 1975. *Themes in the Christian History of Central Africa.* Berkeley: University of California Press.

Read, Margaret. 1942. "Migrant Labour in Africa and Its Effects on Tribal Life." *International Labour Review* 55 (6): 605–31.

———. 1956. *The Ngoni of Nyasaland.* London: Oxford University Press.

———. 1968. *Children of Their Fathers: Growing Up among the Ngoni of Malawi.* New York: Holt, Rinehart and Winston.

Redmayne, Alison. 1970. "Chikanga: An African Diviner with an International Reputation." In *Witchcraft Confessions and Accusations.* Edited by Mary Douglas, pp. 103–28. London: Tavistock.

Richards, Audrey I. 1951. "The Bemba of North-Eastern Rhodesia." In *Seven Tribes of Central Africa.* Edited by Elizabeth Colson and Max Gluckman, pp. 164–93. Oxford: Oxford University Press.

Roseman, Marina. 1991. *Healing Sounds from the Malaysian Rainforest: Temiar Music and Medicine.* Berkeley: University of California Press.

Rouget, Gilbert. 1985. *Music and Trance: A Theory of the Relations between Music and Possession.* Translated by Brunhilde Biebuyck. Chicago: University of Chicago Press.

Rousseau, Jean-Jacques. 1966. *On the Origin of Language.* Translated by John H. Moran and Alexander Gode. New York: Fredrick Ungar.

Ruby, Jay, ed. 1982. *A Crack in the Mirror: Reflexive Perspectives in Anthropology.* Philadelphia: University of Pennsylvania Press.

Schafer, Murray R. 1977. *The Tuning of the World.* New York: Alfred A. Knopf.

Schapera, Isaac. 1982. "Sorcery and Witchcraft in Bechuanaland." In *Witchcraft and Sorcery.* 2d ed. Edited by Max Marwick, pp. 108–18. Harmondsworth, England: Penguin Books.

Schoffeleers, J. 1967. *Evil Spirits and Rites of Exorcism in the Lower Shire Valley of Malawi.* Limbe, Malawi: Montfort Press.

Schutz, Alfred. 1964. *Collected Papers II: Studies in Social Theory.* The Hague: Martinus Nijhoff.

———. 1973. *The Structures of the Life-World*. Translated by Richard M. Zaner and H. Tristam Engelhardt, Jr. Evanston, Illinois: Northwestern University Press.

Segall, Marshall H., Donald T. Campbell, and Melville J. Herskovits. 1968. "Cultural Differences in the Perception of Geometric Illusions." In *Contemporary Theory and Research in Visual Perception*. Edited by R. N. Harber, pp. 678–82. London: Holt, Rinehart and Winston.

Sibisi, Harriet. 1975. "The Place of Spirit Possession in Zulu Cosmology." In *Religion and Social Change in Southern Africa*. Edited by Michael Whisson and Martin West, pp. 48–57. Cape Town: David Phillip.

Soko, Boston. 1984. "Stylistique et messages dans le Vimbuza: Chants des cultes de possession recueilles dans les régions de Mzimba et Rumphi (Malawi)." Thèse de 3eme cycle Université de Paris III.

———. 1987. "The Vimbuza Phenomenon: Disease or Art." Unpublished paper.

Steel, George. 1894. *Native Diseases and Practices among the Ngoni*. London.

Stoller, Paul. 1989a. *Fusion of the Worlds: An Ethnography of Possession among the Songhay of Niger*. Chicago: University of Chicago Press.

———. 1989b. *The Taste of Ethnographic Things: The Senses in Anthropology*. Philadelphia: University of Pennsylvania Press.

Stone, Ruth M. 1985. "In Search of Time in African Music." *Music Theory Spectrum* 7: 139–48.

Tew, Mary. 1950. *Peoples of the Lake Nyasa Region*. Oxford: Oxford University Press.

Thompson, Robert Farris. 1983. *Flash of the Spirit: African and Afro-American Art and Philosophy*. New York: Random House.

Tracey, Hugh. 1948. *Chopi Musicians: Their Music, Poetry, and Instruments*. London: Oxford Press.

Turnbull, Colin. 1962. *The Forest People: A Study of the Pygmies of the Congo*. New York: Simon and Schuster.

Turner, Victor W. 1963. *Lunda Medicine and the Treatment of Disease. The Occasional Papers of the Rhodes-Livingstone Museum*. Lusaka: Rhodes-Livingstone Institute.

———. 1967. *The Forest of Symbols: Aspects of Ndembu Ritual*. Ithaca, New York: Cornell University Press.

———. 1968. *The Drums of Affliction: A Study of Religious Processes among the Ndembu of Zambia*. Oxford: Oxford University Press.

———. 1969. *The Ritual Process: Structure and Anti-Structure*. Chicago: Aldine.

———. 1974. *Dramas, Fields, and Metaphors: Symbolic Action in Human Society*. Ithaca, New York: Cornell University Press.

———. 1982. *From Ritual to Theatre: The Human Seriousness of Play*. New York: Performing Arts Journal Publications.

———. 1985. *On the Edge of the Bush: Anthropology as Experience*. Edited by Edith Turner. Tucson: University of Arizona Press.

———. 1986. "Dewey, Dilthey, and Drama: An Essay in the Anthropology of Experience." In *The Anthropology of Experience*. Edited by Victor W. Turner and Edward M. Bruner, pp. 33–44. Urbana: University of Illinois Press.

Turner, Victor W., and Edith Turner. 1978. *Image and Pilgrimage in Christian Culture.* New York: Columbia University Press.

Turner, Victor W., and Edward M. Bruner, eds. 1986. *The Anthropology of Experience.* Urbana: University of Illinois Press.

Turner, William Y. 1952. *Tumbuka-Tonga English Dictionary.* Blantyre, Malawi: Hetherwick Press.

Twumasi, P. A. 1975. *Medical Systems in Ghana: A Study in Medical Sociology.* Accra: Ghana Publishing Corporation.

Tylor, Edward B. 1920. *Primitive Culture.* vol. 1. 6th ed. London: John Murray.

Vail, Leroy. 1972. "Suggestions towards a Reinterpreted Tumbuka History." In *The Early History of Malawi.* Edited by Bridglal Pachai, pp. 148–67. London: Longman.

Vail, Leroy, and Landeg White. 1989. "Tribalism in the Political History of Malawi." In *The Creation of Tribalism in Southern Africa.* Edited by Leroy Vail, pp. 151–92. Berkeley: University of California Press.

———. 1991. *Power and the Praise Poem: Southern African Voices in History.* Charlottesville: University Press of Virginia.

van Binsbergen, Wim. 1981. *Religious Change in Zambia.* London: Routledge and Kegan Paul.

———. 1991. "Becoming a Sangoma." *Journal of Religion in Africa* 21 (4): 309–44.

Vansina, Jan. 1966. *Kingdoms of the Savanna.* Madison: University of Wisconsin Press.

Wade, Nicholas. 1982. *The Art and Science of Visual Illusions.* London: Routledge and Kegan Paul.

Walker, Sheila S. 1972. *Ceremonial Spirit Possession in Africa and Afro-America.* Leiden: E. J. Brill.

Wendroff, Arnold P. 1985. "Trouble-Shooters and Trouble-Makers: Witchfinding and Traditional Malawian Medicine." Ph.D. diss., City University of New York.

Williams, T. David. 1978. *Malawi: The Politics of Despair.* Ithaca, New York: Cornell University Press.

Williamson, Jessie. 1974. *Useful Plants of Malawi.* Revised and extended edition. Limbe, Malawi: Montfort Press.

Wills, A. J. 1985. *An Introduction to the History of Central Africa: Zambia, Malawi, and Zimbabwe.* 4th ed. Oxford: Oxford University Press.

Wilson, Monica. 1972. "Reflections on the Early History of North Malawi." In *The Early History of Malawi.* Edited by Bridglal Pachai, pp. 136–47. London: Longman.

Yoder, Stanley. 1982. "Issues in the Study of Ethnomedical Systems in Africa." In *African Health and Healing Systems: Proceedings of a Symposium.* Edited by Stanley Yoder. Los Angeles: Crossroads Press.

Young, T. Cullen. 1932a. *Notes on the Speech of the Tumbuka-Kamanga Peoples in the Northern Province of Nyasaland.* London: Religious Tract Society.

———. 1932b. *Notes on the History of the Tumbuka-Kamanga Peoples in the Northern Province of Nyasaland.* London: Religious Tract Society.

———. 1932c. "Three Medicine-Men in Northern Nyasaland." *Man* 32: 229–34.

———. 1933. "Tribal Intermixture in Nyasaland." *Journal of the Royal Anthropological Institute* 63: 1–18.

INDEX

acoustic image, 131, 133–34, 146
acoustical illusions
  and binary oppositions, 168–69
  in consciousness-transformation, 143
  and cross-cultural differences, 156
  in Ewe drumming, 200n. 12
  multistable, 141–51, 155–58
  in rhythmic modes, 147–56
  in transformation of spirit affliction,
    161
  See also drumming, vimbuza; metrical shifting; motto, rhythmic;
    music, vimbuza; rhythmic mode
adepts
  attire of, 105
  as lead singers, 107
  and lucid possession, 29
  as members of the kwaya (choir), 110
  as new moons (mutwasa), 109, 161
  and performance of nkufi clapping,
    85, 97, 115
  relationship to music, 29, 197n. 6
  and smoking medicine, 158–61
  and trance dancing, 12, 158–62
  and vyanusi dance, 154
  See also disease of the prophets; initiatory illness; mutwasa (new
    moon); novices
"African diseases," 51, 61
  etiology of, 41
  European cases of, 40, 52
  See also illness, Tumbuka theory of
African Health and Healing Systems,
  191n. 5
African music
  clapping in, 17

as functional, 77
and health care systems, xi–xii
  historical depth, 191n. 6
  lack of analysis, xiii, 168
hemiola in, 198n. 8
importance of the body in, 131
ancestor spirits (mizimu)
  in categorical opposition to vimbuza
    spirits, 64–65
  as the cause of dreams, 23–24
  classification of, 34, 192n. 16
  demands of, 11, 59–60, 63–64, 71–72
  in dreams, 11, 24, 26, 59, 63, 72
  help in fighting witchcraft, 59
  illness caused by, 11, 59–64 passim,
    71–72
  inability to possess, 30, 65, 93
  paying respects to, 59–60, 72, 105–6
    with cement tombs, 60–64, 105
  role in divinatory trance, 23, 30,
    98–99
  as upholders of traditional values, 55,
    59, 97, 98
  as witches, 55
anthropology of experience, xiv, 4–5
ashes, cooling effects of, 77
Attneave, Fred, 200n. 11, 202n. 27
Aurora, The, 41
authentic existence, 5, 37, 126
  See also being-in-the-world
Azande, xii, 42, 54

ßaßemba (vimbuza spirit), 147, 151–52
ßaßiza (vimbuza spirit), 147
  See also under motto, rhythmic;
    rhythmic mode

215